Sister Woman

by
J. G. Sime

A Critical Edition

Edited by
Sandra Campbell

The Tecumseh Press Ltd.
Ottawa, Canada
2004

Canadian Critical Editions
General Editors
John Moss and Gerald Lynch

Canadian Critical Editions offer, for academic study and the interested reader, authoritative texts of significant Canadian works within a comprehensive critical setting. Where appropriate, each edition provides extensive biographical and bibliographical background, reprints of documents, commentary to illuminate the context of its creation and the history of its reception, new essays written from a variety of critical perspectives, and a biography. These critical editions provide an excellent opportunity for appreciation of the works themselves, for understanding their place in the developing tradition, and for participating in the critical discourse surrounding each work. Making the best accessible, this is the key concept behind the Canadian Critical Editions.

Other titles in the Canadian Critical Editions available from Tecumseh Press

Stephen Leacock, *Sunshine Sketches of a Little Town*, editor Gerald Lynch, 1996.

Sara Jeannette Duncan, *The Imperialist*, editor Thomas E. Tausky, 1996.

Susanna Moodie, *Roughing It in the Bush; or, Life in Canada*, editor Elizabeth Thompson, 1997.

John Richardson, *Wacousta*, editor John Moss, 1998.

A Northern Romanticism; Poets of the Confederation, editor Tracy Ware, 2000.

Early Canadian Short Stories: Short Stories in English before World War I, editor Misao Dean, 2000.

Frances Brooke, *The History of Emily Montague*, editor Laura Moss, 2001.

Stephen Leacock, *Arcadian Adventures with the Idle Rich*, editor David Bentley, 2002.

Titles in Preparation

James De Mille, *A Strange Manuscript Found in a Copper Cylinder*, editor Gwendolyn Davies.

Thomas Chandler Haliburton, *The Clockmaster*, editor Carrie MacMillan.

Charles G.D. Roberts, *Charles G.D. Roberts: Animal Stories*, editor Terry Whalen.

A Northern Modernism: Poets Since Confederation, editor Tracy Ware.

Ethel Wilson, *Swamp Angel*, editor Lei-Ping Geng.

Charles G.D. Roberts' Animal Stories, editor Terry Whalen.

Duncan Campbell Scott, *In the Village of Vigen*, editor Klay Dyer.

Sister Woman

by
J.G. Sime

A Critical Edition

Edited by
Sandra Campbell

The Tecumseh Press
Ottawa, Canada
2004

Copyright © by The Tecumseh Press Ltd., 2004

Canada⁣

*The Publishers acknowledge the financial assistance of the
Government of Canada through the Book Publishing Industry
Development Program (BPIDP) for our publishing activities.*

**National Library of Canada Cataloguing in Publication
Data**

Sime, J. G. (Jessie Georgina), 1868-1958.
    Sister Woman : a critical edition / Jessie Georgina Sime;
editor, Sandra Campbell.

(Canadian critical editions; 9)
Includes bibliographical references.
ISBN 1-896133-39-8 (bound).–
ISBN 1-896133-41-X (pbk.)

    1. Sime, J. G. (Jessie Georgina), 1868-1958. Sister
Woman. 2. Women employees in literature. 3. Working class
in literature. I. Campbell, Sandra II. Title. III. Series

PS8537.I52S57 2004   C813'.52   C2003-907083-2

Cover design by drt.2004, Ottawa

Printed and bound in Canada on acid-free paper.

In memory

of

Lorraine McMullen

(1926-2003)

Professor Emerita
University of Ottawa

Dedicated Scholar of Early Canadian Women Writers

Contents

Editor's Preface. ix
Explanatory Notes to the Text of *Sister Woman* xii

Sister Woman. 1

Biocritical Context
Sandra Campbell, Introduction: Biocritical
Context for J. G. Sime and *Sister Woman* 207

Documentary

Peter Donovan, Review of *Sister Woman*
(1920). 227
Canadian Women in the Public Eye: Miss Sime (1922). . 228

Criticism

Misao Dean, *Sister Woman* as New Woman Fiction
in Canada 230
Gerald Lynch, Fabian Feminism: Sime's Short
Story Cycle. 236
Lindsey McMaster, The Urban Working Girl in
Turn-of-the-Century Canadian Fiction 250
Ann Martin, Mapping Modernity in J. G. Sime's
Sister Woman 277
K. Jane Watt, Cadences of Canada: Georgina
Sime's *Sister Woman* 283

Bibliography 293

Editor's Preface

For scholars of women's writing, in Canada as elsewhere, the need to recover and republish women's writing of the past is a truism of the field. J. G. Sime's 1919 short story cycle *Sister Woman* has been a particularly satisfying example of the value of republication ever since Tecumseh Press reprinted the text in 1992 in its Early Canadian Women Writers Series under the general editorship of Lorraine McMullen. Sime's subject in *Sister Woman* is the social and sexual lives of a fictional selection of middle- and working-class women in the Montreal of World War I. Georgina Sime created her characters as representative women caught up in an era of urbanization, industrialization, and concomitant changes in women's lives. Sime's literary techniques are as sophisticated as her view of women's lives in her creation of a cycle of twenty-eight stories interrelated thematically and technically. As a result, in the last decade, *Sister Woman* has been read by literary, women's studies, and historical scholars from different perspectives.

There is a certain irony in this flurry of interest in *Sister Woman* at the beginning of the twenty-first century. When Sime's short story cycle appeared at the beginning of the twentieth century, Canadian reviewers were rather taken aback at Sime's avant-garde interest in lower-class women's lives, including their sexual natures. Canadians were not used to reading about charwomen, munitions workers, and even prostitutes in a text that foregrounded their perspectives on life, even as told to a middle-class narrator. As Lindsey McMaster's article in this volume points out, Canadians of the day seemed reluctant to accept social criticism as part of Canadian literature, unlike historical or rural romance. *Sister Woman* sold less than 250 copies in Canada after its 1919 publication. By contrast, for some twenty-first century readers, Sime's text is significant precisely because she is a pioneer in Canadian writing in presenting ideas about feminism, about modernity, about urban life, and about men and women facing rapid societal change, all the while writing with an acute consciousness of variables like gender and class. Sime's sensibility strikes more of a chord today than her work did in 1919, at least with reviewers and book buyers.

Accordingly, the aim of this critical edition is to make available the text of the 1919 edition of *Sister Woman* published by London publisher Grant Richards (the only edition in which the book ever appeared, although copies for the Canadian market carried the imprint of Toronto publisher S. B. Gundy), in company with a sampling of the range of critical commentary book and author have inspired between 1920 and the present. The background material begins with a biographical and critical essay on Sime and her text updated from my introduction to the 1992 reprint of *Sister Woman*. Next, to give an idea of the way Sime was viewed by her contemporaries, the Documentary section reprints a 1920 review of *Sister Woman*, as well as a 1922 article about Sime published in *Saturday Night*. The Criticism section provides a selection of recent critical appraisals of the book, including both articles and book excerpts. These critical pieces are arranged in chronological order, ending with two articles written especially for this critical edition. The selections are intended to introduce the student and other readers to the book from a range of perspectives valuable to one reading the book for the first time. The Bibliography at the end of this critical edition invites the reader to follow up and examine the entire body of material devoted to *Sister Woman* to date.

The critics of the last decade whose work is presented here show how varied the analyses and debates over *Sister Woman* can be. Sime's text is rich with possibilities for interpretation. Misao Dean addresses the book as "New Woman" fiction, in an analysis that dissects the tensions and contradictions between traditional domestic/maternal ideology and the social changes of the period for women. Gerald Lynch incisively analyses the form of the book as short story cycle and its links to Fabian Socialism and to other works of Sime. Lindsey McMaster breaks ground by setting *Sister Woman* in the context of the fictional and historical figure of the working girl in early twentieth-century Canada, looking at Sime's book in relation to three other novels of the era which, unusually for the fiction of the period—which tended to shy away from urban social engagement—featured the working girl. Ann Martin considers the meaning of the symbolism of space in *Sister Woman* and links it to Sime's presentation of modernity.

Jane Watt—who has done pioneering research on Sime's life and work and recovered some of her papers—analyses the work as a "disharmonious reading of Canadian nationhood" and argues that its tensions and subversions derive from Sime's views about Canada, art, music, and women and from the influence on Sime of the ideas of English social reformer Edward Carpenter (1844-1929).

In closing, I wish to thank the publishers, Frank Tierney and Glenn Clever of Tecumseh Press, and Gerald Lynch and John Moss, co-General Editors of the Canadian Critical Edition series, as well as Janet Shorten for their support and assistance in this project. Gerald Lynch fielded my queries about the critical edition and deftly adapted his analysis of Sime from his book on Canadian short story cycles for inclusion here. All contributors speedily sent material and obtained permissions, for which many thanks. My husband and fellow academic Duncan McDowall generously helped with computer matters, as did Marianne Keyes, a computer help specialist at Carleton University. Laura Brandon, curator of the Canadian war art collection at the Canadian War Museum, kindly helped with the cover illustration.

Explanatory Notes to the Text of Sister Woman

p. 32   *Carmagnole*...A popular song and dance of the French Revolution, subsequently associated with eruptions of popular discontent.

p. 33   Harry Lauder...Scottish music hall comedian (1870-1950), famous for his Scottish ditties.

p. 45   *vade mecum*...Latin phrase (literally "go with me") — a book for ready reference; here, a catchword.

p. 57   Edward Carpenter...English writer and social reformer (1844-1929), author of works on the relationship between the sexes, including *Love's Coming of Age* (1896); popularly viewed as a prophet of "free love."

p. 60   Athanasius...Byzantine monk (c. 920-1000) who founded communal monasteries on Mount Athos.

p. 81   Una without the lion...The beautiful heroine and her protector in the first book of Edmund Spenser's sixteenth-century epic poem *The Faerie Queen.*

p. 83   like Dick Swiveller's "Marchioness" with her orange peel and water...Character in Charles Dickens's *The Old Curiosity Shop* (1840).

p. 86   *sal hepatica*...liver salts

p. 115   Æsculapius...Greco-Roman god of medicine.

p. 157   Mr. Granville-Barker...Harley Granville-Barker (1877-1946), British dramatist, critic, producer, and proponent of theatrical nationalism.

p. 193   *Nessun maggior dolore*...Quotation from Dante's *Inferno* (V, 121), the first phrase of a famous passage:

> There is no greater sorrow
> Than to be mindful of the happy time
> In misery.

SISTER WOMAN

MISS J. G. SIME
(From a Drawing by Gertrude DesClayes)

SISTER WOMAN

BY

J. G. SIME

Then gently scan your brother man,
Still gentler, sister woman.
BURNS.

CONTENTS

	PAGE
PROLOGUE	7
ALONE	9
ADRIFT	17
MUNITIONS!	26
LOVE-O'-MAN	33
ALEXINE	39
WAITING	46
AN IRREGULAR UNION	53
MOTHERHOOD	62
JACQUOT AND PIERRE	74
MR JOHNSTON	81
THE CHILD	96
THE COCKTAIL	101
THE WRESTLER	106
BABY BUNTING	110
LIVIN' UP TO IT	113
UNION	116
THE LAST HOPE	123
THE DAMNED OLD MAID	129
A PAGE FROM LIFE	133
A WOMAN OF BUSINESS	141

CONTENTS

THE SOCIAL PROBLEM 145

A CIRCULAR TOUR 152

ART 157

ROSE OF SHARON 163

THE CHARLADY 173

POLLY 185

THE BACHELOR GIRL 191

DIVORCED 198

EPILOGUE 205

PROLOGUE

"YOU women don't know what you want," he said. "Perhaps not," I said, "but you be sure we won't be happy till we get it."

He laughed.

"Be articulate then," said he.

"Did you ever try," I said to him, "to be articulate? It's not so easy as it sounds."

"You talk plenty, anyway," said he, "you women."

"Yes," I said, "that's the way we're learning to be articulate."

"It's a wearing way," he said, "for other people."

"Granted," said I. "But it's the only way. You have to talk to find out what you think, when you're a woman. Besides that, if we didn't tell you men, and keep on telling you, you'd never find out that anything was wrong with us."

He sat and puffed.

"Don't think," I said apologetically, "I'm complaining. I'm not. I think you men are patient—wonderfully, extraordinarily patient—with us. But—"

"Now," he said, "for the grievance!"

And we both laughed.

"Suppose," he said, after a bit, "suppose you try and be articulate yourself. For me—just for my benefit. I hate to have you women discontented—it makes a world that's not worth living in. And more than that, I hate to see *you* with a private grievance of your own—oh yes, you have one sometimes! Stop being antagonistic. Be articulate and tell me. Perhaps it's something I can fix. Perhaps," he said hopefully, "it's something I would *like* to fix . . ."

He sat puffing.

"Perhaps," he said, "it's yours already, only you don't know it."

"You're very nice," I answered him. "You really are." And then I said: "It's not so easy!"

Then I said: "Shall I try?"

"Do," he said.

He puffed, and I sat looking at him.

"Well," I said, after a long pause for consideration, "I'll—I'll skirt the question if you like."

"The Woman's Question?" he inquired.

"The woman's and the man's," I said. "It's the same thing. There's no difference."

"That," he said, "sounds hopeful. That's the most articulate thing I ever heard a woman say."

At that we laughed again. When people like each other and are happy they laugh easily.

"When," I asked him— "when shall I begin?"

"Now," he said, "this minute. State your grievance, madam!"

I took the cover off my typewriter and sat down before it. . . .

ALONE

HETTY GRAYSON waked up in the very early morning—and she learned what it means to open one's eyes to loss and sorrow and an aching void. She lay looking out into her little room through a mist of misery.

The first greyness of dawn was coming through the window. The room was just faintly lighted—and as the rays of light got stronger and reached farther, one familiar object after another started, as it were, into consciousness. The dressing-table with its chintz-covered chair before it—the chintz he had chosen; the bookcase with the books in it that he had given her; the pictures that he had hung up with his own hands for her; the trinkets on the pincushion that he had brought home one by one when he had been away from her—all his choice. It was his room really, not hers. It spoke of him in every inch of it. It was their room. And he lay dead downstairs . . . and she not even with him.

She lay there, and before her tired eyes her past life flitted by in restless pictures. Her home in England—how long ago, that! And then her father's death and her mother's death, and her coming out to Canada. She had come against all the ideas and wise counsel of her friends; but she was tired of them and their way of life. She wanted a change—more room. She had come to Canada and she had got it—her change.

She thought of her first days in Canada. She remembered the wonder, the infinite surprise of that first new country she had seen—the sunshine and the unexpected heat, the intensity of the burning summer days, the queer, unfinished look that gave a sort of zest to life because it made you feel how much there still was left to do, and the soft, slurred Canadian accent all about her. She had roamed to and fro, here, there and everywhere, with a girl friend she had picked up on the boat, and they had explored and made discoveries and wondered and laughed to their hearts' content. Odd, cheap, delicious meals they had had—delicious only because they were odd and different from staid old England. And she saw a picture of the Chinese restaurants and the impassively smiling, slant-eyed waiters . . . and all sorts of other lovely unexpectednesses; and she remembered how they had laughed in the warm Canadian summer sunshine. She thought of it all and she wondered if that girl was really she. Had she laughed like that lightheartedly at nothing just these few years ago? Was it possible?

And then the girl acquaintance had gone on farther—out West, to seek her fortune. And Hetty, left by herself, had turned her thoughts to work and money to live on. And almost at once she had come—here.

She thought of the evening when she had come after the place. She remembered how she had stopped all alone in the street to laugh as she wondered what the aunts at home would think if they could see her tramping along to apply for a cook-housekeeper's place. She had laughed and laughed till a man had said to her: "Come and laugh with me, dear!" And then she had stopped laughing and gone her way. And other would-be cooks and housekeepers had answered the advertisement, and while she sat waiting with them in the hall downstairs—she had wondered. And then she had come in to interview the advertiser . . . so she had met him.

She remembered his face as he sat there in his study, his eyes, and the queer sense they gave her of familiarity. Could they have met? How? Impossible! And yet she felt as if ages and ages ago . . . somewhere . . . only half-forgotten—How could it be? Impossible.

He had engaged her as his housekeeper. That was the beginning of it all. He had engaged her there and then. She had her English training in Domestic Science well behind her; the theory of how to keep a house, at any rate, she knew. He had asked her questions—how she came, and why? What relations she had left behind? And she had told him quite simply that she had come out to get a change—because she was tired of the life back there . . . and that she had no one. Only friends who disapproved . . . no one, really, at all. And then their eyes had met . . . he had engaged her.

She opened her eyes and she looked at the room. It was almost light now. The world was getting ready for the sun to rise. In a little while the room would be flooded with light. Another day. How could she bear it?

She sat up and glanced at the clock on the table by her bed—that little clock! One of the very last of all her treasures. And it said just after three. Then she'd been asleep—not three hours! *That* was why she ached . . . and her eyes ached . . . And perhaps why her soul too ached in her like that.

He lay dead downstairs. And she couldn't go and lie beside him because there were other people in the house now, and his sister was sleeping just below. She had to keep it a secret . . . even now. He was dead. She was alone. She had nothing and nobody . . . and there was nothing anywhere, ever any more. And the sun was rising on a new day.

She lay back on her pillows quite still; and in a moment those incessant pictures began again.

How she had worked at the housekeeping—to please him! When she had found the Science she had paid to learn quite insufficient for his needs, how she had worked to add to it and bolster it up and turn it into comfort for him! How he had laughed at some of her first meals . . . and then, how kindly he had told her he would take meals at the club till she had time to learn. And then, what a *furor* of cook-books—and trying! And that first *good* meal of his at home, that he had liked . . . and praised her for!

She thought how she had loved her work, and how easily it had come to her; perhaps just because she loved it. To arrange his house! To choose the meals he liked! And then to serve them—almost as he might get them at his club! She had loved it . . . and how she had treasured any scrap he had told her of pretty, elaborate meals he had had somewhere else so that she could give him just as elaborate at home. Such fun, all of it—such happiness! And behind, all the time, always that sense of having met . . . somewhere—that sense of deeply knowing him.

He had allowed her a perfect liberty from the first. She had elected to have no one else to live there, but just a Chinaman to come daily: John Ling, who had done the heavy work—the actual cleaning; and the personal things, the actual ministering to his wants, she had done herself. The folding his clothes, the putting them away, the little mendings and darnings that she used to do for him . . . she remembered how sometimes she was puzzled at her joy in doing them. There was something new in all of it; and yet, behind, somewhere, it all felt infinitely old.

As she lay there it seemed to her as if she *felt* his things again between her hands. And the faint, human scent of them . . . great tears for the first time rolled down her cheeks.

The room was brilliant now with sunshine. It poured in everywhere. Every chink and cranny seemed full of sunlight. It was unbearable.

Then came that evening when the old, past, dimly remembered intimacy and the quite new, unexpected, undreamed-of love met and seemed to blend into one. And after that night the sense of having known him somewhere faded away in the wonderful miraculous present. There was no room for any more than that.

She had gone into his study with some message, no thought in her mind but happiness in being near him, sheer delight in being useful to him—and she had stood there waiting while he wrote out some instruction for her. And as he wrote she stood looking—and looking, not thinking about him, not appraising him—just watching him—drinking him in . . . and her whole personality had seemed to take flight away from her so that it could come home . . . in him.

When he had handed her his written memorandum their hands had met. And then she had come home.

Never at any time had the thought of any wrongness troubled her. She was his, and it was right that she should be. It not only never troubled her, she had never so much as thought of it. She was his, and it was a miracle that she was his, and at the same time it was a matter of course. It had to be. In some mysterious way it always had been so. She was absolutely happy.

The first months and the first year or two went by like that. She was happy. She had never thought about herself—not consciously; if she thought at all, it was to make herself more acceptable to him. She had planned little new ways of arranging her hair, and she had suddenly got clever at sewing, making dainty things that surprised herself . . . and sometimes as she put the dainty things on, she would look at herself in the mirror with a new kind of curiosity. It was not herself she saw there, it was how he would see her if he could be looking through her eyes. And once she had the dainty things on she would look into his eyes to see what he thought of them—look eagerly—and see that he loved her.

Life had gone on like that for a long, long time. The days raced past. She kept the house and looked after Ling the Chinaman and taught him English, and read with him sometimes; and she grew to be a skilful cook, almost an artist. And when he had some men friends in, then she would show her artistry . . . and Ling would come and wait. And after they were gone he would smile at her and tell her she ought to be the *chef* at the club. And she would say to him: "But did you *really* like it? *Really? Did you?"*

She was absolutely happy so. She asked no more of life. She lived in him. It was complete.

She lay there. And the tears rolled slowly down her cheeks. And now and again a great unexpected sob shook her from head to foot. And then she impatiently felt for her handkerchief . . . tried to stop. And she heard a voice she didn't know saying sometimes: "Oh, I can't bear it . . . I can't bear it. . . ."

These were good years—unclouded. She knew no jealousy because he was so evidently fond of her. And she knew no loneliness because she had so wrapped herself in him. She lived cloistered and yet busy. Going her little daily round of shopping for his needs . . . chatting with the people in the shops . . . getting the house pretty for him . . . arranging . . . waiting for his return . . . lost in love for him. She had only one idea: how she could minister to his comfort, what more she could do to show her love.

She put up her hands to push her hair away and she felt the great coils of hair tight round her head. And then she remembered. Last night . . . after . . . she had come up and thrown herself down just as she was, and from sheer exhaustion had slept an hour or two. Yesterday . . . last night! He had said: "Hetty—"

When she took out the hairpins one by one and threw them from her, her thick dark hair came tumbling all about her and fell over her face . . . that hair he used to kiss! . . . And she threw herself back on her pillows and lay there quite still, and it seemed to her as if her heart was breaking . . . as if she could feel it breaking there, inside of her.

Then after a bit she turned over on her face, and with her hands over her ears she shut the world out . . . and the pictures came again. They shifted rapidly, unbearably before her shut eyes. And now and again she moved as if the bed was red-hot under her.

For now she saw pictures of the time that came . . . after. That time she was sorry for now . . . so sorry . . . so sorry! How could she have been so unreasonable! How could she have treated him so . . . been so unlike herself! Her low sobbing came quick and she was breathless . . . she lay there struggling. And then, after a bit, she lay quiet again, just looking—looking at what went passing before her eyes.

It was the baby did it. Her baby! The baby she couldn't have. Of course, she couldn't have it: she saw that. It couldn't be. It was a choice between it and him . . . it couldn't be, of course. How could it? But she hadn't thought she should mind . . . so much.

She saw the journey away . . . and it was done. And then she saw herself come home again. Home! Well, it had to be, of course. She wasn't questioning that. But it changed everything.

She loved him more—if that was possible. More, and differently. But the laughing time was over. The days seemed long when he was out, and lonely . . . and while she sat sewing she would think and think, and wonder why such things should be . . . and why a mother can't have her child . . . just because people will talk about it. And she had learned what it means to have small hands at your heart . . . small hands tugging. She had learned the longing of the woman to give her breast to her child. She had had days and days to learn it in.

After such days as that when he came back she would sometimes greet him coldly . . . hardly speak . . . keep away. And weeks and weeks like that. It wasn't that she didn't love him . . . but she couldn't bear to have him touch her, somehow. She was sore. And then, after those lost days, passionate repentance . . . reunion . . . and the longing to tell him what she could never make clear.

How good he had been always! She remembered. How patient! How he had welcomed her back when the bad fits were over; how he had kissed her and kissed her, and said: "Never mind, Hetty . . . never mind, dear." And how she used to answer between her sobs: "Oh, but I *do* mind. I do mind. . . ."

The baby! That was the crux of it all. If she hadn't ever . . . had to lose it . . . there needn't ever have been any trouble. But that changed everything. The little dinners . . . those were a torment now. She was jealous of them; jealous of the men that came; jealous of his sister who sometimes came there . . . miserably jealous of everything that happened when she couldn't be

by his side. And how could she be? How *could* she? She hated
herself, she despised herself as she lay there . . . and she knew
that if it had all to be gone over again she would be the very
same. Yes, the very same. For she wanted to be his *openly*. The
secrecy, which had made her laugh at first, the delicious secret
between the two of them that she had loved to play with like a
toy . . . she was sick of it. Her heart turned from it. She loathed
it. Sometimes she wanted to climb out on the leads at the top of
the house and cry out, as loud as she could, to the whole world:
"I'm his. Do you hear? . . . I'm his!" And she couldn't breathe it
to a living soul.

She got restless. Long, lonely days . . . and sometimes
evenings still more unhappy. Those evenings when she had said
things . . . Oh, if she could unsay them! If she could have those
evenings back again! Just one of them. What was wanting? She
had him. She had him there close beside her . . . loving . . . full
of love for her . . . patient like that just because he was so full of
love. . . .

He lay dead downstairs.

She sat up, bolt upright, stiff from head to foot, and she
pushed her hair out of her eyes and strained it back from her
brow, and she sat there thinking with her head between her
hands.

He was dead and her baby had never been born. She was
alone.

The pictures stopped while she sat there thinking. He lay
dead downstairs. He was dead. He could never speak to her any
more . . . she could never hear him say again: "Hetty, Hetty, if
you could only be half-happy—"

He was dead.

She took her hands away from her eyes and she sat there. A
ray of sunlight landed on a picture of a child he had given her . . .
after: a boy with rings of fine silky hair, and downcast eyes, and
a pouting mouth. She had loved it. And now she pushed the
very sight of it away from her, passionately, with both her
hands, and she turned away from it and sat looking through her
window into the sunny world outside.

What if—?

She slipped out of bed, and mechanically she went over to
the mirror. She had to see a human face, if it was only the

reflection of her own. Could *that* be Hetty Grayson in the miror?

The face looked at her. It was stern and white, and its cheeks were wet with tears, and its swollen eyes looked at her as if from a great distance. Of what use was life to a face like that? Those days when she felt his arms warm round her . . . and when he had taught her miracles . . . life was worth while then. And afterwards . . . even then! When she had forgotten herself and her sorrow for a moment, and had lost herself in him again, and life in his arms had seemed a more wonderful thing than ever, just because of all she had suffered . . . *then* it was worth while to live. But now?

What was before her? A new place somewhere . . . wages . . . exactitude . . . the employer and employed. What else?

The brilliant sun came pouring in. It lighted up the stern white face in the glass. And the swollen eyes looked out at her—questioningly. She stood like that for a long while.

And then suddenly the eyes changed. There was no longer any questioning in them. And in the glass Hetty Grayson saw the figure raise its arms and coil up the heavy hair that hung all about it, and make itself neat . . . rapidly . . . unself-consciously. She seemed to be just watching it; she had no connection with it. And then she saw it pause a moment with its closed hand at its mouth. And she saw its lips move, and she seemed to see— or was it hear?—the words somewhere: "And then it'll not be a secret any more!"

Hetty Grayson unclasped the chain that hung about her neck, and she took a ring off it, and she clasped the chain again. And she slipped the ring on to one of her fingers, and lifted it to her lips, and kissed it . . . and kissed it. And her tears rained down upon it. And once she said: "My baby. . . ."

She went over to the door of her room and she opened it softly and she listened. And then she slipped out into the quiet-ness, and ran downstairs noiselessly, in her bare feet. And as she went she kept whispering to herself: "They'll find us together. It'll not be a secret any more. . . ."

When, at last, she could lie down beside him, she reached up and took his hands in hers, and she laid her warm face close to his—and waited.

ADRIFT

S HE came in to sew for me, but she wasn't that awful infliction—the woman who comes in to sew by the day. I liked her and I liked to have her. There was something about her blue eyes that it gave me pleasure to look at; and she had that most charming and rarest thing in woman—a merry laugh. How she had kept it, God only knows. Life had taken hold of her and twisted her all askew; she had gone as wrong as woman can go, and she had suffered correspondingly. Yet she had kept her laugh. A child's laugh! A long, low, rippling sound like happy water falling, falling over clear, clean stones in the sunshine. Such a pretty thing, a laugh like that. I loved to hear her.

She could sew. Sewing had been her original profession; but by the time she came to sew for me it was not her profession any more. She had left it for a sadder trade. Her young body was for sale to any man that cared to buy. And her clever hands were idle.

I had come to know her quite by chance. She had been in hospital, and once as I was passing up the ward to see some other patient, her blue eyes met mine. I stopped and spoke to her, and we talked a little—a very little. It was her blue eyes that kept talking, saying all kinds of unsayable things to me. They had seen life on its difficult side.

And when they met other eyes that could understand—they spoke.

When she was well enough to come out of hospital I asked her to come and sew. She had told me of the old dressmaking life, little anecdotes about it; little reminiscences; when she found that I knew Paris, *her* Paris, she was only too ready to speak. Paris as she knew it, Paris before the war, full of all the things the Newer World is destitute of, Paris at night with the river winding through it like a serpent, and the lights reflected! . . . She loved it. As she talked of it, her thin face would light up, and her blue eyes would stop saying unsayable things, and she would grow young again, and her face would be irradiated

with a smile. Willingly she came to me, and I looked out things
for her to sew: enough to keep her busy till she was strong
enough to go back to—work.

She sewed well. She had that instinct for sewing that one
finds in certain women. Why she cut and stitched as she did she
could not tell you; she only knew she had to do it that way—she
created her little wares as a poet creates his; half-unconsciously,
as a thrush throws out its notes. As she worked she would stop
sometimes and hold the thing off from her a little and eye it; and
with her head tilted back so that she could see it better, she
would talk to it. "C'est beau, ça!" she would say; "c'est bien la
chose!" Or to me, perhaps: "Regardez, madame. C'est un joli
mouvement, ça, n'est-ce pas?" And when I said it was indeed a
joli mouvement, she would flash out a sudden smile at me—
happy, radiant: "J'aime les jolies choses, moi!" she would say.
And if I left her alone for a bit I would hear her singing to herself in a low little voice, crooning over her work as she turned
and twisted it in her supple fingers.

She was happy, working in my little flat. She would look
round her sometimes and say involuntarily—it seemed as if the
words came out of her by their own force: "Comme vous êtes
bien ici, madame! C'est si joli. Et comme c'est bon d'être chez
soi!" If I asked her where *she* lived she evaded answering me.
"One lives where one can," she said once. Even her address she
would never give me. "No," she would say to me, shaking her
head; "no; tell me only when to come. I come, madame, trust
me. It is better this way." And when I fixed the day she would
assent at once with no remark; and on the appointed day, as the
clock struck, she would ring my bell. "Bonjour, madame." In
she would come, smiling, rubbing her hands: "Comme il fait
froid, mon Dieu!" And even before she took her things off, she
would run to her work of yesterday to see if it still retained the
joli mouvement that had made her happy. "Oui, c'est encore
joli," she would say. And then she would trill out her low,
delighted laugh just like a merry child.

At lunch-time we dropped work and came together into my
little kitchen. Then was Émilie in her element. "Can you cook?"
I had asked her once while she was still in hospital. And with a
little shrug she had answered me: "Oh oui . . . une bonne cuisine
bourgeoise. Rien d'extraordinaire. . . ."

Une bonne cuisine bourgeoise—that was what it was. Good, simple savoury France, brought out to Canada. *Omelettes, biftecks, côtelettes—pommes de terre frites.* The way I always think of Émilie is frying French potatoes. *Pommes de terre frites!* What joy! What ecstasy! "They don't know the way to fry them here," she would say to me. "Ah, ces grands morceaux! Ces gobets!" And she would fall to slicing her potatoes carefully, delicately, lovingly. "Comme ça!" And then immerse them in the boiling fat and watch them tenderly. "Oh, comme c'est bon chez soi!" she would say again to me. And her blue eyes would speak . . . and speak.

For a long time we discussed merely—things. She had the natural intelligence of her country-women, and we talked quite comfortably of—things. She passed her criticisms frankly on the newer land she had come to live in. "Voilà des barbares, n'est-ce pas?" she would say to me. "Des vrais barbares. Comme les femmes crient!" And in her prettily modulated voice she would tell me tales of men and women in the houses she had roomed at—ugly, unsavoury tales of uncleanliness and dishonour. If I cried out at her: "Émilie, how can you live there? How can you live like that?" she would meet my eyes gravely with her blue ones. "One lives as one can," she would say.

One afternoon late in November the snow was falling— falling. The whole world was blurred with it. And the wind kept driving it against the window-panes as we sat there working together. Émilie sat in her chair close up to the table bending over the sewing in her hands: and the light of the lamp fell on her fair hair in such a way that it seemed to make a halo round her face. She was thin yet and there were little lines at the sides of her eyes. And round her mouth there were other lines. She was twenty-three years old, and her face was full of past experience.

"How droll, madame," she said suddenly, "the way we love these clothes of ours. Look, it is pretty," and she held the little thing—the last garment of mine she had to make—from her at arm's-length, and looked at it.

I looked too. "It is pretty, Émilie," I said.

"Yes," she said; and stopped a minute. "But it is droll that for such things as that we women sell our—souls."

"Do you want pretty things so much, my dear?" I said.

She shook her head.

"Not now," she said. "That was the beginning."

Then, that last afternoon that we spent together, she talked. Not just of things, but of herself. She talked in a low tone as if the things she spoke of were asleep and she didn't wish to disturb them overmuch. And sometimes she would glance at me, and her eyes would finish anything she left untold. As she spoke she worked; and now and then she would interrupt herself to ask me something: how I liked it; if I would have it this way or that. And then she would go on with her story again in that low voice: "We were poor," she said, "always poor. Papa was ill as far away as I remember. He drank, Papa—then he was too ill to work. And Maman kept a little shop where we sold . . . des choses."

She glanced up at me.

"Des choses," she said; "sugar, des pâtes, candies"—in her vocabulary she had some words in the New World tongue— "newspapers . . . que sais-je? Tout ce qui fait argent. A gé-né-*ralle* store. Little bits of everything."

She sewed.

"Maman," she said, "was hard. Dure!"

She thought a minute.

"When one has nothing one is hard, perhaps," she said. "And," she went on, "there were children!—c'était Papa ça. I was the first, then there was little Jeanne and David, then Berthe . . . how many more! Always a baby to take about. Something to care for always—never a moment."

Again she sewed. And then began again:

"Maman worked. She worked the whole day long. She cleaned the house and cooked, and tended Papa and sold things in the shop. She worked. When Maman had her babies then it was I who had to clean and cook, and tend Papa and sell things in the shop. . . ."

She stopped a minute.

"And every day all the year round," she said, "I it was who took the papers to our customers."

Over her work she sighed and shook her head a little.

"Ah, qu'ils sont lourds," she said. "Papers to sell! Ces maudites choses! I had them in a bag slung at my side, like this. . . .

Up she sprang.

"Look a moment, look, madame," she said to me; and half-way across the room she trailed as a bird trails brokenly when it is winged.

"See," she said, "to one side. All bent. Comme ça. . . ."

She sighed again. Her eyes met mine.

"Each day," she said. "Comme ça—et ça fait mal. And for five papers sold only one sou of profit. And as you sell your paper, each time—thank you! Merci! Il le faut."

She sat and took her work again and settled to it with little rapid movements of her hands.

"Five times," she said. " 'Merci, monsieur! Merci, madame!' Five times for every sou you earn!"

Her eyes met mine again.

"I never meet a child to-day," she said, "who carries papers, but I share my gains with it."

She sewed.

"That," she said, "was mon enfance. Sometimes I suffered. But if I told Maman I suffered she would say, 'Tais-toi. Ce n'est rien, ça.' "

She glanced out through the window at the driving snow.

"Maman was hard—dure," she said again.

She sewed a little without saying any more. Then in her soft voice she went on.

"When I was twelve years old," she said, "I went to learn to sew. 'It is full time,' said Maman, 'that you earn. Jeanne is old enough to take your place. Earn, you. Gain and bring money home.' "

She stitched a moment and the lamplight fell on her.

"Believe me, madame," she said, "I earned nothing—and Maman knew I would not earn. Before her marriage she had been couturière; she merely spoke that way to spur me. I was the trotter—and they sent me trotting. I ran from shop to shop. I matched. I carried samples and I brought back things . . . I ran! And if I had a minute's time they set me sewing. I worked—I worked. And on my way to trot I carried newspapers each morning—still five to sell to earn one sou. At night when I got home again there was little Jeanne to help. . . ."

She looked at me and laughed—that pretty laugh!

"Ce n'est pas gai vivre comme ça," she said; and into that little phrase she put all her apologies for grumbling.

"When they found out that I could learn to sew," she said, when she began again, "I ceased to trot."

Émilie's eyes met mine.

"Sewing came easily—"

I nodded.

"And," she said, "I loved it. It was a big atelier that I had come to work for. Such orders! And such robes! Such—ah, madame, tant de beauté! I loved the work. I loved it. . . ."

She stopped to find her words.

"Do you know, madame," she said, "the way it feels to love to do a thing? Not for what you get from it—not to gain anything—just to love to do it?"

"Yes," I said.

Émilie smiled.

"That was the way I loved to sew," she said. "The richness of the stuffs between my fingers—the softness of the silks. I loved to feel and touch and watch things growing as my fingers worked on them."

She drew a deep, long sigh.

"C'est beau," she said, "un sentiment comme ça!"

When she said that, I knew the reason why I loved to watch her hands at work—knew why I loved to see Émilie manipulate a drapery—taper off a seam. Once when I went to see a sculptor long ago in Florence I loved in the same way to watch him work. Such delicate workmanship—such loving care!

"I loved the work, madame, believe me," Émilie went on, "and yet—and yet—I gained so little. They pay so very, very little. At home Papa suffered always. Maman had to tend him more and more. Adolphe was in hospital—comment dire?—épileptique. And Jeanne, my little sister, worked—worked always. Ah," Émilie said, "what a home! Five thank-yous for a sou. That is not life. . . ."

She paused at her work, then held it out to me.

"Tiens, madame," she said to me, "comme ceci—ou comme ça? Lequel préferéz-vous?

"Five years I worked like that," she said, when I had made my choice, "five years. And then Jeanne came to work, and in the mornings we carried the newspapers between us."

Émilie looked across at me. Her eyes had grown quite soft.

"Jeanne," she said, "was so pretty—like a flower. And gentle . . ."

She smiled.

"Sometimes," she said, "she was so pretty that when we passed the kiosks I used to buy her muguets—lilies, do you call them?—with the money for my lunch."

Still she smiled.

"A spray—one only. And she loved it. But when I pinned it in for her she used to say to me: 'Ah, Émilie, ça coûte dix fois merci!' "

Émilie laughed a little.

"That," she said, "was the way we counted all our money."

She sat there silently. She said no more.

"Émilie," I said at last, "why did you leave the dressmaking, my dear?"

Still she was silent for a minute.

"Madame," she said at last, "it was like this."

She stopped again, but this time it was only to collect words to speak with.

"Sometimes," she said, "I was happy. But sometimes— sometimes that other feeling would come over me—that I too must live."

She sewed a while.

"I was clever," Émilie said. "I could not only use my needle, I had the—the *feeling*. I was quick—I learned. And when they noticed, then they let me come downstairs and help to fit the robes. . . ."

She looked at me.

"Downstairs," she said, "I saw such lovely things. Ladies came dressed as flowers are dressed—vraies femmes du monde. And I would lend a hand and touch those lovely things—like clouds at night—like flowering trees! Things that would ripple . . ."

Émilie looked at me intently.

"Madame," she said, "things like that are beautiful!"

"Were you not happy then," I asked her, "just to be amongst them?—just to lend your hands?"

She hesitated.

"At first," she said, "but then—"

Again she hesitated.

"Sometimes, madame," she said, "there would come actresses—des femmes entretenues—que sais-je? These were no richer than myself when they began . . . and perfect—"

She stopped.

"I, too, had things to sell," she said.

She stopped again.

"Madame," Émilie said, "did you ever think? We were up with sunrise and before it—just to work. We left our papers on our way to work—and all day long we worked. And we came back at night to work again. We worked—it was our life. For what?"

She stopped her sewing.

"We were young," she said.

She looked at me. Her eyes looked into mine—they had begun to speak again.

"And," she said, "on our way to work men spoke to us. They spoke—they offered . . ."

She stopped.

"Jeanne," she said, "was so pretty; like a flower. . . ."

She sewed again.

"You see," she said, "you make yourself a dress—a little robe. You make it. How? You have no money and no time. And yet you make it."

She drew her breath.

"You make a dress like that because you *want* it."

She drew her breath again.

"You make yourself a little robe like that," she said, "because you have to have it."

She sewed a while.

"And the first time you wear your dress, perhaps," she said, "some other woman comes—a woman no better than yourself— and dressed superbly. You look at her—"

She stopped a second, then went on rapidly:

"You look at her—like starlight—perfect! And you—with the same things to sell as she—"

Suddenly her eyes filled with tears.

"Ah, madame," she said, "my little dress. Cette petite robe! Rien—rien du tout! Et je me suis donné tant de peine. . . ."

She sewed. Then suddenly she looked up.

"From then to now I have not sewed," she said to me.

"Émilie," I said to her, "you have sold yourself into slavery, my dear."

Her eyes looked into mine.

"What is that word?" she said.

"*Esclavage*—slavery, my dear," I said to her.

"Ah," she said; and sat and thought a minute.

"Yet," she said, "always to see those things. Always to wish and wish—and gain so little. No change—no chance. Marry—and lead a life like Maman? Esclavage, ça! No. . . ."

Her eyes kept looking into mine. They said things.

"To-night," she said, "I am ill . . . Oh," she said, "I am ill."

The lamplight fell on her. She looked old.

"One way," she said, "you go on wishing—longing. The other way—you *know*. It is a choice."

"Émilie," I said, bending over to her and laying my hand on hers, "let me find you work to do—sewing . . .!"

She shook her head.

The snow came drifting up against the window-pane.

MUNITIONS!

BERTHA MARTIN sat in the street car in the early morning going to her work. Her work was munitions. She had been at it exactly five weeks.

She sat squeezed up into a corner, just holding on to her seat and no more, and all round her were women and girls also working at munitions—loud, noisy, for ever talking—extraordinarily happy. They sat there filling the car with their two compact rows, pressed together, almost in one another's laps, joking, chewing tobacco—flinging the chewed stuff about.

It wasn't in the least that they were what is technically known as "bad women." Oh no—no! If you thought that, you would mistake them utterly. They were decent women, good, self-respecting girls, for the most part "straight girls" —with a black sheep here and there, to be sure, but where aren't there black sheep here and there? And the reason they made a row and shrieked with laughter and cracked an unseemly jest or two was simply that they were turned loose. They had spent their lives caged, most of them, in shop or house, and now they were drunk with the open air and the greater freedom and the sudden liberty to do as they liked and damn whoever stopped them.

Bertha Martin looked round at her companions. She saw the all sorts that make the world. Here and there was a pretty, young, flushed face, talking—talking—trying to express something it felt inside and couldn't get out. And here and there Bertha Martin saw an older face, a face with a knowledge of the world in it and that something that comes into a woman's eyes if certain things happen to her, and never goes out of them again. And then Bertha Martin saw quite elderly women, or so they seemed to her—women of forty or so, decent bodies, working for someone besides themselves—they had it written on their faces; and she saw old women—old as working women go—fifty and more, sitting there with their long working lives behind them and their short ones in front. And now and then some woman would draw her snuff-box from her shirt-waist and it would pass up and down the line and they would all take great pinches of the brown, pungent powder and stuff it up their noses—and laugh and laugh . . . Bertha Martin looked round the car and she couldn't believe it was she who was sitting in it. It was the very early spring. The white March sunshine came streaming into the car, and when Bertha, squeezed sideways in her corner, looked through the window, she saw the melting snow everywhere—piles and piles of it uncleared because the men whose job it was to clear it were at the war. She saw walls of snow by the sides of the streets—they went stretching out into infinity. And the car went swinging and lurching between them, out through the city and into the country where the factory was. There were puddles and little lakes of water everywhere; winter was melting away before the birth of another spring.

Bertha looked. She looked up into the clear—into the crystal clearness of the morning sky. It was the time of the spring skies of Canada—wonderful, delicate, diaphanous skies that come every spring to the Northern Land—skies the colour of bluebells and primroses—transparent, translucent, marvellously beautiful. Bertha looked up into the haze of colour—and she smiled. And then she wondered why she smiled.

It was the very early springtime.

Just five weeks before and Bertha had been a well-trained servant in a well-kept, intensely self-respecting house—a house where no footfall was heard on the soft, long-piled rugs; where the lights were shaded and the curtains were all drawn at night; where the mistress lay late in bed and "ordered" things; where life was put to bed every night with hot bottles to its feet; where no one ever spoke of anything that mattered; where meals were paramount. There had Bertha Martin lived five long, comfortable years.

She had gone about her business capably. She had worn her uniform like any soldier—a white frock in the mornings and a cap upon her head, and her hair had been orderly, her apron accurately tied. She had been clean. There were no spring skies in sight—or else she had not looked to see them. She had got up—not too unreasonably early—had had her early morning cup of tea with the other servants, had set the dining-room breakfast, waited on it—quiet—respectful—as self-respecting as the house. And in the afternoons there she had been in her neat black gown with her cap and apron immaculate—her hair still orderly and unobtrusive—everything about her, inside and out, still self-respecting and respectful. She had "waited on table," cleaned silver, served tea, carried things everlastingly in and out, set them on tables, taken them off again, washed them, put them away, taken them out again, reset tables with them—it was a circular game with never any end to it. And she had done it well. "Martin is an excellent servant," she had heard the lady of the house say once. "I can trust her thoroughly."

One afternoon in the week she went out. At a certain hour she left the house; at another certain hour she came back again. If she was half-an-hour late she was liable to be questioned: "Why?" And when she had given her explanation then she would hear the inevitable "Don't let it occur again." And Sunday—every other Sunday—there was the half day, also at certain hours. Of course—how otherwise could a well-run house *be* well run? And down in the kitchen the maids would dispute as to whether you got out half-an-hour sooner last time and so must go half-an-hour later this—they would quarrel and squabble over the silliest little things. Their horizon was so infinitesimally small, and they were so much too comfortable— they ate so much too much and they did so far too little—what could they do but squabble? They were never all on speaking-terms at one time together. Either the old cook was taking the housemaid's part or she and the housemaid were at daggers drawn; and they all said the same things over and over and over again—to desperation.

Bertha Martin looked up at the exquisite sky—and she smiled. The sun came streaming in, and the girls and women talked and jabbered and snuffed and chewed their tobacco and spat it out. And sometimes when the car conductor put his head in at the door they greeted him with a storm of chaff—a hail of witticisms—a tornado of personalities. And the little French-Canadian, overpowered by numbers, would never even try to break a lance with them. He would smile and shrug and put his hands up to his ears and run the door back between himself and them. And the women would laugh and clap their hands and stamp with their feet and call things to him—shout. . . .

Bertha turned to the girl next her—nearly atop of her—and looked her over. She was a fragile-looking, indoors creature—

saleslady was written all over her—with soft rings of fair curled hair on her temples, and a weak, smiling mouth, and little useless feet in her cheap, high-heeled pumps. She was looking intently at a great strap of a girl opposite, with a great mouth on her, out of which was reeling a broad story.

"My, ain't she the girl!" said Bertha's little neighbour; and with the woman's inevitable gesture, she put her two hands up to her hair behind, and felt, and took a hairpin out here and there and put it in again.

She turned to Bertha.

"Say, ain't she the girl alright? Did you hear?"

Bertha nodded.

The little indoors thing turned and glanced at Bertha—took her in from head to foot with one feminine look.

"You gittin' on?" she said.

"Fine!" said Bertha.

The eyes of the women met. They smiled at one another. Fellow-workers—out in the world together. That's what their eyes said: Free! And then the little creature turned away from Bertha—bent forward eagerly. Another of the stories was coming streaming out.

"Ssh! . . . ssh!" cried some of the older women. But their voices were drowned in the sea of laughter as the climax took possession of the car. The women rocked and swayed—they clutched each other—they shrieked.

"Where's the harm?" the big strap cried.

Five weeks ago and Bertha had never heard a joke like that. Five weeks ago she would hardly have taken in the utter meaning of that climax. Now! Something in her ticked—something went beating. She smiled—not at the indecency, not at the humour. What Bertha smiled at was the sense of liberty it gave her. She could hear stories if she liked. She could *act* stories if she liked. She was earning money—good money—she was capable and strong. Yes, she was strong, not fragile like the little thing beside her, but a big, strong girl—twenty-four—a woman grown—alive.

It seemed a long, dim time ago when all of them sat round that kitchen table to their stated meals at stated hours. Good, ample, comfortable meals. Plenty of time to eat them. No trouble getting them—that was the cook's affair—just far too much to eat and too much time to eat it in. Nothing to think about. Inertia. A comfortable place. What an age ago it seemed! And yet she had expected to spend her life like that—till she married someone! She never would have thought of "giving in her notice" if it hadn't been for Nellie Ford. How well Bertha remembered it—that Sunday she met Nellie—a Nellie flushed, with shining eyes.

"I'm leaving," Nellie had said to her. "I'm leaving—for the factory!"

And Bertha had stopped, bereft of words.

"*The factory* . . .!" she had said. That day the factory had sounded like the bottomless pit. "The factory . . .!"

"Come on," Nellie had said, "come on—it's fine out there. You make good money. Give in your notice—it's the life."

And Bertha had listened helplessly, feeling the ground slipping.

"But, Nellie—" she kept saying.

"It's the life," Nellie had kept reiterating; "it's the life, I tell you. Come on, Bert, *sure* it's the life. Come on—it's great out there. We'll room together if you'll come."

Then Nellie had told her hurriedly, brokenly, as they walked along that Sunday afternoon, all that she knew about the factory. What Agnes Dewie, that was maid to Lady Something once—what *she* said. "It was great!" That's what she said. "Liberty," said Agnes Dewie, "a room you paid for, good money, disrespect to everything, nothing above you—freedom. . . ."

Nellie had panted this out to Bertha. "Come on, come *on*, Bert," she had said; "it's time we lived."

And slowly the infection had seized on Bertha. The fever touched her blood—ran through it. Her mental temperature flew up. She was a big girl, a slow-grower, young for her years, with a girl's feelings in her woman's body. But Nellie Ford had touched the spring of life in her. After that Sunday when Bertha looked round the quiet, self-respecting house—she hated it. She hated the softness of it—the quietness—hated the very comfort. What did all these things matter? Nellie Ford had said: "It's time we lived."

Bertha gazed upward through the window of the car—twisted and turned so that she could look right into the morning blue. The car was clear of city life. It sped along a country road.

Fields were on either side, and only now and then a solitary house. Great trees stretched out bare branches.

Then in that far-off life came the giving in of the notice. Bertha remembered the old cook's sour face—that old sour face past every hope of life and living. Could one grow to look like that? Can such things be? "You'll live to rue the day, my lady!" said the cook. And Bertha remembered how the lady at the head of things had said: "Do you realise that you'll *regret* leaving a good place like this?" And then, more acidly: "I wouldn't have believed it of you, Martin." And as she turned to go: "If you choose to reconsider—"

Regret! Reconsider! Never again would she hear bells and have to answer them. Never again would someone say to her: "Take tea into the library, Martin." Never again need she say: "Yes, ma'am." Think of it! Bertha smiled. The sun came streaming in on her—she smiled.

Liberty! Liberty to work the whole day long—ten hours at five and twenty cents an hour—in noise and grime and wet. Damp floors to walk on. Noise—distracting noise all round one. No room to turn or breathe. No time to stop. And then at lunch-time no ample comfortable meal—some little hurried lunch of something you brought with you. Hard work. Long hours. Discomfort. Strain. That was about the sum of it, of all that she had gained . . . but then, the sense of freedom! The joy of being done with cap and apron. The feeling that you could draw your breath—speak as you liked—wear overalls like men—curse if you wanted to.

Oh, the relief of it! The going home at night, dead-tired, to where you had your room. Your own! The poor, ill-cooked suppers—what a taste to them! The deep, dreamless sleep. And Sunday—if you ever got a Sunday off—when you could lie abed, no one to hunt you up, no one to call you names and quarrel with you. Just Nellie there.

What did it matter if you had no time to stop or think or be? What did anything matter if life went pulsing through you amidst dirt and noise and grime? The old life—that treading round with brush and dust-pan—that making yourself noiseless with a duster: "Martin, see you dust well *beneath* the bed." "Yes, ma'am." And now the factory! A new life with other women working round you—bare-armed—grimy—

roughened—unrestrained. What a change! What a sense of broadening out! What . . .!

Bertha Martin smiled. She smiled so that a woman opposite smiled back at her; and then she realised that she was smiling. She felt life streaming to her very finger-tips. She felt the spring pass through her being—insistent and creative. She felt her blood speak to her—say things it never said when she was walking softly in the well-ordered house she helped to keep for five long, comfortable years. "Selfish to leave me." That was what the lady of the house had said to her. "Selfish—you're all selfish. You think of nothing but yourselves."

Well—why not? What if that were true? Let it go anyway. That half-dead life was there behind . . . and Bertha Martin looked out at the present. The car went scudding in the country road. There was the Factory—the Factory, with its coarse, strong, beckoning life—its noise—its dirt—its men.

Its men! And suddenly into Bertha Martin's cheek a wave of colour surged. Yesterday—was it yesterday?—that man had caught her strong, round arm as she was passing him—and held it.

Her breath came short. She felt a throbbing. She stopped smiling—and her eyes grew large.

It was the very early spring.

Then suddenly the flock of women rose—felt in the bosoms of their shirt-waists for their cigarettes and matches—surged to the door—talking—laughing—pushing one another—the older ones expostulating.

And, massed together in the slushy road, they stood, lighting up, passing their matches round—happy—noisy—fluttered— not knowing what to do with all the life that kept on surging up and breaking in them—waves of it—wave on wave. Willingly would they have fought their way to the Munitions Factory. If they had known the *Carmagnole* they would have danced it in the melting snow. . . .

It was the spring.

LOVE-O'-MAN

ELSIE came to see me—Elsie, that old cook of mine, of whose eloquent eyes and fluent conversational powers I have always cherished such a fond remembrance. She was on a week's holiday, she told me, and half-an-hour of that holiday she chose to lavish on me. It may have been the interval since I saw her last that made her seem more Scotch than ever; but this morning it seemed to me as if Harry Lauder himself would lilt with an Englishy clip if I listened to him after her.

Elsie had seen bits of the world, here and there. She started life in the West Country somewhere, I believe: loved, married— but not the lover—and became a widow there; and only left it, I fancy, because her restless spirit yearned for "mair than whit Scotland had tae gie her."

Ten years ago, at any rate, she came out to Canada and learned, as the immigrant has to do, from the bitter winters and the mellow summers of the New World: then, when she had absorbed her share of Canada, she passed on to the New England States to see what *they* would do for her.

Elsie has been, and still is, a handsome woman. Her hair is white, her skin is lined, but her dark eyes are soft and velvety as a girl's. Her forehead is ample, her mouth is sensitive, her slightest gesture is alive with vital energy. She has seen; she is as keen as seven or seventeen to see more; so will she be at seventy.

"The warld's big," said she to me to-day, "and me naught but an auld wife . . . yet mair wad I ha'e o't afore I turn up my taes tae the flowers, mem. I wadna dee jist yet awhile gin I could ha'e my w'y."

"You won't," I said, with certainty; "you'll live, Elsie, and work your way to seeing plenty yet."

Under her hat-brim her dark eyes looked out at me enigmatically.

"And to begin with," said I, "when are you coming back to us in Canada?"

"Never that, mem," said she, "and nevermair. Ye maun aye gang forrit, ye ken. And I'm no sayin' but there's a generosity like," continued Elsie, " 'at comes at ye for yer wark i' the States, mem, when a's said and dune. Ye'se hairdly credit, mebbe, at me pittin' past my twa hunderd dollars . . . and no there my twa years yet. And it's lang ye'se wark i' the auld land," said she, "afore ye'se pit past sic a like siller as yon for your bairn."

"All that you save is for your daughter, then?" said I, and as she nodded yes to me, I added: "Yes, you're right, Elsie . . . the Old Country's not so generous as all that comes to, I'm afraid."

"No' that generous nor no' that free," said Elsie.

"They're no druv tae mak' sae muckle o' ye back there, ye ken, guid wark bein' easy come by at ony turn i' bonnie Scotland. But the States," said she, "i' the States, mem, they'se fair forced tae mak' a democracy like, as they ca' it, guid wark bein' that scarce and haird tae light upo'. And wi' democreetical w'ys," said Elsie, "there's nae sic a like sweepin' o' ye up wi' the dirt, mem; they're that afeared tae loss ye. But mair an extry dollar bill mebbe, and whiles a sweet word wi' it, comin' on-expected like at ye for the sairvice o' yer hands. . . ."

"Then," said I, with most officious friendliness, "then I suppose you're settled down for life where you're so lucky?"

She paused and took a thought.

"It's a dilennium like," said she at last. "Whiles thinks I tae mysell, I'll mebbe better rest my banes . . . and whiles sic a like thocht as yon'll fair stick i' my craw. For the warld's a braw sicht," said Elsie," and fain am I, mem, tae get my share o't!"

"But perhaps you've got all that you're meant to get already," said I unfeelingly.

"Mebbe aye," said she, "and yet, for a' that, mem, whatever comes my w'y yet . . . I'll tak'."

She sighed.

"And gin it's God's wull," said she, "I'll settle . . . and me no bearin' Him ony grudge like for His deceesion. For gin a woman's anest past the flower o' her youth, mem, ane place is the spit o' anither for the likes o' her. There's nae man, no' the very man o' her heart and him at her side ance mair . . . that'll tak' heed o' her goin' out . . . na, nor yet o' her comin' in again gin her heid's like the snaw. . . ."

"Elsie," said I," that's the second time you've talked of being old. What do you mean by it? Two years ago you never used to talk like that."

"It's no' 'at I'm that auld," said she, "but I'm no' that young. Fine ken I that, mem, by the e'e the men-folk disna cast upo' me as I gang my w'ys. A body'll mind the glance o' the man's e'e as it rests upo' the lassie," said she, "and weel does a body mind the feel o' the lassie's heart as her cheek grew rosy wi' the pleasure o't."

"Elsie," I said, "you know too much!"

"I ken whit I ken, that's true," said she. "For I'se nae auld lass, mem . . . it's a woman 'at I am. And there's a differ!"

"What kind of a differ?" said I.

"Weel, gin ye speir at me," said Elsie, "an auld lass kens mebbe the taste o' her meat and the peace o' her sleep . . .! But a woman's kent the feel o' a man's airms haudin' her close and the warmth o' his mouth upo' her ain."

She stopped, and her velvety eyes looked back into the years. "Ye'll mind yon," said she. "And gin ye dinna mind . . . ye kenna whit it means tae be a woman."

"Elsie," said I, "was it your husband?"

"Na," she said, "it wasna him, mem . . . kind body 'at he was tae me! Marriage wasna mair nor kill or cure wi' me, mem. And it wasna for the love o' my guidman 'at I bore him a wean . . . na, nor kent the feel o' the wee mouth at the breist. It was Jamie, mem . . . afore I was mairried on ony man. Jamie it was . . . Jamie 'at garred me grow the woman I'se warkin' out the noo."

"But how, Elsie?" I said—"working out what?"

For I saw that in the mood that was on her I had only to ask to know; and I had always wanted to know what lay behind the velvety softness of her eyes.

"Warkin' out i' yer ainsell whit's anither's," said Elsie, "is ane o' thae things that ye dae mair than ye ken how tae speak mebbe. . ."

She stopped and pulled her mind together, as it were, before clearing it out for my benefit.

"Ye'll mind," she said at last, "how the woman sleeps i' ye at the first . . .?"

She paused to consider how she could make it strong enough.

"Ye'll mind," said she, "when ye kent nae mair than the sun shinin' doun upo' ye . . . and you lo'in' the warmth o't?"

She looked inquiringly at me and I nodded, and the nod,

apparently, carried conviction with it, for she went on with a more certain note in her voice.

"There's some," said she, "and no that few neither, 'at gangs back tae the gerse kennin' nae mair than jist about whit that comes tae. They'll ken 'at the sun's yelly and the mune's white . . . and then they'll tell ye they ken whit life is!"

She nodded slowly once or twice at me and I nodded back at her.

"Mem," said she, "there's but the twa things 'at learns the lassie and wakes the woman i' her breist—and them twa things is a man and a wean. Gin it's the mither 'at sleeps i' the lassie, it's the turn o' the quickened wean and the saftness o't as it sleeps i' her airms 'at learns her. And mebbe," said she, "the maist o' us learns mair frae the like o' yon than whit we'll learn frae we'r ain heids."

"That's so," said I, and as our eyes met we saw straight down into one another's souls.

"But there's anither kind," said she, "and her mebbe no jist the mither lass. And for yon," she said slowly, "it's no the suck o' the wean's bit mouth 'at gars her ken . . . it's the sweetness o' whit the man has tae gi'e her."

She considered for a moment.

"I lo'ed my wean," said she, "bonnie wee wifie 'at she was. And yet I could find it i' my heart tae pairt wi' her. It's true I waited lang and lang tae see her safe mairried on her man, and him her ain lovin' choice . . . but I left her wi' him at the last. And think you, mem," said Elsie, " 'at I could ha' pit an ocean twixt my Jamie and mysell. . . .?

She looked far back, down into Jamie's eyes.

"He used me ill," she said. "He had me and he flung me aff . . . he left me by my lane tae wark out my bitter wae. He kent ither women, aye, he kent yon the very while 'at I was a' his ain. This very day I'se tellin' ye, mem, he'll no mind as muckle as the sound o' my lovin' voice at him . . . na, nor the warmth o' me, mebbe, as I lay close in at his side."

She looked out past the naked trees and through the driving snow far back to Jamie.

"But it's Jamie," she said, "it's Jamie lives i' me the day. It's Jamie's e'en I see through, and me wonderin' whit w'y he wad speak gin I had him at my side. It was him 'at lay at my heart

through my lang mairried nicht . . . it was him I kissed when I
felt my nursin' wean. It's Jamie glints at me frae out this far
sunshine . . . it's him blinks at me through the winter's snaw."

Her dark eyes shone softly like stars.

"It's a' Jamie," said she, "and me aye wonderin' whit lovin'
word he wad speak gin his heart was beatin' upo' mine."

Her mouth quivered.

"He had me first at the turn o' the year," she said. "He'll be
the last thocht at the end . . . and the first when I waken tae
anither warld."

As I looked at her, every line in her face spoke to me.

"Oh, Elsie," I said, "you've suffered long."

"Aye," said she, "I've had my share, it's true. But I had him,
mem, as he had me. And that's warth it . . . warth mair than a'
the grief and wae he's cost me syne. Jamie wasna mebbe a' he
micht ha' been . . . but he's mine. He canna tak' hissell back. It's
him 'at warks i' me . . . it's him 'at rives my body on and on. It's
no 'at I'd speir at God tae let me see him, and me but an auld
wife the noo . . . and my Jamie lo'in' whit's bonny and young."

She stopped, trying to make it clear in words to me.

"It's jist," she said, "when the warld comes new like at my
e'en . . . that's ane thing mair, thinks I tae mysell, for me tae
tak' tae Jamie at we'r meetin'."

"Meeting, Elsie!" said I; "what meeting . . . where . . .?"

"Wha kens when or whaur," said she, "but a meetin'll come
at the twa o' us yet. It's no for jist the ance I met my Jamie . . .
that couldna be."

She looked at me.

"My guidman's sleepin' fast," said she; "my bairn's happy
mairried on a man, and bears her weans tae him. They twa's
been and gane for me. . . ."

The years fell off her as she smiled at me.

"But Jamie . . .!" said she. "Me and Jamie's hairdly started.
Me and Jamie'll get thegither yet, mem, ance we're deid, and
him mair lovin' mebbe then . . . and me jist happy tae be neist
my ain ance mair."

She began to draw her thick woollen gloves over her work-
worn hands.

"It's been a clash betwixt the twa o' us," she said, "and me
ne'er thinkin' tae speak the word i' life. But there's naebody the

like o' you, mem, when a's said and dune. Ye're a leddy born, it's true . . . but ye're a woman too. And gin woman meets wi' woman, mem, she'll clash o' whit lies neist her heart . . . and there's nae eddication'll stand atwixt the twa o' them."

She rose, buttoned her long winter coat, settled her hat, shook herself ready for departure in the eternal feminine way.

"Ye'll ken, mem," said she, "how it is wi' the likes o' women. Gin he was here the noo, and auld and frail, I wad but lo'e him mair and mair the mair there was tae tend. But wi' the maist o' men . . . they'll turn frae the whiteness o' a woman's heid or the sickness o' her body . . . they canna help theirsells. And I fear but Jamie couldna dae his lo'in' wi'out the brightness o' the lassie's e'e!"

She looked straight at me with those understanding eyes of hers—ever so much lovelier than the lassie's innocence, if Jamie did but know enough to see it.

"Sae that's whit mak's me fain tae wait a bit and see the warld," said she, "jist tae ha'e mair tae gi'e him at we'r meetin'. And mebbe then I'se get my share o' shinin' Bible raiment . . . and wi' that," said Elsie, "wi' that, mem, I'se surely see the love-look back i' Jamie's e'e."

She smiled at me with eyes and mouth.

"That's whit I'se waitin' on," said she. "I'se waitin' jist on that, mem. Tae see the love-look back i' Jamie's e'e . . . and bid him welcome hame."

We kissed at parting, and I nearly wept to let her go. For it is queer how differently one sees a woman when one knows the spring she works by. To me Elsie is no longer only the cook who baked and boiled and roasted for me for a given wage; she has become a sister creature too, hoping and fearing like myself, trusting more faithfully than I shall ever do—and loving so well that the very bitterness of her grief has passed into a sort of second happiness.

ALEXINE

I HAVE a shrewd suspicion that in her own country Alexine used to be all things to all men, or a good many things to a lot of them—but I don't know that that specially matters. What does matter is that I like to see her come in at the door and am sorry to see her go out again. If you feel that way to anyone you may reassure yourself as to her possessing or not possessing all the essential Christian virtues. Be satisfied that any of them she does not possess may quite safely be put in the Museum—price ten cents admission to see them.

Alexine is not a wealthy person—not at all. Perhaps that may account in some measure for her niceness. She is what is called poor—I mean she hasn't much actual money in the hand. But she has such a lot of talents in the bush that I don't know that *that* matters specially either—to anyone but Alexine! After all, it isn't the actual money you possess—is it?—it is whether you know how to spend the money you have; and *that* Alexine knows to perfection. She has brought the spending of a very little money to a fine art. Why, I have seen her come in at the door looking as if "Your Grace" was the only suitable way to address her—and fifty cents would have bought her as she stood. If any woman knows as much as that, she deserves her golden crown somewhere or other, and as she isn't likely to get it in this world we will set our hopes on what is to come. For my part I hope, I am sure, that it—I mean the world to come—is going to be some different (as we are in the habit of saying here across the water) from what we are enjoying now.

The country Alexine hails from is France. The country she has come to is Canada. And she only left France—long before the war—because there were so definitely no golden crowns going there that she found it hard to get even the fifty cents wherewith to make herself look like a duchess. Just like any other immigrant, she came to Canada—to make money. I wish I could say she had succeeded.

"To tred," as they say in Scotland, and over and above her supernumerary "tred" of making herself pleasant to the male persuasion, she is a dressmaker. She has no establishment of her own—"Bad debts!" she says to that, with a shrug of her expressive shoulders; she merely employs her own ten fingers, and these she takes out with her to any customer who is willing to pay her a dollar and a half for the use of them. There was a time when Alexine made a push for two dollars a day, but the customers (the only women who form an efficient Trade Union without any organisation at all) wouldn't stand for it, as they themselves said. They declared to a woman that ten hours' skilled labour wasn't *worth* two dollars a day, and they would die rather than pay it. Alexine, who only formed an inefficient Trade Union of one, was obliged to climb down. She climbed back to her dollar and a half with—apparently—the same good-humoured nonchalance with which she had tried to emerge from it; for she is one of those who know not only the buttered side of life but also how life tastes without any butter at all. If she is vanquished she is too wise to show rancour . . . but I don't know if that necessarily means that she has forgotten.

The chief topic of Alexine's conversation when she brings her ten fingers in for the day is—Man. She is frankly interested in Man, or perhaps I should rather say that she is interested in him in so far as he touches Woman. In Political or Scientific or Philosophical Man Alexine is only perfunctorily interested—so long, I mean, of course, as he is in his public and professional capacity. In his off-moments—when he is just man like any other—oh, then Alexine is as keen on him as if he were the hero of a French novel of twenty years ago, with nothing to do in life but flit from one woman to another, behaving to each—as the hero of a French novel of twenty years ago would naturally do.

Alexine has few reticences. She regards life as a thing to be spoken of and discussed, and when its seamy side comes uppermost she merely shrugs her shoulders. Yet, with the curious tact and discretion of the French-speaking peoples, Alexine doesn't say things that set one's teeth on edge—no, not half so much as she might and very probably would if she were a worthy, entirely straight-going individual. She has a way of flitting about her subjects much as the hero of our novel used to flit amongst the ladies of his acquaintance; and, like him, she attains her result. You understand perfectly what she would be at when she hasn't said anything at all; and when she is flitting around the direst complexities of life she is simplicity itself. It is a gift, I suppose—or perhaps she has reduced her knowledge, like any other eminent specialist, to first principles. She isn't pretty at all—not in the very least. If you were to take Alexine to pieces (as we say) I doubt if you would find a decent feature in her face, though you might find many a decent bone in her body. She has vivacious black eyes, with a slight squint in them, and what skin you can detect through the powder is fine in texture. She wears a wig (perhaps I should call it a transformation) on the principle, I suppose, that it looks nice, and of course we all have a right to our opinions. I think myself that Alexine would look nicer without the wig, but I am sure she would die rather than pluck it off and cast it from her. It is a frizzly kinky production, and it looks to the uninitiated eye as if it were made of horse-hair. In colour it is a sort of faded drab— possibly it started life as pure gold and wilted in the furnace of Alexine's experiences. Alexine's hands are her strong point. They are plump and dimpled and small, and there isn't a bone showing anywhere. As they don't wear powder, the fine texture of their skin is evident; they are soft; the nails are pretty and well-tended; and the hands and nails together can do pretty well anything they want—poor little Alexine, her hands are all the fortune she is ever likely to have this side of the grave, and all they can manage to bring in, as I said before, is a dollar and a half a day. However great an adept you may be at the spending of money, you can't launch out on what Alexine calls a *luxe effréné* on that. As to Alexine's figure, it is not unlike that of a pouter pigeon, if you can imagine a pouter pigeon dressed in the height of the mode. Apart from these things, she is always clean and sweet, and she smells very nice. Where she finds the money to buy her perfume with I don't know—perhaps she ekes out her precarious income with more experiences, or perhaps she makes scent out of the dandelion leaves that she tells me she goes out to pick each Sunday after Mass. "It is all there is to do in this country here," Alexine says, "cueillir les feuilles. Voilà comme on s'amuse le dimanche en Canada. Quel pays!" For Canada and the Canadians Alexine cherishes a deep and dire contempt. "Franchement," she says, "ce sont des barbares, n'est-ce pas?" And if I try to put a word in for the Canadian: "Ne dites rien, s'il vous plaît, madame," she says; "les

Canadiens ne savent pas vivre. Voilà la vérité. Dieu—they do not know the way. . . ." And once on this tack, Alexine is impossible to stop.

"Ces femmes," she says (Alexine's clients move in the highest social circles) "regardez moi seulement ces riches Canadiennes. Quelle vie, mon Dieu! They talk amongst themselves, they lunch together, and they dine toutes seules. . . ."

Alexine shrugged her shoulders.

"For what do they buy toilettes?" she said.

"To wear," said I.

"Bah!" Alexine said; and after a moment: "And often they cannot even wear them—these toilettes we make for them in Paris. Ces femmes ne savent rien du tout."

She went on working at her *joli mouvement*, as she liked to call it.

"They have no aim, madame," she said, after a bit, "ces femmes."

"What kind of aim?" I asked her.

She stopped an instant—then she glanced at me and smiled. But what a smile!—what depths—what oceans of experience lay behind it!

"Chez nous," she said, "en France, rich or poor, it is quite otherwise. We have an aim, nous autres. We meet, we talk, we women work together, it may be; we even like to be together sometimes. Mais ce n'est rien, tout ça. With us there is the man. He may be at our side, our man—in front of us if we are young . . . or else it may be that he lies behind us. But he is there. He governs our toilettes—he rules our way of speech—he animates our thought—our gesture. C'est une préoccupation pour nous— cet homme. Il est notre vie de femme."

She smiled at me again. She tilted back her head a little, shook her finger at me.

"Oh, par exemple, il est toujours là, notre homme," she said.

She went on sewing at her *joli mouvement*.

"Here," she said, "in your New World—there *is* no man. L'homme travaille tout simplement. He stays at his business— works—makes the money. The woman spends that money. Bon! They spend their lives apart, he and she—n'importe if they share one house, one foyer, they remain apart. Their lives are separate—and why, madame? Because your New World woman no longer knows the préoccupation that I speak of. She has loosed her hold—let go—her man is lost to her. . . ."

Alexine paused a moment. Her lip curled.

"C'est vrai," said she, "that sometimes still they speak par téléphone. C'est presque tout ce qu'il y a entre eux. Yet still she thinks he loves her . . . oh, she has yet to learn that she has lost her man, your New World woman.

"Oui," said Alexine, "elle l'a perdu, son homme. C'est là ou gît le lièvre!"

She turned her *joli mouvement* in her hands and held it off from her to look at it.

"Yet," she said, "what, madame, can be more of interest to the woman than the man? He is her life—c'est bien vrai, n'est-ce pas? If she stands there and merely watches him—if she is preoccupied with her own life and herself—he goes. He leaves her—wanders. Then he makes business life his home, perhaps. He wastes life—makes money only—seeks knowledge. Oh, mon Dieu . . ."

She shrugged her shoulders.

"How can one guess what men will do when women let them go?" she said.

Then as she went on working she began to smile.

"Ah," she said, "to hold a man, croyez-moi, madame, the woman gives her life. She must absorb herself in him—yet," Alexine said, "she must not let him see all her préoccupation with him. No; he must not know she holds him. C'est une préoccupation sans préoccupation qu'elle doit faire. Ah!"

She paused.

"She makes herself," she said, "if she will hold him fast, his—friend. She is his fellow-labourer if he wishes it. She is his wife—keeps his house—makes a foyer for him—gay, elegant, amusing. She makes his wife, if she can manage it, the most amusing thing that he can find . . . If she is wise, cette femme," Alexine said, "elle se fait même maîtresse un peu. . . ."

She held her *joli mouvement* off a little bit again—she poised it on her pretty, busy fingers—looked at it.

"Comme ça the man comes home," she said. "Comme ça il y a une vie de femme."

She sighed a little. "Ah," she said, "l'amour! What you call love . . ."—then in a second she went on.

"But in your New World here," Alexine said, "there are toilettes and evermore toilettes—and no préoccupation with the man. There *is* no man. Here women meet—they talk amongst themselves . . . of what? Bêtises. They dress, these women, spend their money— rich and poor they spend what money they can get . . . et voilà tout. Where is their man? Away!—their lives are separate. . . ."

For a moment she considered.

"Et c'est une vie vide, ça," she said at last; "ça ne vaut rien, cette vie—c'est vide."

She sewed a bit in silence.

"Alexine," I said, "isn't there something more?"

"Ah," she said, and raised her pencilled eyebrows, "vie de famille—hein? Des enfants?"

I nodded to her.

"Yes," I said, "what about all those New World women who have children?"

She hesitated for an instant.

"Ça," she said, "ça, c'est bien autre chose, n'est-ce pas, madame? I speak only of the man."

Again she hesitated.

"Mais," she said, "même ça—même les enfants! What worth, madame, have children if you have not préoccupation with the man you bear them to?

"If with one's child's father one has the intimacy of the télé-phone—" She laughed and shrugged her shoulders. "Bah!" she said, "what use toilettes—gaiety—children—what use life, enfin . . . if first of all you have not préoccupation with the man? He is the thing on which a woman builds. If she has not him to build on—"

"Then," I interrupted, "then she builds her house on sand. Is that it, Alexine?"

"Oui, c'est ça," Alexine said; "c'est bien ça."

She looked at me and in her slightly squinting eyes was something enigmatic.

"In your New World," she said, "si on est femme on est déplacée. . . ."

Then with her charming smile she said: "Pardon, madame . . ."

The subject was complete.

Once—a long time ago—I used to know a highly proper youth who, if you said that the wind was blowing or that you hoped it wouldn't rain, or that the sun rose east and had a way of setting west, used to reply with infinite gravity: "There's *something* in what you say!" He made this same remark to the most intimate confidence with which you entrusted him or the most transient trash you had to offer. It was his *vade mecum.*

"Something!" he would say. And then he would repeat: "Yes, *something* . . .!"

I wonder if he would have said it to Alexine, and what she would have thought of him—as a foundation for a building site!

WAITING

SHE came to the Doctor's office sometimes—she came just as often as she dared—always carrying carefully in her hands some little gift. It might be a couple of pears, or perhaps a peach or two when peaches were very, very plentiful, and as the season drew on it would be half-a-dozen apples—for apples are cheap and you get more for your money. And as she held out the fruit to him she would say, in that clear-cut, rigorously English voice of hers: "Just a little offering, Doctor!" And then, as he took it from her she would add hurriedly and doubtfully: "You may care, perhaps, to refresh yourself with a little fruit in the intervals of examining your patients." And he would thank her cursorily and hand the fruit over later to anyone who would take it—the house-maid, or the typist; or he would merely leave it lying unheeded on his desk.

She was old—old. She had outlived everything there is to live for—husband, child, friends, money, health. She had out-lived all these. Death had forgotten her. And those younger than herself, whose duty it was to care for her, thought of her merely as a weight to carry, a load to be borne, a something to be kept alive somehow till Death remembered his duties and came and took her away with him.

As things dropped away from her she expected less and less of life. The first things that went—father, mother, husband, son—to say good-bye to those rent her heart. But after she had let her son go the other things went easily. She let go without a struggle once her boy had left her. She had lost her son. What are money or friends, even health, compared with a son?

The friends dropped off, one by one—some in the Old Country which she had left so many, many years ago; some in the new land to which she had never thoroughly acclimatised herself. She heard of this one going, and of that one going—and she sighed a little; and then her thoughts would go sweeping back to that other death-bed that had cut her life in two. And her old eyes would fill with slow, painful tears.

When the money went she had to leave her home—that home where she had known what married life means—the home where motherhood had come to her, and then widowhood—and then barrenness again. She had to leave that home, where she was lodged as a snail is lodged in its shell, and go to an alms-house—a place where gentlewomen, unfortunate like herself, were herded together to hate one another. There she lived, suffering at first, and as the years passed by, merely bearing—just taking one day at a time and bearing that; and then taking the next—and the next—and the next—interminably—and bearing them all. The days were long, but each one came to an end. "I have borne yesterday," she used to say to herself; "I can bear today and tomorrow. Why not?" And she bore them. As the days went on and on they got to seem longer and longer, for even her eyesight was taken away from her—almost. First one eye went completely, and then the other faded and faded imperceptibly till all life outside it was a mere shadow. But a glimmer of sight was left to her. She could distinguish, if not faces or the print that had used to make the days seem shorter, still tables and chairs indoors, and carts and automobiles outside. It was still possible for her to get about. Her glimmer of sight gave her her permit to go about still—to go about as she wished and where she wished. And where she went—it was the only place left to her—was the Doctor's.

She had come to know "the Doctor," as she always called him, in her old age, after—long, long after she had lost one by one the treasures of her life. She had been taken, after the days of the alms-house had begun, suddenly and violently ill. There had had to be an ambulance and a hurry-rush up to the hospital and an emergency operation—to save her for a little longer space of desolation. And when the operation had been successfully performed, her convalescence had been so slow that she had had to remain in the hospital months and months—almost six months she had been there: four of them because she *had* to be, and the last two because the Doctor—her Surgeon—out of sheer good-nature didn't turn her out. He let her stay because she was old and pitiful and he thought a hospital was better for her than an alms-house.

And it was. In her old age that hospital was the one bright spot. There was so much going on all round her—such bustle, such opportunities to hear little bits of things that make the time pass quicker. She was a public ward patient, of course; but she wasn't like the patients round about her, and, once the Surgeon had shown her a little kindly favour, the nurses were willing enough to do their part in helping her to make the best of it. There was a sort of old-world gentility about her that placed her apart—that, and a little reserve she had, and a gentle way of speech. Soon the Surgeon would make a point of stopping beside her for a little chat each time he made his rounds, and after a chat or two he took to ordering for her little extra luxuries—an early morning cup of tea, another in the afternoon, and such-like. For to those who had eyes to see she was attractive—beautiful in her extreme old age, with her parchment skin the colour of old ivory, and her features sharpened to an extreme refinement, and the lines carved deeply in her face as time carves lines on an ancient tree-trunk. She stood out in the ward amongst the younger flesh and blood like a bit of cunning workmanship that has learned to defy time—merely by shedding superfluities.

She gave no trouble. She was peaceable, and soon became a favourite with the nurses—good-natured girls for the most part, who took pleasure in smuggling a piece of cake or a sweet biscuit to her with her cup of tea. Each time the trays were brought to her she treated them as a fresh surprise; each time she expressed her formal thanks as for something wholly unexpected. "I must thank you, Nurse, for your delicious cup of tea," she would say; then add, with a stiff, unbending sort of courtesy that was a part of her: "I find it most refreshing." And the nurse would say: "Sure, Mrs MacNeyder!"—and, with the sort of amusement a child takes in touching up its doll, "fix" the old-fashioned nightingale her patient wore over the thick, ungainly hospital night-gown, or smooth the poor old faded wisps of hair back under the pleated nightcap.

She lay there quietly. And as she lay, or later, when she was able to be up in the wheeled chair for a bit each day, or later still, when she could feebly take the length of the ward and back again, leaning heavily on the nurse's young, strong arm, she thought of one thing and of one thing only—her Doctor. She loved him. She loved him as a dog loves its preserver. He had given her life—without his knife she must have died. And though the little bit of life that he had snatched for her was hardly worth the snatching, yet, just for saving her, she loved him. All that had been so long pent up in her she lavished on him. The love for her child, the sorrow and loneliness of her later life—all this seemed merged in her great feeling for him. As the months went on she gradually came to give the Surgeon something more than love—she gave the sort of adoration that we give to God. If she recognised his step her face would brighten, and she would call a nurse, take her by the arm, pull her down and whisper tremulously: "Nurse . . . is my cap straight? I hear the Doctor." And they would laugh good-naturedly together and say she was in love with him.

When she left the hospital "cured," then it was she started her visits to the Doctor's office. As she was leaving he had said to her: "Going? Well, good-bye. Take good care of yourself." And as an afterthought he had added: "Let me hear from you— come and see me at my office." She took this invitation home with her and treasured it in her heart: and, just as soon as she was strong enough, she groped her way once a fortnight down from the alms-house to his office, happy just to be near the Surgeon who had given her a little longer lease of life.

For hours on end she would sit there in the waiting-room amongst all the other patients who came from every quarter to consult him, and sometimes she would speak to whoever was sitting nearest her and ask if it were growing dark yet. And then she would explain that her sight was dim and that she was afraid to wait till it was night, and that just as soon as it got dusk she must be moving. "If the Doctor," she would say, "is too much occupied this afternoon to see me I can come again. His time is taken up—I have no claims on him. I can come again." And she would add sometimes: "My visits are purely friendly. Pleasure visits merely!" And then, having made a start, she would go on, if only the other would consent to listen, and tell about her time in hospital and how happy she had been there, and how marvellous the Surgeon was—and then, in a whisper, for age unlocks reserve, she would tell how he had given her a picture of himself and how she kept it in her room and prayed to it at night. "I don't know what he looks like," she would say, "for I am almost blind. But he is good—I know he must be beautiful. He saved me." And when the patients would smile to one another across her she would know nothing of it.

Sometimes she would try and knit a gift for him—a muffler or a pair of muffatees. But she had no one to cast her stitches on and no one to pick a stitch up when she dropped it, and when she had spent whole days and sometimes weeks knitting and pulling down and knitting up again, then at last the wool would get all teased and tangled and she could do nothing with it. Then she would put it all aside "till she could get somebody to help her," and fall back on the gifts of pears and peaches and apples and bananas.

To get the money to buy these gifts she stinted herself of the one luxury of her poor life—the cup of tea that a few pence could bribe the alms-house maid to bring her. Before the hospital time this cup of tea had been her luxury. It came between the early noontide dinner and the evening meal at half-past six, and it had been the thing she waited for, the thing she longed for and enjoyed: without it there stretched a desert of an afternoon, hour upon hour of loneliness. But after hospital a greater luxury had come her way—the luxury of giving. The daily cup of tea transformed itself into the little parcels she carried so carefully to the Doctor's office.

After a bit the Surgeon, driven and overworked and worried, began to regret his kindly invitation. And when his office nurse would say to him: "Mrs MacNeyder is here this afternoon," he would reply impatiently: "Can't you get rid of her?" Then, as he turned the pages of his case-book to make a fresh beginning for the day, he would call after the nurse as she went out: "Tell Mrs MacNeyder I can't see her. Send the first patient in." And the nurse, in her immaculate white uniform, would make her way into the waiting-room, and pass amongst the throng of waiting patients, and come to Mrs MacNeyder and say to her: "The Doctor is sorry he can't see you. Next time perhaps—" And she would assist the old lady to her feet and help her to fasten her old-fashioned dolman cloak, and take her by the arm and lead her along the passage to the doorway. And to the nurse, impatient to be rid of her, it seemed a waste of time that Mrs MacNeyder should turn and sweep an ancient curtsy to the waiting patients, whom she could not see, and say to them: "Ladies, good afternoon. The Doctor is busy, so I shall not wait to-day. I hardly expected I should see him—mine is a purely friendly visit." And a worse waste of time that, as they passed the closed door of the consulting-room, Mrs MacNeyder should stop, and with a radiant face and an uplifted finger, say: "Ssh! Hush, my dear—the Doctor! Listen." And the worst waste of all that she should linger there listening for a mere echo of the Surgeon's voice.

After she had got the old lady safely down the steps and on to the side-walk, and had turned her with her face towards home—the alms-house—the nurse would run up into the house again and say to anyone in hearing: "That old thing! They never ought to let her out alone. It's a disgrace." And then she would hurry to her waiting patients—and forget. But the old lady went her way remembering. As she went groping home she would repeat over and over to herself "He's busy. He's so busy. He's a busy man!" And when she reached her lonely room at last she would begin to count how many days must pass till she could go to him again.

As time went on her mind grew blurred. She apprehended life, just as she saw it, not clearly any more, but through a mist. She grew less tidy in her person. She mislaid things. Hours— whole days sometimes—she spent hunting for things she had put down somewhere, she could not remember where. Then she took to losing her little bit of money—the few poor pence that came to her each month—and she could buy no more gifts. She could no longer go into shops and ask for pears and peaches and take away with her the damaged goods that they thought good enough for sightless eyes. And she grew suspicious. She suspected—she knew not exactly what. Only she knew that life was not as it used to be, and she dimly thought it must be those about her who were stealing it away from her. Instead of packets of fruit she started taking her little possessions to the Doctor's—first her photographs, her husband and her son, and then the picture of the Doctor himself—to ask him to keep them for her. "Give him these, my dear," she would say, when the nurse came for her; "ask him to keep them safely for me." And she would pause and then add in a whisper: "*Very* safely. Tell him Mrs MacNeyder begs him to take care of them." And sometimes, as they went along the passage—for she very seldom had a chance of speaking to the Doctor now—she would reach up and whisper in the nurse's ear: "One must be careful with one's precious things. Sometimes one is surrounded by those who are not so trustworthy as one would wish to see them." And she would nod with infinite meaning and gently pinch the nurse's arm. And over and over again she would repeat: "Careful—very careful. You'll not forget—" And now the nurse said: "Why, that old thing's crazy. How *can* they let her out alone?"

One by one she took all her things and left them at the Doctor's: shawls, little bits of extra clothing, stray books, old faded photographs of friends, a dilapidated album—anything she could lay her hands on. She would set off early in the afternoon and sit in the waiting-room hours and hours, hugging the little parcel close to her, and only breaking silence now and then to ask, in her clear-cut, English voice: "May I trouble someone to tell me if it is getting dark yet?" And if it was a kindly voice that answered her she would go on to tell a scattered anecdote or two about the hospital, or the Doctor's picture, or the untrustworthiness of human nature.

At last an edict went forth in the alms-house that she was not to go out any more alone—she was completely blind. Then she sat day-long and week-long and month-long—waiting. There was nothing else to do. She sat in her room alone and waited. And each day as she waited she remembered a little less of life—she dropped her memories as a tree sheds leaves in autumn. She thought dimly of life as it had gone past her. Vague memories floated round her of her old childish home in England, of her married life in Canada, of the hospital life—her son—the Surgeon. And as she sat day by day watching the memories float by her, the Surgeon and her son grew intertwined so that at last she hardly knew which was which. The one had come to open up life for her when she was young, the other had saved a scrap of life for her when she was old. She loved them both. Hour after hour she would sit there, leaning her head back and her poor eyes closed—just loving them. And gradually, as the days went over her, the lines of weariness and suspicion and petulant anger were all smoothed out and her face was full of peace. If they asked her what she was thinking of as she sat there she would reply: "My boy!" and smile.

So she sits, loving life away. One day Death will remember.

AN IRREGULAR UNION

PHYLLIS REDMAYNE sat in her little room that was
drawing-room and dining-room and study and bedroom
all in one. It was a pretty little room—pretty in spite of
its not costing very much. It had its dining-table and its plain
chair close up to the table, its easy-chair, its cot-bed masquerad-
ing as a couch in the day-time; it had its pillow or two covered
in silk, and a vase of flowers; and, in the best light the room
could give, close up by the little high window that looked out
straight on the sky, it had its inevitable typewriter. Phyllis
Redmayne was the ubiquitous Business Girl of our time, and
she earned the money she lived on by the sweat of her brain.

But just at the moment she wasn't looking at her typewriter,
or thinking of it, or working at all. She sat in her chair close up
by the table and she looked at the telephone. She looked at it
and she looked at it; her eyes were fixed on it, and the eyes of
her mind were fixed on it too. She was just sitting there thinking
of the telephone. She was longing for it to speak.

It is a bad business waiting for a letter, but it is a worse business to wait for the telephone. The telephone is there before
you—it may be going to speak any minute; and minute after
minute passes by and changes slowly into hour after hour—and
it doesn't speak. And you sit and look and long. And when the
bell goes clang at last and you take the receiver in your hand—
most likely it's the wrong number or someone you don't want to
speak to or some triviality or other. You just say what you have
to say and hang the receiver up, and you sit there again, sick at
heart, waiting.

When that has happened to you over and over again you
grow, not so much accustomed to it, perhaps, as patient—
passive—resigned; but that attitude of mind doesn't come all
at once. You only grow like that with the years. And this was
the first time Phyllis Redmayne had had to sit and watch the
telephone—sick with impatience and apprehension and unable
to ring up and ask what she longed to know. It was the first time
she had had to sit with her heart torn with anxiety—and just

wait. It is currently said that waiting comes easy to women. I wonder why that is currently said.

The thing that Phyllis Redmayne was waiting for was a telephone message to say whether the man she cared for was better or worse. He was in hospital, this man she cared for, and once every day she had a message, not from him but from his nurse—just a professional bulletin of his condition—a calm, noncommittal: "Mr Radcliffe is rather better to-day," or "Mr Radcliffe has had a bad night and is not quite so well," as the case might be. And then the telephone rang off. And Phyllis Redmayne had that much to live on till the same time to-morrow.

That isn't a very easy proposition when you are young and not used to wait—and when you care very much. And Phyllis cared—she cared very much indeed; in fact, she didn't care for very much else except for this man who lay in hospital ill and away from her. She had just one idea of happiness in life and that was to be with him, to be with him always, to take care of him and to be taken care of by him—to look after his interests—to work for him—to be close beside him all the time and help . . . and to have him there being helped, and at the same time looking after her and sheltering her and protecting her. As you see, there was nothing at all new or original about Phyllis Redmayne and her views. She was just the old traditional woman clothed in a Business Woman's garb. For all that was unexpected in her ideas, her typewriter might just as well have been a kitchen stove—or a cradle. She looked on Dick Radcliffe as Eve looked on Adam. She thought the same old things that women always have thought, though she gained her own living and imagined she was independent and free and modern and all the rest of it.

Dick was the head of the office where she worked—he was her "bawss," as the girls in the office called it. And she was what people call his mistress. There was nothing new in their relation—nothing whatever. It was the same old thing. He had seen her and seen that she was pretty—and she had seen him and seen that he was strong. The rest followed. What *was* a little bit new perhaps—or the way that Phyllis looked at it was new—was that though she gave herself very willingly and went on and on giving herself, she took nothing in exchange. I mean that she went on earning her own livelihood and supporting herself just as she had done before the episode—the episode was something over and above in her life, as it were, just as it was in Dick's. In plain words, she didn't take any money for the gift of herself.

It is a queer thing how a little practical fact like that can make an old episode seem new—a new thing in the history of the world; and that Phyllis Redmayne felt as she did only goes to show how this present-day life of ours is based and rooted on money. The little insignificant fact that she was able to "keep herself," as it is called, changed for her the whole complexion of her love episode. It gave her confidence and self-respect. She could feel with perfect accuracy that she was not a "kept woman." She had years of supporting herself behind her and she had every justification for feeling that in the years to come she would always be able to go on making ends meet. She could feel, in one word, independent—and it is extraordinary how deep into a woman's soul that desire for independence goes, when once she has had a taste of it. If Phyllis Redmayne had been Phyllis Radcliffe I doubt not at all that she would have felt quite differently. The fact of being a wife, of sharing house and home, bed and board, changes the most independent woman's point of view. She feels then that she can go shares with a good conscience—the children that are in the back of every woman's mind, children who will bear their father's name when they come, make that all right. But in the relation that Phyllis Redmayne bore to Dick Radcliffe—it is different. There is a sensitiveness—a lack of security perhaps—on the woman's side. She isn't a wife, and however much she may protest that she doesn't want to be, there are moments when she almost certainly does want it very much; and then, besides that—well, besides that, there is the tradition of centuries past and gone to fight against; there are all those thousands—millions—of women who *have* been "kept women"—mistresses and women who have borne harder and more contemptuous names than that . . . they have to be taken into consideration. And a Business Woman, a modern Business Woman, working for herself, quiet and decent in her life, independent, doesn't want to be mixed up with things like that. No, she doesn't—she doesn't. She feels herself different and she *is*: different. Why, Phyllis Redmayne would hardly take even a present—the most she would accept were little valueless things at the rarest intervals. Though she wouldn't allow it even to herself, this uncertainty of her relation to Dick Radcliffe got on her nerves at times.

Just at times. She was at the period of loving him so much that nothing else seemed to matter. And when life was going on its normal lines, nothing *did* matter except that she could see him day after day—work with him—help him with that active, trained brain of hers; and see him sometimes too in the little home she had got together with her own money—her very own earnings. There was something rare and wonderful in having a little home where she could welcome him as her treasured guest. It was something that nearly made up—that sometimes far more than made up—for their not living and sharing a home together.

When things were going normally Phyllis dwelt entirely and always on the good side of their relation. She looked consistently on what is called the "bright side." She hardly admitted to herself that the shield had a reverse that wasn't quite so bright. Remember she was young. And their relation to one another was young too. The fear of the possible child, of Dick's tiring of her, the possibility of his caring for some other woman as well as for her, the dread of detection—of sickness . . . of all these possibilities none had pressed on her yet. She simply basked in love. Dick manifestly did care for her and she—she cared for nothing in the whole world but him; the world, indeed, hardly seemed to her to exist at all, except just as it revolved round Dick Radcliffe as its axis. There was joy in going to the office—there was infinite joy in the knowledge that she was useful . . . and she knew that she was: and there was joy unspeakable in welcoming him home sometimes—making him free of her little domain—spreading it out for his acceptance—preparing little fêtes for him. What was there in the world to worry about or to regret? Nothing.

And now Dick was ill. He wasn't ill so that he was going to die. No—not ill like that at all. But he was ill, and pretty sick too, laid low, suffering—and she wasn't able to be beside him and take care of him. He was in hospital, as the New World way is, and he had a special nurse, two special nurses, in fact—one for the day and another for the night—and she, Phyllis, who would have given ten years of her life to be near him, was shut out, shut out absolutely, not even able to take the receiver off the telephone and call up and ask how he was.

It was while Phyllis sat at the table with her eyes on the telephone that the first doubt of her way of life entered into her mind. She had thought—thought sometimes a little defiantly perhaps—that theirs was the better way of life. Such a union could never grow "stuffy," she would say to herself—she had read Edward Carpenter, and she borrowed the word from him. She had dwelt on all the advantages of their union. Dick was free. She was free. Nothing bound them together but their love, and if that were to fail they were free to part. But away back in—well, in her heart, I suppose it was—she said to herself at the same time that nothing could ever make them *want* to part. They were one and they would stay one. Sometimes she would tell Dick how free he was, impress it on him: "If ever you choose another woman, if you grow tired of me," she would say to him, "you are free. You're absolutely quite free, Dick. I sha'n't say a thing." But even as she said these things, and she honestly thought she said them sincerely, something within her said: "He never will want another woman. Why should he? Aren't you his friend as well as everything else? Can't you satisfy his brain as well as his heart—why should he *want* to part from you . . .?"

She had been very happy for those last three years. Yes, she had been happy. Hardly a doubt had assailed her about anything. She had just taken the moment as it passed, enjoyed it, made the most of it, caressed it almost sometimes—and then taken the next moment as it came along. She was happy in her work—happy, perhaps, rather in her usefulness to Dick—and she was happy in her little home. She was young enough and strong enough to be able to cope with her double work, the working of her brain at the office and the working of her hands at home. But most of all she was happy because in her love for Dick she was carried wholly, utterly out of herself. She never thought of herself; she hardly knew that such a person as Phyllis Redmayne existed. For her, Dick was the Great Reality, and her whole life was her gift to him. I have said that, in spite of her brain and her modernity, she was just the old, old thing.

But now as she sat with her eyes fixed on the telephone the first doubt assailed her. She took on that road her first step— that costs. She sat there longing with all her soul to know about the man she loved; and she couldn't know. She just had to sit and wait. Twenty-four hours had passed since she heard last. Of all those hours she had merely slept uneasily two or three; all the rest she had spent—longing is a weak word for it. She had yearned and craved to know how he was. She would have prayed if she had had the least idea that she would get an answer. She thought of telepathy and she felt it was a fraud— she longed to project her spirit and it wouldn't go. There was nothing for it but to wait, harrowed and devoured by anxiety. He wasn't going to die—she said that over and over to herself; but for all that he was ill—suffering—and she wasn't beside him. Phyllis Redmayne felt it wasn't fair.

Yes, that was how she felt. She said to herself as she sat there that there was nothing wrong in what she craved. She didn't want to worry him, to bother him, to show him love at the wrong time. She merely wanted to be beside him, to tend him, to read his slightest gesture so as to be of use—*that* was what she wanted, just to be of use. And when she thought of the nurses being with him, giving him intimate care, touching him, raising him, looking after him in the sleepless watches of the night—when she thought of this and visualised it, her hands clenched under the table and she felt the hot tears rising to her eyes. That was *her* place—it was her place to be with him. It was her privilege to lose her sleep so that she might soothe him. It was her right—yes, it was her right to tire herself, to wear her body out, if need be, that he might have one moment's rest and peace. Why should he be given over to indifferent paid nurses when she, *she* would give anything, anything in the world, just to be allowed to tend him?

What she felt to be the injustice of the world came on Phyllis Redmayne all of a sudden as she sat in her little room. It was growing late. The sun was away past her window now, and that meant that it would soon be evening. Why were they so late in ringing her up to-night? Was it possible that they had forgotten her—if so, was she to sit there another twenty-four hours wait-ing? Or was it possible—was it possible that he—that some-thing had happened . . . her hand went out towards the receiver. Could it be—oh, could it be, that the doctors were wrong, that he was seriously ill, that he might—*die*? Phyllis Redmayne felt her heart leap—and then she felt a sickness—she felt grey. . . .

After all, it wasn't as if she was asking anything *wrong*. She only wanted to know—and she mightn't ring up and ask.

Suddenly the secrecy of the thing struck her as horrible—hateful. She felt that she loathed it—she wanted to go up to the hospital openly and boldly, just as she was, and demand that she should be let in to nurse her—Her what? If she went up to the hospital and demanded to be allowed in to nurse her lover it wouldn't advance her cause much.

It began to dawn on her dimly, the mess she was in. There was nothing wrong in the relation itself—that she would swear. No wife that ever was could look on her husband with eyes more loving than those with which Phyllis Redmayne looked on Dick Radcliffe. And—she kept saying it to herself as she sat there—there was no question of money between them. There was nothing sordid in their relation. She earned her bread as she had earned it before she ever knew that a Dick Radcliffe lived in the world. She was true to him with every shred of her. She wasn't his only in her body, she *was* his in all her heart and soul. She was devoted to him. She—she adored him. The only thing that was wrong about it all was that she had to keep it a secret, and to keep it an effectual secret she had to tell lies. She had to act lies too. Her life was more or less a lie—but that was all anyone could bring against her. And she wasn't lying for any advantage of her own . . . it was just to keep the bare bread and butter coming in that she had to lie. She felt that she was justified—yes, she felt that down to the nethermost depths of her soul. And at the same time she knew that the world would not call her justified, and dimly, reluctantly, almost against her better judgment, she felt that the world had something on its side. There was no harm in her loving him. There could be no harm just in her wanting to be beside him now that he was sick. In longing to be of use to the man she loved, was she not proving herself to be a woman? Yet she couldn't go to him—he would be furious with her if she went and gave him away; and the world, the little bit of it with which she came into daily contact, would never forgive her if she were to give it away. There would be no one to stick up for her at all—not one person that she knew could be made to understand that she, Dick Radcliffe's mistress, had kept her self-respect, that she was an independent creature—she detested the word mistress, and she didn't feel that it applied to her . . . and yet she knew that it *did* apply to her and that her poor, pitiful little plea about earning her own livelihood and keeping herself decently wouldn't have any weight with anyone at all anywhere. As she sat there gazing at the telephone she felt like Athanasius against the world—and the world looked big and heavy.

What if he were ill—seriously ill? What then? How long was she supposed to go on sitting there just waiting for a message? If they went on forgetting her might there not come a time when she would be justified in going and—not demanding at all—just asking—pleading—begging for some scrap of news? Would it be possible that they would shut her out if he—if he—was *dying*? . . .

Suddenly the telephone cried and clanged. It was speaking. Phyllis Redmayne gave a great start and she took the receiver in her hand, and in a vague, uncertain way she was astounded to feel that her hand was shaking so that it would hardly hold the receiver in its fingers. She put the other hand up to steady it; she pressed the receiver to her ear. "Yes," she said. And then she repeated it. "Yes, hello!" she said again. She hardly knew that dim, unsteady voice. "Mr Radcliffe a-asks me to 'phone you up and say he's feeling some better to-night. He guesses he'll sit up to-morrow for a spell. . . ." That was the message. Phyllis Redmayne's heart gave a great leap—it leaped up nearly into her mouth, and when she tried to speak she could hardly get the words out for breathlessness. "Is his temperature normal to-night? Is he tired?" The questions poured out as water gushes out of the neck of a bottle when the cork is removed. "How did he sleep last night? Do you think he seems like sleeping now? Is he eating? Can he talk? Is he able to—?"

Phyllis Redmayne hung the receiver up. Everything that she had thought and feared as she sat waiting dropped again out of sight, out of touch, out of thought. Dick was better! He wasn't so very, very ill. He wouldn't die—what nonsense! The doctors were right, of course, he wasn't in any danger of dying, not even thinking of it. And as this certainty flooded Phyllis Redmayne's being, nothing else in the world seemed to matter. She was carried out of herself once more. Love spread its broad, strong wings and lifted her up—lifted her up above herself— above what the world might think or mightn't think. As she sat there looking at the telephone that had brought her the good news her heart seemed to swell in love and gratitude. She felt happy. She felt blessed. What if she couldn't be beside him? Wasn't he being taken care of and looked after so that he would be given back to her well and strong again? She felt that she had far, far more than she deserved. Mistress seemed to her the loveliest word in the language. Oh yes, she was Dick's mistress, and soon he would be well and able to come to her. She glanced round her little room, wondering how she could beautify it for his coming. There passed rapidly, tenderly through her mind the little meal she would give him to eat. She would welcome him soon—see him sitting there again—watch him eat. She would be able to see with her own eyes what havoc sickness had wrought in him—she would be able to touch and feel him—she could kiss him as he sat there and be sure that he was no spirit but dear flesh and blood.

She looked out through her little window at the early evening sky. She sat watching the lovely evening clouds going their majestic peaceful way. And suddenly—no one could be more surprised than she herself—she laid her head down on her two outstretched arms—and she sobbed and sobbed.

MOTHERHOOD

MARION DRYSDALE lay in her hospital bed. She had a private room, the very cheapest private room available; still it *was* a private room, and she had it—but not alone. She had a little bedfellow.

She was not allowed to have him always. He was brought to her, left with her while she nursed him, and then he was taken away again—up to that great nursery which he shared with the little bedfellows of other women; little bedfellows who were brought and taken away again, just as he was. There they lay in a row, some with pink bows on the tops of their bassinettes and some with blue, sleeping away the days and nights, waiting for the time when they could walk and speak and grow into human beings—new and unexpected, every one of them, and at the same time old and, each one, exactly like what has been before. It was a grief to Marion Drysdale that she might not have her little bedfellow with her all the time—close, close beside her so that she might feast her eyes on him all day long. But hospital laws are as the laws of the Medes and Persians. It is not good for a babe to be with his mother all the time. It is better for a mother to be quit of her babe now and then—they must meet and they must learn to part. It is the law of life.

"You won't *mix* him, will you?" Marion would say anxiously to the nurse. She said it indeed almost every time the white-capped, white-aproned kindly piece of officialdom came to fetch him away again. "You won't mix him, will you? I should know, of course, if you did," said Mamie Drysdale, "but it might make trouble—so don't—don't . . . will you?"

The nurse would laugh and take the babe up expertly—think of the hundreds of babes that passed through these expert hands in the course of a year! "That's what all the mothers say to us," she said. "They're all afraid of the babes getting mixed up in the long nurseries into a jig-saw puzzle and never coming right again." And she laughed and pointed to the baby's tag with his name—or his number!—on it.

But Mamie Drysdale didn't laugh. She didn't laugh at all.

She looked earnestly at the nurse and her eyes travelled back to the baby.

"Oh," she said, and her voice was as earnest as her eyes, "you ought to be *mothers*, every one of you baby nurses. If I was your principal or your matron, or whatever you call her, I wouldn't let a nurse in—not to nurse, I mean—if she hadn't had a baby."

The nurse would only laugh again "Don't you worry," she would say, and then she would disappear with the babe, shutting the door softly behind her. And it would seem to Mamie, lying with the spring sunlight streaming in on her, as if the sun had hidden his face for good—as if black night had descended on her. She would lie there and long—and long—and long—for the sun to come back again. Her baby!

She hadn't been long through her woman's work. Just five days old the baby was. But Mamie had come through well—she was young and strong, full of vigour and life and hope. Such women do their work well. They bring forth their children in joy.

Not that Marion Drysdale had done that exactly. Hers had been a hard row to hoe—and there were other rows ahead of her still harder. Life, as she lay looking at it, seemed uphill, and an uphill road is hard to tread with a child in your arms: you must have courage. To begin with, Mamie had had to come into hospital with a name that was not hers. She had entered herself as Mrs Middleton and her name was Marion Drysdale—Miss Marion Drysdale. It had to be, this taking of another name. She knew it. But for all that she kicked against the pricks.

"I don't *want*," she had said, "to go in and have my child—our child, Davy!—with another name. I want to go in frankly and openly, and bring our child into the world with its mother's name if it can't have yours."

And when David Winterford had kept saying to her: What did it matter—such a little, unimportant thing as that—she had only kept on saying: "But I don't *want* it . . ."

And she had seemed to him once more unreasonable.

For what *did* it matter? Marion Drysdale had so many lies to tell in her way of life that one more was neither here nor there. It was all in her day's work to tell lies; it had been that way for so long that she ought to have got used to it by now. But she wasn't used to it. Each lie was a new prick to her soul. She never got used to them—though she told them fluently enough. And now there was a third person—something new, quite, quite new—and she felt as if it were a shame to start it in life with a lie. A child ought to come into the world royally—hoped for, prepared for, welcomed—yes, welcomed with reverence. To bring it there in any sort of a hole-and-corner way . . . it wasn't right. No; it wasn't *right*.

Mamie gave up arguing the matter. It was just one of those things that she and Davy couldn't agree about. Usually they understood one another perfectly—they were as one mind about most things. But now and then there would crop up a thing—something—and as luck would have it it was almost always one of the things that *mattered*—that they didn't think alike about. And the more they talked, the less alike they seemed to think. The end of arguments like that was tears—passionate, unwilling tears on Mamie's part, and a little anger, perhaps, on his. She consented to the Mrs Middleton and there was a conspiracy with the doctor about it, and she was entered in the hospital books in that name, and came in as Mrs Middleton, with the plain gold ring, that she usually kept hidden, conspicuously on her finger—and she was known only in that way. But she was continually afraid she would forget—wake up suddenly perhaps—forget to respond—give herself away somehow before she realised what she was saying. And deep inside her she resented having to be afraid like that.

Mamie lay in her straight little hospital bed and looked out of the window. She was high up on the top story so that she was far above the street, and the noise of the street cars as they went clanging by. She seemed far away from everything. All she could see out of the window was the sky; and as she lay on that early March afternoon watching the drifting clouds—she thought.

She was weak yet—too weak to enjoy sitting up. She lay flat, with her dark head low in the pillow; and her dark eyes looked out and far out, right into the sky beyond the window—right into the big world that is just outside every one of us. It was a long time since she had heard from Davy, so it seemed to her, and she knew that there was another long time to come before she could hear from him. By an abstruse and roundabout piece of work he had been told that he had a son—a son! But she didn't know yet how he felt to that son. She didn't know if he was pleased or excited—if it changed his whole outlook on life, or if he was just sorry that his son wasn't dead . . . as they had agreed would be the easiest way.

Yes, they had agreed that together; and Mamie, as she thought of it, couldn't believe that it was she who had even acquiesced in such a thing. Wish their son dead! She wish her baby still-born—she—his mother! She drew a great breath as she lay there and she shook the thought from her for ever.

She turned a little on her pillow and she thought of the past—that past between her and Davy before the baby was. And now that past—that sacred thing of her life—presented itself just as something that had led up to this—their child. She remembered her first sight of Davy. He was standing talking— he had had his profile turned to her. And she remembered that queer, inexplicable feeling that came over her of some past intimacy with him—and the rush of feeling that swept through her and seemed to penetrate into every tissue of her being. It hadn't been a thing thought of, considered, their love—it had been a sudden flame and she had been caught up in it as a leaf before the wind is caught up by the blazing bonfire. She had loved him, yes, she had loved him that first day before she had even spoken to him. She had loved him—and she loved him now. Davy was to her the one man in the world—the only thing that mattered—the one *real* thing there was. As she lay there looking up into the sky and back into the past she remembered her blank astonishment at this love of hers—her amazement at the way it had taken hold of her—and shattered her.

For that was what it had done. It had shattered the old Mamie Drysdale whom she knew—and a new Mamie Drysdale had come into being whom—whom sometimes she shrank from. The old Mamie had been a straight girl, gaining her own living, hardworking, conscientious. She had meant to go straight all her days, had the old Mamie—till she met Davy; and then things had changed. He couldn't marry her. That was the first thing. He loved her—that was the second. And she loved him—that was the third. Mamie Drysdale hadn't been able to go straight any more.

And so they had—not drifted into it, not at all. They had entered perfectly open-eyed into an irregular union: into one of

those unions with which our whole society is honeycombed to-
day. Marion Drysdale had gone on working. She had taken
nothing from David Winterford but his love. As a free gift she
gave herself—he gave himself. There were two to the bargain—
they loved one another—they came to meet each other freely.
So they had united. So they became one.

They did become one—for they loved one another very
much. He, who had always jeered a little at women, was
astounded to find in Mamie a human being as well as a woman.
He was frankly amazed to come across something so like himself and yet so entirely unlike himself—a woman who gave
freely all she had—gave and gave—yet one that he could not
take from unless she chose to give.

Mamie remembered his naïve astonishment.

"You're different, aren't you?" he had said to her once, "*different . . .*"

And she remembered, too, his incredulous look at her once,
when they were walking together on grassy cliffs, with a grey,
grey sea far below them, and she had said to him: "I don't *want*
to marry you, Davy. I like it better this way—better—"

That was a while ago.

She thought of it, lying there. She thought of their physical
union—her surprise. Her surprise at herself—at this undiscovered life she felt surging up and up in her. "Where is this leading me?" she would ask herself. There were moments when she
used to feel afraid of these waves of life that surged up in her—
and came back and back on her. She remembered times when
she felt inclined to put out her two hands and keep the waves
off—push them away.

That time of love—that early time! How had she worked at
all? How had she managed to go about and look just as usual?
How had she kept their secret, when inside her all day long
there had been that tumult—and those great waves surging up
and up in her and breaking down every landmark she had lived
by! She remembered their first morning, for they had stolen—
with what infinite deceit and pains!—a day or two together . . .
and she remembered how, as they passed out into the freshness
of the May morning, she had somehow let fall a note—a fifty-
dollar note—out of the bosom of her dress. And she had just
watched it drift away from her on the spring wind without even

stooping to pick it up—it hadn't seemed to matter. Yes, she, the practical business girl, the woman who had earned her money and had had to live on what she earned, she who had pinched and scraped and struggled—she had stood there and watched her fifty-dollar note drift away from her, when by merely stooping down she could have picked it up again. Think of it! What confusion—what chaos—what a dazed brain! They had laughed together about it since . . . but that confusion, that chaos of her mind was to lead straight to this: to this bed in a hospital—and her boy! Her breath came quick and fast.

When that stolen day or two of love was over, then working-time had come. And they had settled down to work—or seemed to. But Mamie, lying there, remembered the struggle of it. There was the work to be done—that work that she had always done well and thoroughly, that same work that had seemed all-important to her before she met Davy—it was still there to be done as before. She had been a good business woman: prompt, punctual, never absent-minded, trustworthy to the smallest item. She had been working her way steadily up when she met Davy. She had even had ambitions.

But the day she saw Davy's profile, as he stood there on the hearthrug—waiting for her, as it had seemed to her—her ambitions had vanished. They had just passed away from her, as she remembered seeing pictures pass away from her at a dissolving view. She asked herself if she really ever had had those ambitions! Or had she only thought that she had had them? She wondered. Yet they had seemed real enough at the time.

After she had met Davy—after they had been away together, at any rate—there had seemed no room for ambitions any more. Mamie had found herself suddenly full to the brim of confusing, surging, growing things—things growing at such a pace that sometimes they had seemed to her ill weeds threatening to overgrow anything that was good in her. She loved Davy—but at that time she loved him with a passionate, absorbing, narrow love, a love that would have kept him for ever at her side; a love that grudged him to anyone else—anything else; a love that was engrossing. selfish, that hated to have him absent from her an hour, a second . . . but she loved him. She remembered once hearing his voice as she came into the office hall—listening to him as he talked quite unself-consciously through the telephone

receiver. "Well, good-bye," he had said, "good luck to you—
ring up again some time. . . ." And as she listened she remembered how the thought had gone dashing through her: "Will the
day ever come when I shall hear that voice and it won't go
through and through me—like this!"

The day had never come. She had gone on always loving
him more and more—more intensely and always more
intensely, partly perhaps because of the enforced secrecy of
their love. Love, like any other thing, needs an outlet. It must
react and be reacted on. Store it up, pack it close, force the door
on it, turn the key—why, you might as well try to pack away
growing life and ask it to grow healthily. But Mamie Drysdale
hadn't known plain and ordinary truths like that in the early
days—and, lying quietly on her hospital bed, she remembered
outbursts, explosions . . . and then she remembered how she had
thought herself wicked and ungrateful when such explosions
came—she had accused herself of selfishness, of not loving
Davy. She had wept in those early days—she had felt ashamed.
Oh, she had wept!

Then came the time of danger when the fear pressed on her.
A child would separate her from Davy—she couldn't have them
both; she knew it. She must tear herself away from Davy—or
she must cast away her child. And after the first year or two of
love she had longed for a child—and at the same time she had
feared it with all her soul. Whole days she had passed tossing
between desire and fear. She had wanted her child; it had
seemed to her as if their love was incomplete without a child . . .
and she had dreaded the moment when she might find it was
coming. Her life had become torn. She remembered how she
used to feel sick sometimes with longing—and the next moment
sick with fear lest her longing should be realised.

Her work had suffered. How can one go about with one's
mind full of such things as that—and work? Work seems a pal-
try thing when you put it in the scales with life. Life and making
life—what is the adding up of figures, what is the balancing of
books compared with that? Yes, her work had suffered. She had
done her best. She was conscientious—she had tried and tried
again, but her work had suffered. It had grown incorrect,
slovenly, almost in spite of her. She called to mind the times
when she would pull herself together, make a great, great effort.

"I must do better—I must try harder," she had said to herself; "I *can* do better if I can only try . . ."—and she would try. But her mind would be rent asunder again by fear—and through the fear the longing would spring up in spite of everything she could do to keep it under. And her resolutions would all melt away as the snow melts before the spring sun, her work would slacken again and fall back—and then something in her would feel ashamed. She felt as if she *ought* to have strength to help it—she couldn't forgive herself. She hadn't told Davy much about these things— never more than she could help. But sometimes, and usually at the wrong moments, they would burst out of her . . . and he didn't—he didn't seem able to understand. He was impatient sometimes of things like that.

Then came conception. She found herself with child; and she was happy. Yes, against her reason, against her judgment, against all that her common sense could say, she was happy. Suddenly—it was owing to her unreasoning happiness, perhaps, that she felt like that—it didn't seem to her that this need separate her from Davy! Why need it? Why mightn't she have both man and child? She had an unreasonable feeling that something could be done—that something must and would be done to make things go all right; and she expected, as a matter of course, that Davy would feel the same. She expected him to feel just as she did, that a miracle had happened, and that when miracles happen they change our commonplace, everyday life and turn it into something golden and beautiful and—quite different. But he didn't feel like that. David Winterford didn't feel like that at all. He wasn't happy as she was, he wasn't even pleased for a second. He just thought it an unmitigated nuisance . . . and he had all sorts of suggestions to make that she wouldn't so much as listen to. No. The child was there. She would give it birth; after it was safely in the world, then they could think what they would do. "But I can't leave you, Davy," she had kept saying, "I can't leave you, dear, remember . . ."—and she had thought that she couldn't leave him. She had imagined that even after the birth of her child she would cling to the man. She remembered how it had passed through her mind then—while she was telling him she couldn't leave him—that her child could be nothing to her in comparison with the man who had given her her child. It had seemed to her that woman's love for

man must surpass any love she can have for the child she may
bring into the world.

Yes, she had thought that. She had actually thought that. She
had fancied that once she had brought her child safely into the
world she would be content to place it safely somewhere—pay
well for it with Davy's money and her own too—visit it—see to
the very best of her ability to its bringing up—be sure that it
was healthy and well cared for. She had imagined that she could
desert it so—she had even thought that the knowledge of its
being there and away from her would steady her perhaps. It
might be that she would be able to care for Davy a little differently, perhaps even more, but more sensibly . . . and that the
babe would just be a responsibility in their two lives, something
that she and Davy had brought into the world, something they
had to see to. It was only at the last, just at the very last when,
for the first time, she had felt a little desperate—that she had
agreed with Davy that it would be the best thing if their child . . .
well, there was no use thinking of that. That was past.

The night before she came into hospital she had said good-
bye to Davy. And as she stood with her eyes on his face and her
hands on his two shoulders, she had said to him: "Davy, it will
be all right, my dear. I sha'n't be very ill. I know it. I'm
strong—I'll be out in a week or two . . . and then I'll be beside
you again. We'll house it somewhere and make it comfortable—
if it's really there—and then you and I will work again as we
used to." And she remembered how she had drawn closer to him
and said: "You'll miss me, won't you, Davy? You'll be glad to
have me back again . . ." And they had said good-bye. And
Davy, for the first time, had been—upset, poor boy.

Now the child was there—actually there, something to touch.
It was no longer something invisible, hidden, something you
thought about all day and all the night-time you were awake,
something you thought about continually, but something nevertheless that it was hard to believe in as a reality. It was there
now. You could touch and feel it. It was a child—a living,
human creature, five days old.

Marion Drysdale lay looking up into the sky. She lay quite
quietly, without moving at all. Her mind was no longer in a
tumult. There was no confusion or doubt or hesitation in her
soul. She knew that she loved Davy just as she had always

loved him. She knew that she loved him even more now that he was the father of her boy . . . and she knew that she would leave Davy and stay with her boy. She knew quite certainly that there was nothing else for her to do—that she wanted to do nothing else. She had known this the first time she had heard her child give its little wailing cry.

As she lay quietly there her mind suddenly caught on to practical things. She lay calculating how she could best provide for her child. She lay counting the cost of living—counting the money value of her brain—wondering just what she could make—how she could best spend it—how she could arrange her whole life—for the baby. There was no danger now that she would slacken, find her work beyond her, that she would add her figures wrong, mix her book-keeping up. Never again would she see a fifty-dollar note go drifting before her in the spring wind and not stoop to pick it up. No. She felt her brain steady and determined. She felt able for work—greedy for work and for the money work could bring her. And far down in her she felt those old ambitions—those ambitions that a little while ago she had found herself wondering if she had ever really had—she felt them stir in her—not the old ambitions quite, perhaps, but still ambitions. With all the force of her heart and soul she wanted to have strength to do for her baby, so that he might grow to be a man—a big, fine, strong man with ambitions of his own. As she lay there she realised all of a sudden that her point of view had shifted. She loved Davy deeply, tenderly, passion-ately too, perhaps; but she loved her son as one loves the future. She saw the possibilities of the future in that tiny creature that she had carried in her womb for nine long months. She saw in him the possibilities that long ago, as it seemed now, had dimly stirred in her for herself—and she felt that everything she had to give was not enough to give, if only it could help those possibil-ities to grow into actual fact. She lay counting and calculating. What does a child need? How can I do what is best for him? How can I get him everything and all things that he has a right to ask from me? How can I bring him up that he may be a man—how can I make him strong and well . . . and *good*? These were the things that Mamie Drysdale asked herself as she lay in her hospital bed. The difficulties in front of her were plain, but she felt in herself the strength to override them. Davy, her one preoccupation since the day when she first set eyes on him, had—not vanished, but taken second place in her thoughts. This little one, this tiny thing that needed her—*he* was what Mamie lay thinking of—he was what filled her mind to overflowing. It was as if all her life had led her up to this moment—as if everything that had happened to her had brought her up to this open door. A child! Hers and Davy's. "We have made a man," she kept murmuring to herself, "a man! When his father sees him he will understand. He couldn't want to keep me—I have to go with the boy. Davy couldn't want to keep me—when he sees the child. . . ."

And just then the door opened and the tall, white-capped, white-aproned nurse came in. In her arms she carried something, carefully, solicitously—she carried something small and human and infinitely precious. "I've brought you your son, Mrs Middleton," she said, and she raised Mamie up on her pillows and laid the tiny bundle of preciousness in her arms. "He's a fine boy," said the nurse, as doubtless she said it to every mother who made her way in and out of the portals of the hospital. "He's a fine boy, Mrs Middleton. I guess he'll do you credit all right."

And Marion Drysdale was conscious of holding in her arms something that was immensely her own—something that, as it lay across her heart, seemed to belong to her as the heart itself did. She looked down at the tiny face, at the small, round, soft, soft head, at the tiny, restless hand, at the living eyes—and she put her child's mouth to her breast. "It's mine," she thought; "it's ours—Davy's and mine. We've made it, we two—and God. God made it for us out of our love for one another." And she looked down at the little wrinkled face, at the busy mouth, at the tiny, constantly-moving hand, and a waft of that first spring morning that she and Davy had stepped out into together seemed to come across her. She saw again the laburnums raining their golden blossoms—she smelled the sweetness of the lilac—she saw the spring sky overhead.

"It was for this we went away together," she thought—"for this."

She looked down at her child—she felt great tremors of love going through and through her as it sucked at her breast. Her love for Davy seemed to be embodied in her arms. It was drawing life and strength from her body.

Marion Drysdale looked up at the nurse and she smiled—she smiled.

"He'll forgive me. Davy will forgive me for going," she thought. "He can't *help* forgiving me when he sees the boy."

And when the nurse had left her alone again she kept saying over and over to herself: "Our son. Our son. Little Davy. . . ."

She felt infinitely happy.

JACQUOT AND PIERRE

MADAME L'ESPÉRANCE comes now and then to mend my rugs. She is a Française de France, as they say in Canada: no French-Canadian, but the real, genuine thing. Such come to the New World to push their way; to make money is frankly their ambition. Dollars! That, after all, is the sum of every immigrant's ambition. Perhaps the very worst that can be said of transatlantic life, indeed, is that, in spite of one, it fixes one's attention all too exclusively on dollars. Life in newer lands is something to be bought and sold—never a thing to be enjoyed. And that philosophy leads—downhill.

Madame L'Espérance is the Frenchwoman typified. She is bourgeois France. She has the self-possession of the Frenchwoman, the knowledge of the world, the *savoir vivre*—where do they get it?—that all of them seem honestly to come by. She has the mental compactness, too, the intellectual view of life, that her countrywomen have; she accepts the world just as it is—and cheerfully. Extraordinarily, for she has had hardly anything of what we call "education," she *knows*; not only does she know *her* world, the world of seamstresses and manual workers generally, but she knows other worlds as well. She reads—newspapers, books, whatever she gets hold of; and she observes. She makes use of the two eyes God has given her, and what she sees with them she thinks about—weighs—reasons out—decides upon. She is finite, certainly. But if she has limits, within those limits she moves freely—and which of us can say as much? In talking to her I always feel that hers is a point of view—not, as one so often feels in talking, especially to women, that what they think is simply nonsense and not a point of view at all.

Madame L'Espérance knows her work and does it. For that work she charges the maximum fee, but then she earns her money honestly. Punctually to the moment in the morning she appears, punctually to the moment in the evening she goes away again. Nothing would induce her to give more than the market rate of time. "If," she said to me once, in a moment of unwonted confidence—"if my ladies keep me to do something a little extra for them—on purpose, madame, see you, if so they think they have me"—with one of her rapid gestures she sketched a person prostrate, bound—"then the next morning"—she shrugged her shoulders—"I come by so much the later." She feels that she can tell me things like that because she knows I never try to take advantage of her. She knows her human nature well, does Madame L'Espérance! She sizes us all up and treats us as we deserve, and if she will not give us extra time—why should she?—at least she will not cheat us of a minute. She comes to us to work and she works hard; what she does is done—not done so that it falls to pieces in a week again, as is the New World way of work. No; Madame is thorough. She accepts Canada's views on "getting on" perhaps, but she retains her own original views of work. Why is it that of all the immigrants who come to Canada the French and the Chinese are the only ones to keep their accuracy and their thoroughness? Why should the French and the Chinese hold to their faith—why should the Scotch and English slacken, fall into slovenly ways, and in the end often outdo the New World itself in lack of honest workmanship? Why? I have no answer—I merely ask.

Then Madame L'Espérance is frankly unsentimental— French again. She views the world from the rational economic point of view; and if for a moment she chooses sentiment as her medium, it is a sentiment riddled through with laughter. Yet she has feeling. She is an absolutely faithful wife—faithful, I am sure, in deed and word and thought. She views her husband a little with the maternal eye, perhaps—but lovingly. He is in Champagne—fighting. She is in Canada—waiting. Never in his three years of absence have I known her grumble—say one word that even hints at loneliness—at missing him—at wishing him back again. What Madame L'Espérance feels she keeps intact inside herself. She makes no show of grief, and yet she feels. You know it by the way she brings a letter sometimes from her husband, by the way she shows it you, unfolds it— feeling is like murder, it will out; and as she reads a sentence here and there her voice betrays her. "Ce pauvre garçon," she says, and glances up at you apologetically, "he speaks like that because he misses me! . . ." She passes from the endearing words to business—such details as the Censors let wives have.

She lingers as she reads—she hesitates—you see that she is loath to put the letter by again. How many wives all the world over are doing things like that to-day?—living on letters, staying life not by bread but by the written word. The letter-carrier has turned into the most important thing in all the world. Crowned heads are nothing to him.

One day Madame L'Espérance, when she had folded up her letter and put it by, began to talk.

"He is big," she said, "and simple. He would have stayed in France and worked for nothing all his life. I it was who brought him here."

She stopped her work and glanced out through the window for a second. It was April, and the world was waking up.

"Why," she said, "should one always work for nothing? Why must we give our lives, we others who are poor? For what?"

Just for a moment I saw a reflection of the women of the Revolution in Madame L'Espérance; something fierce and merciless—a sense of deep injustice seemed to stir in her. After a moment she went on.

"We came here," she said. "We left France. Richard found work to do in Canada. Good work. Well paid."

She smiled. The woman of the Revolution was gone again.

"They like him everywhere," said she. "Richard is good. Simple—big—like that—"

Her tone was motherly.

"But," she said, "see you, to be good and simple, that is not the way that one makes money. No, madame; one must keep guard—suspect—be hard—if one would have success. And that is what one comes to Canada to do."

She looked at me. I nodded. She went on.

"Bien"—she settled to her story. "We found work," said Madame L'Espérance, "we were en train to make a home—a foyer. Then came the war. And Richard went. He went—nothing could keep him. 'Why should you go?'—I said to him. He answered me: 'Our country is at war.' And when I said: 'Let them fight,' he only answered: 'They have need of me—I go.'"

Madame L'Espérance hesitated.

"What can one say," she asked; "what—?

"To me," she said, "it seemed that he might stay perhaps. See, madame, we have known life hard. We have worked all our

lives—for nothing. Now . . . we are here in Canada, we work—
we make a home. We, who never have been able to have children—how can one have children where there is no money?—
now, we could found our family, have a child. . . ."

Once more she hesitated.

"That, madame," she said, "was why I wished to keep him.
One wants children. It is nature. One wants to replace oneself—
to go on living in the world in one's own child."

Again she glanced at me. Again I nodded. She went on.

"See," she said, "here, madame, is my ambition. To replace
oneself—to replace one's husband and oneself, a daughter and a
son. And then, perhaps"—she hesitated—"another little son" —
she laughed—"un petit extra."

She paused a moment, shifted her position, threaded her needle, started on another rent.

"Such," she said, "is my ambition. For that I waited."

She sewed.

"Then," she said, "came the war."

She sewed.

"He may come back," I said. "You may have your husband
safely back again."

"He may come back," she said; "he may—"

Outside it was sunny. The trees were budding. The leaves
were pointing—breaking through their sheaths.

"He went," said she. "I had to let him go. I it was who sent
him off at last."

She paused a second, but when she spoke her voice was
absolutely steady.

"He said: 'Do not weep.' I did not weep. And if the tears
were even in my voice Richard would say to me: 'Do not
weep!' and hold his finger up as if I were a child." She laughed
at that—a tender little laugh; yes, she was maternal to her husband. And then she said: "I did not weep." And then she sewed
again and we were silent for a while.

"Madame," she said at last, "how strange this longing that
we have for children! Why do we want them so? For what reason? Is it merely planted in us, this great longing, that we may
replace ourselves?"

She looked at me. She shook her head.

"I do not think that is the reason," Madame L'Espérance

said; "we would not have that longing in us day and night for that."

She sewed, but one could see she sewed mechanically.

"It is a longing," Madame L'Espérance said; "one wants a child. Life is an empty thing without a child. Life is without reason if one has not got a child. Yet why—"

She was so evidently not thinking of me that I made no answer; and in a moment she continued, in another voice. "Tiens," she said, and shrugged her shoulders, "we cannot all have children. One makes the best of it. . . ."

She laughed a little.

"If one longs," she said, "one borrows. One shares, mon Dieu, a scrap of other women's children. Voilà what one does!"

Her face took on its ordinary, cheerful, eminently rational look.

"Mais oui," she said, "one borrows—voilà tout." Once more she shifted her position, took another corner of the rug, settled to it.

"Above me," she said, "lives a friend, a Madame Benoit— Lina is her name of baptism. She has two children"—and suddenly into Madame L'Espérance's face there came an intimate look—"yes," she said, "she has two sons, Jacquot and Pierre."

She glanced at me and raised her hand with one of those gestures so absolutely, so wholly and entirely French.

"She has replaced," she said, "her husband and herself. There remains for her the little daughter—her petit extra."

She smiled at me.

"Comme ça, c'est bon!" said she.

I like to watch Madame when she looks like that—so rational—so cheerful—so kindly and so pleasant.

"There they live," said she, "they and their mother. Their father fights for France."

"How old," I said, "is Pierre?"

"Pierre," she said, "is five. He is a boy already. But Jacquot is yet a baby; he is fifteen months."

She glanced up from her rug. Her eyes met mine.

"You, madame," she said, "love babies?"

"Yes," I said; "I love them."

She drew the rug closer to her, turned a corner where my foot had worn it, and set to work.

"With Pierre," she said, "one knows already. He is a boy—he will be a man. He asks questions: 'What are the stars? Where does the wind go to when it does not blow? Who makes the clouds?' Such things as that continually he asks."

She laughed.

"Ce Pierre," said she, "il est impayable!"

Her face grew pleasanter and pleasanter.

"One knows," she said, "that such grow into men—and so one loves them. But with Jacquot—"

She paused. She raised her smiling eyes to mine.

"Jacquot," she said, "is yet a baby. You, madame, know how we women when we see a baby see no baby but a miracle. We say: 'Here is no man, perhaps. Out of that may grow—who knows!' "—she laughed a little—" 'some kind of angel!' "

She made another of those gestures so exquisitely, inimitably French.

"Such foolish things as that one thinks sometimes," she said; "all women think like that just for one moment when they see a baby that they love. 'There,' we say, 'is something new. What if there grew there something that has never grown before—all things are possible—' So to think is in us women, is it not so, madame?"

"Yes," I said.

Her thread went done. She took another and she sewed with it.

"And then," she said—once more she laughed a little—"our angel speaks. It says: 'What are the stars? Where does the wind go when it is not blowing?' And we know that there will be a man like any other.

"One loves it better so, perhaps," said Madame L'Espérance. "It is a man."

She sewed a little while.

"When I come home," she said, "I eat my supper and I run upstairs. Jacquot is there, not yet in bed, perhaps. I take him in my arms, there in my lap he sits—warm—good to touch—solid. Sometimes he sleeps."

She sewed.

"Ce petit lapin bleu!" she said—and suddenly she dropped her sewing. "Mais pensez donc, madame," she said, "une fois on a tapé Jacquot, et j'ai pleuré, moi—"

She laughed again a little.

"Tiens," she said, "c'est ridicule, n'est-ce pas? Comme c'est absurde!—j'ai pleuré, moi, parce qu'on a tapé Jacquot!"

She took her rug again and sewed.

"Last night," she said, "Jacquot spoke."

"Philosophy?" said I.

"Oui, madame," she answered—and what English or Canadian sewing-woman could have answered me like that?—"oui, toute une philosophie. He said: 'Maman!' "

She laughed again—the tender sort of little laugh that she had given when she spoke of keeping back her tears before her husband left her.

"Comme ça," said she, "we know he is a man. Jacquot will grow a man like all the rest—he is no angel.

"Tiens, tiens!" said Madame L'Espérance. After a bit she said: "Ce petit bonhomme . . ."—and then she snapped her thread and smoothed the rug—her work on it was done.

"Comme ça," she said, "we borrow scraps of happiness, we others."

She shrugged, it seemed to me, not so much her shoulders as her soul.

"C'est la vie, mon Dieu," she said—and rose from her hands and knees.

She stood there, faced me, spoke in quite another tone—her ordinary business voice: "Que voulez-vous, madame," she said, "que je fasse maintenant . . .?"

MR JOHNSTON

SHE is pretty and not very wise. In fact she isn't wise at all except for a sort of unexpected flash now and then of the kind of wisdom that comes of rubbing up against the hard proposition of earning your own living in this big, big world— the kind of wisdom, I presume, that Solomon was alluding to when he remarked that there was much grief in it. She has been earning her living by rubbing up against the world for quite a number of years—too many years considering how little old she is; and in certain ways, there is no denying it, she knows a lot. "Well," she says to me sometimes, "folks says this ole world is a-all a ba-ad kind of a place. But come to think, *I* ain't seen nothin' ser ah-ful ba-ad. Not to ca-all ba-ad," she adds reflectively; and forthwith she proceeds to tell me something that makes my hair stand up on end. "Ain't ut the limut, eh?" she says after that—and then she adds: "An' *tha-at's* not the worst *I* seen!" And complacently she resumes our casual conversation.

But she is pretty—oh, she is pretty! Just to look at her brings all sorts of adjectives arising to the surface of your mind. Dainty, charming, tempting, delicious—words like that she makes you think of. And when she comes in at the door, of an evening, looking in her elegant slimness for all the world like Una without the lion, it is hard somehow to believe that her path has been so thorny and uphill all the way.

She has had a hard time. There have been lots of occasions when the lion would have come in handy. Young women who look dainty and charming and tempting and delicious don't have a very easy time of it on life's journey if they have nothing to protect them but their own sense of decency and fairness. And young women in stores who also serve by standing and waiting all day long suffer not only from sore and swollen feet—they suffer in their self-respect too. They get bumped up against and hustled and hurtled: they are either too sharply or too sweetly spoken to. If they don't get themselves into a mess they deserve, to my mind, everything that is going—for, take it all in all, they have a pretty poor time.

Altabelle—for that, I am sorry to say, is her name—serves in a drug store; one of the kind that is called "cut-rate"—cheap, cheap and exceedingly nasty at the price. She is a young lady clerk there (pronounce, please, just as it is written), on a salary of five dollars a week. She is due at the drug store at eight-thirty in the morning, and there she stays till six-thirty p.m., with a short space of time off for her dinner—or her lunch, as Altabelle prefers that it should be called. Three evenings a week she is back at the store by seven-thirty p.m. and comes away again at eleven. On Saturdays she has to stay till midnight, and on alternate Sundays she is "on duty" all day long. It is the species of store that has printed on its window: "All Night and All Day Service." When that is the legend, someone has to be there to make it come true.

Altabelle's work is various. First of all she "makes sales," and she likes that very much. She is more or less of a genius at it. Her pretty face tempts customers and her winning manner tempts them to buy. She has a way of recommending wares, in fact, that makes everyone want to buy them on the spot, and her secret is that she more than half believes in them herself, though the less than half of her knows very well that everything she sells is pretty much of a fraud. When she leans over the counter and says to you, in a low, persuasive voice: "Jes' try ut. It's a fine article. It'll a-act da-andy on you, b'lieve *me*!" why, then, you feel that life has been incomplete without that particular drug and that only as soon as you and your fifty cents are parted will you begin to live. "It's a *fine* thing," says Altabelle, as she does up your knobbly parcel, with the aid of the bad paper and the worse string that the cut-rate stores provide; and off you go with your parcel under your arm—happy till you try it. The odd thing is that the next time you go back and Altabelle leans over the counter and says to you in exactly the same voice: "Say, tha-at's a swell production. It's ideal!" all your previous experience vanishes from your mind and once more you buy, with the self-same human hope as before springing eternal in your breast. Altabelle's name ought, of course, to have been Circe . . . but Altabelle has never beard of Circe, and if you were to tell her the story of the changing of Ulysses' followers into hogs she would only say: "Git a-an! —you ca-an't stick *me*" or words to that effect.

When Altabelle isn't making sales she is "going over stock." In other words, she is cleaning and dusting the goods that later she intends to palm off on an unsuspecting humanity. She doesn't like that. First of all, it makes her as bla-ack as a pa-at, and then she has to mount on a ladder to get at the top shelves, and the gen'lemen below can see up her legs. " 'Tain't right," says Altabelle. " 'Tain't the thing for a young lady. And," she will add, with a good deal of heat, " 'tain't as if a young lady ca-an afford to wear her sheer hose every day neither. Tha-at cleanin' pra-aposition ain't *right* . . . it's a ma-an's work," she will go on repeating with energy.

Granted these working hours there isn't much time left over for anything else. Altabelle "rooms." She lives all alone in a garret, for which she pays two dollars and fifty cents a week. She hasn't "kitchen privileges," but there is a gas-ring in the corner over which she cooks her breakfasts (I mean she makes a cup of tea before she gets out of bed and takes gulps at it and hasty bites at a piece of bread and butter while she is waving her hair); and when she gets home at night she makes another cup of tea and eats another piece of bread and butter—with possibly a second-grade quality of egg or a third-rate grade of kipper. On the nights that she is due back at the store by seven-thirty this meal is as hurried as the first one of the day; and usually on such occasions, when she returns at night, she makes *another* cup of tea and drinks it in a leisurely manner after she gets into bed. Tea is cheap and stimulating. Altabelle never does without the accompanying milk and sugar if she can help it, but sometimes when funds run completely out she has to drink it "clear"; and then, like Dick Swiveller's "Marchioness" with her orange-peel and water, Altabelle has to make-believe very much before it tastes quite nice—normally she likes three lumps of sugar to the cup and a generous supply of milk. The midday meal Altabelle always takes "out," because there isn't time to get home to the gas-ring. It is more a problem than a meal. If you deduct two dollars and fifty cents for your room (light extra) and fourteen meals of tea and bread and butter with seven accompanying second-grade eggs or third-rate kippers, and then add on to that your car fares for the times you sleep in and start late, and the clothes you would love to buy and do buy some-times, though you know you can't afford it—well, you will find there isn't much over. However, Altabelle takes a sangwitch with her in a general way for this midday meal of hers, and she buys a cup o' cawfee to wash it down, or sometimes she has a ten-cent salad and a roll, or sometimes just ice-cream. And when funds run out altogether she takes a walk in her lunch-hour and looks in at the shop windows, and thinks what stunning high-heeled pumps she would buy if she only had the money.

Sundays make a change. The Sunday she stays at home she usually stops in bed till the early afternoon to "rest up"; and then she drinks her cup of tea and dresses herself in everything she has and goes for a wa-alk with a friend. I mean a young lady friend. "I take no sta-ack in beaus," says Altabelle; "beaus, from wha-at *I* can see, jes' leads a young lady right straight into trouble." She goes for a walk, therefore, with a young lady friend, as I have said, and for want of any place else to go they sometimes turn into a church at the conclusion of the walk and join in the singing of the hymns. Other days, when they have ten cents apiece handy, or one of them has twenty cents to treat the other with, they step into a movie and watch the show. "It wa-as real roma-antical!" Altabelle says, speaking of the latter. If I ask her how she liked the church she usually replies: "Oh, it wa-as la-ats o' fun."

On the Sunday when Altabelle has to wait on customers at the store all day she treats herself to a "full course meal" in the middle of the day. It is an ah-ful extravagance, but she does it on principle. She feels it to be her due. "Ef I ha-ave to wait on tha-at mean ole crowd all day, Sunday," she says to me, "I mean to ha-ave my lunch *good*. I'm jes' *goin'* to," she says. And she does. At one-thirty precisely she repairs to the restaurant adjoining the store (and under the same management as the store), and she goes there because the employees are allowed a discount—a slight discount—a very slight one indeed—on their bill. The full meal costs thirty-five cents and the employees are allowed to get it for thirty—that is all. Still, five cents is five cents, and Altabelle's lovely face and sweet, dear smile is so popular with the waitresses (also young women struggling with life on an income of five dollars weekly) that whenever the Manageress isn't looking they slip extra dishes and best helpings and even double portions on to Altabelle's plate. The Manageress herself, indeed (coping with the world on a salary of seven), has so fallen under Altabelle's spell that she takes care always to be looking the other way when that is desired of her; so Altabelle does well at her fortnightly dinner. "Guess I ha-ad a fifty-cent meal a-alright yest'day," she tells me triumphantly on the Monday evening. "Say, them wa-affles tasted *good!*" "I ha-ad spring la-amb yest'day," she will say to me on another occasion perhaps. "Yes, sir, and new potatoes! An' I ha-ad a-all the ice-cream I could git around. Tha-at waitruss there is a lovely young lady . . ." I think those dinners are what keep Altabelle up to the scratch. She eats enough every other Sunday to last till every other Tuesday anyway, and the other twelve days she passes not too disagreeably—wondering what the menew will be on the next occasion. I have not been to the caffay myself, but I understand from Altabelle that it is *the* thing a-alright, and the way the ladies dress there is swell.

The way Altabelle dresses is one of the riddles of the universe—anything the Sphinx could possibly have to offer would be child's play compared with it. Altabelle has, as you see, nothing whatever to spend, and no time to spend it in if she had, and yet she looks like the Countess of Malmesbury every time. She next to never can buy anything at all. The best she can do, as I have said, is to walk along in her lunch-hour thinking what she would buy if she had the money. She buys nothing—and she always looks well. She has the faculty of wearing her clothes. She is, as she says, easy on 'em. Her black suit (you have to wear black in the store) goes on from year to year. Its peplum is taken off in the winter and then the coat is a bodice, and there is Altabelle in the full draught of the constantly opening and shutting door in her black frock with a white collar at her neck and a string of sham pearls glistening above it. In the spring the peplum is sewn on again and there is the suit as before—and Altabelle in the hot August days looks cool and refreshing as a gurgle of water on a hill-side, in her old black skirt and a white Jap silk blouse that she washes and irons herself in the dead of the night . . . while her coat and Merry Widow hat hang up safely amongst the cockroaches in the sanctum provided by the management for the lady employees and known as "the rest-room." This goes on till—well, till another suit has to be screwed out of the five dollars a week—somehow. It is somehow, too. But it is screwed out when it has to be, and the cups of tea at such periods are "clear" for such an indefinite period that by the time you have got your suit and are able to go back to your milk and sugar, you almost like your tea better without. Man—and also, to a modified degree, woman—is a creature of habut, as Altabelle says, and if you had to live on blubber exclusively you would soon think, I suppose, that it had a rarefied taste, and would prefer it on the whole to salmon. Once Altabelle had salmon at her fortnightly lunch. and not even the fact that it and unlimited cucumber and vinegar made her extremely ill can take away from her the joys of remembrance. O happy day that fixed her choice! is the way Altabelle feels to *that* occasion.

All this time I have never said what Altabelle looks like. She has red-brown velvety eyes like a gazelle, and her hair is immensely soft and thick and fine—fine as a baby's—and it is of the shade that centuries and centuries of blondes have vainly struggled to attain to. It isn't golden and it isn't auburn and it isn't ash-coloured. It is a shade that you see sometimes in clouded amber—a colour subtle and exquisitely refined. That is what Altabelle's hair is like—and at her temples it goes of its own accord into little tendrils, and if Altabelle could only be decoyed away from her Marcel wavers her hair would wave itself with a curve like a sea wave breaking on the shore. But Altabelle doesn't admire that. She says it "ain't reg'lar enough." So she waves her hair into a mathematical problem that no wave of the sea ever attained to yet. She likes it better that way. As to the rest of her, she has the most idyllic little nose—did anyone ever notice how rare a thing a really pretty nose is?—and her smile is worth going a long way to see. Her face is an oval like an early Madonna's, and she looks you straight in the face just as an early Madonna would do if she were selling you *sal hepatica* in a cut-rate drug store with All Day and All Night Service. When it comes to "and ceteras," as Altabelle says, she takes five-and-three-quarters in gloves and three in shoes, and about the greatest sorrow of her life is the fact that her feet are "spreading" on the soft-wood flooring of the drug store. She doesn't grumble a bit at the stiffness and soreness; she takes that as all in the day's work; but the fact that her poor little feet may spread to size four—say C or D—instead of remaining at size three, A, gives her acute anguish. "Say, ain't ut jes' too ba-ad," she will say to me, "tha-at *mean* ole store! I don't wa-ant to go squishin' around there. . . ." This possibility of a broadened foot is one of the very few grudges that Altabelle cherishes against life. If I suggest that a fallen arch would be a more serious matter to fight she merely replies: "I'll take my chanst o' tha-at!" and dismisses the possibility. But when she says "that-at *mean* ole store!" her voice is full of feeling. A four pump D!—that, surely, is the first step down to Hades.

Altabelle serves in the drug department in comp'ny with three gen'lemen, each of whom gets his twenty dollars in the week, while Altabelle gets five. Yet Altabelle is, as I have said, a good saleswoman. Right straight opposite the drug department is the ice-cream-soda fountain, where the young gen'leman in charge told her she could come and ha-ave a free treat any time the manager's back was turned. "I s'pose he thinks I'd do ut too!" says Altabelle. "What did you say to him when he asked you?" I say, perhaps. "Jes' give him a look," says Altabelle— and apparently it was enough. At the right hand stands the young lady who manages the candy department. Altabelle has a poor opinion of *her*. "I ha-ave no truck with tha-at young girl," says Altabelle, "she's *loose*. I see her with my own eyes tickle one of the young gen'lemen on the ankle as he was goin' up the ladder to fetch down a bottle of sarsaparilla." There was no more to be said about the young lady who manages the candy department. "She *is* no young lady," says Altabelle. "She's nothin' but a girl." That finishes her. The cashier however (in the cage as you go in to your left) meets with Altabelle's approval. "*She's* a young lady," Altabelle says of her; "guess she knows how to take care of *her*self a-alright. I see one of the gen'lemen try an' kiss her," Altabelle says further, "and I tell you she give him wha-at for." Of this Altabelle approves highly. "You jes' *got* to show those gen'lemen you won't sta-and fer no nonsense," she says, and then meditatively: "But ye ca-an't come ut over 'em too strawng or they'll git ba-ack at you. Ye jes' ha-ave to keep 'em on the string . . . and you *ca-an*, too, ef 'tain't the bawss gits a-after ye. . . ." Altabelle gave a kind of sniff when she said that. "Ef it's the bawss," she said impressively, "*look out!* You'd best git out ef it's the bawss. Quit!" she said, making an end of it.

"But say," she goes on sometimes when she is in a talking mood, "say, ain't ut true, ye ca-an't sla-acken up a minnut when there's gen'lemen around? Why, tha-at young lady in the kodak section she ga-at ta-alkin' bus'ness yest'day. When she ga-at through with wha-at she ha-ad to say, wha-at do you s'pose she done? She reached up so she pretty near touched the gen'le-man's cheek and 'Say,' she says to him, 'you look at *me* some now. How is tha-at fer sixteen cents?' says she."

"What did she mean?" I ask at that.

"Why, *don'-you-know?*" says Altabelle, all in italics. "Say, tha-at's the latest out. It's *good*! 'How's tha-at fer sixteen cents?' you say."

Altabelle gave that soft, musical laugh of hers.

"It's witty, ain't ut, eh?" she said, and then returning to the young lady in the kodak section: " 'Say,' she says to him, 'you look at my ca-amplexion some!' " Altabelle tilted up her nose. "An' say," said she, "don't it strike yer some as tha-at's no kind of way fer a young lady to behave? She's some girl, eh? Wha-at do you s'pose she'll get ef she ta-alks tha-at way when there's gen'lemen around!"

Altabelle gave her head a toss.

"*She* ga-at lef' tha-at time anyway," she said. "She ha-appened on a nice young gen'leman. He's our assistant ma-anager—he's a fine young fellah. *He* don't go round kissin' the young ladies. No *sir*!—he's a *good* fellah. Mr Johnston is a very fine young gen'leman."

"Does he wait on customers there with you?" I asked her.

Altabelle stopped short a minute before answering—it wasn't like her.

"Why, yes," she said; "he's our assista-ant ma-anager right in the drug department there. An' he's a-alright."

She paused.

"He's *a-alright,* Mr Johnston is," she said; "he's a re-turn. He ga-at hit in Fra-ance there, so he ca-an't git back to work on wha-at he'd used to . . . an' I guess he is superior a-alright. He is right there in the drug de-partment. Mr Johnston's our assista-ant ma-anager."

She paused again.

"Say," she said, "don't it strike yer he's a-alright? He's fine. He's da-andy, Mr Johnston is. He ain't the sporty kind. No, sir, he keeps his ha-ands awf the young ladies. He's a *nice* young fellah."

She gave a sigh. I never heard her sigh like that before.

"Don't it seem kind o' mean to you," she said, "tha-at ole store rakin' in the plunks and Mr Johnston gittin' twen'y? *I* think tha-at's *mean!*" said Altabelle. "We a-average pretty near a thousan' dollars Sat'days," she said, "and then they pay a fellah twen'y! . . . How's tha-at, I wa-ant to know? How's Mr Johnston goin' to live the way he should? Why," said Altabelle, "it's a dawg's life fer a young fellah in the drug de-partment there. An' ef he hadn't got himself crocked up, why, Mr Johnston oughter . . ."

She stopped.

"He oughter ha-ave the dearest little home," she said, "I guess . . ."

"Altabelle," I said, "you like Mr Johnston, don't you?"

"Why, yes," she said, "I guess I like um. He's *a-al*right. He's a *good* young fellah."

She was quiet a minute.

"He's *good*," she said, "he's *fine*, tha-at's wha-at he is. He's lovely. . . ."

The time she came to see me after that—she comes in sometimes in the evening when she isn't working in the store—she was more discontented than I have ever seen her. Altabelle takes life easily as a rule. I couldn't think what was wrong with her that evening.

"Aren't you well?" I said to her.

"Oh, I'm a-alright," she said. "I'm a-alright."

She paused.

"Sometimes I guess," she said, "as I'll git workin' in a Departmental Store. There's more young ladies workin' there. Seems to me as if it would be kinder more re-fined, p'r'aps, ef you could work with ladies."

She paused again.

"Gee-whiz!" she said, after a bit, "tha-at streak me an' the bunch o' gen'lemen works in there is narrer! We're kinder bound to bump when the crowd's a-an."

She paused.

"I wa-ant you to understa-and," she said, "as them young fellahs there is perfec' gen'lemen. I've never ha-ad one bump aginst me yet but wha-at he ha-as excused himself. 'Pardon *me*!' he'll say. Or sometimes when the crowd's ga-at sla-ackened up he'll find the time to say: 'Won't you ex-cuse *me*, lady, please?'"

She paused.

"I don't say but wha-at they'll kinder bump sometimes . . ."— and there she came to a full stop—"but Mr Johnston don't," she said; "he ain't acquainted with the pawin' up young lady bus'-ness. No, he ain't. *He* knows enough to let young ladies be, an' I will say as I 'preciate tha-at. He's—"

She stopped.

"Say," she said, "wha-at do you s'pose! Ef I set out to climb tha-at da-arned ole ladder, Mr Johnston, *he* ha-aps up and gits ut fer me. Ain't tha-at da-andy? Gits ut every time, sir . . . an' it ain't ser easy climbin' ef you're a-all crocked up." She shook her head. "Don't make no difference ef he *is* a cripple. He's a nice young gentleman, is Mr Jo—"

She stopped again—this time for a considerable period.

"I kinder guess at times," she said, "as I'd best go and work in the De-partment Store p'ra-aps. There is young ladies workin' in the dry goods section there. It's more re-fined, I guess."

She sighed and went away.

But the next time she came she had a radiant face. She hardly got inside the door when: "Say," she said, "will you ima-agine, please, wha-at Mr Johnston ha-as to say!"

"What?" said I.

"Says he guesses I'm the daintiest thing he ever seen!" Altabelle smiled a very sweet and innocent and charming and triumphant smile. "Quite a re-ma-ark, eh?" said she.

She paused.

"Oh, he's a-alright," she said. "He's *a-al*right, you ca-an bet your life on that. He's da-andy, Mr Johnston is."

"When did he say it, Altabelle?" I asked her.

"Why," she said, "when we wa-as workin' Sunday aft'noon he kinder opened out. And then he tole me—"

She smiled again—a little shyly this time.

"We wa-as tha-at hustled on till a-all o' four o'cla-ack," she said; "we didn't git a bite to eat."

She laughed.

"So, say," she said, "ima-agine! I jes' didn't ha-ave no full meal Sunday. Them full course meals is awf at three."

She laughed again.

"So tha-at wa-as one on me a-alright!" she said.

"What did you do?" I asked her.

"Oh, it wa-as fine—we done a-alright," said she. "We ha-ad a sangwitch at the ice-cream-soda fountain, him and me done, and we ha-ad a sundae a-after, and he said I ha-ad to ha-ave my cup o' tea.

"It tasted good a-alright," said Altabelle; "we done fine." She hesitated.

"Say, listen here," said she. "I tole him as I ha-ad the Dutch treat habut with the gen'lemen."

She stopped.

"He kinder seemed—"

She stopped.

"Oh, well, I let um pay," she said, "but—"

She broke off and sat gazing into space. When I spoke to her she started.

"Why, yes," she said, "I guess there wa-as no ha-arm to tha-at. Tha-at Mr Johnston is a perfec' gen'leman. *He's* a-alright, I guess."

And she sat gazing into space.

"An' Mr Johnston says," said Altabelle, "he kinder loves to see a lady lookin' nice."

She sighed.

"He's fine," she said, "once't he gits ta-alkin'. Why, you ca-an't b'lieve the things he seen! And say!—them things he done," she said, "is ah-ful. An' he got lef' when he wa-as hit."

Her eyes filled up with tears.

"Him lyin' there!" she said. "He must ha-ave been a *fine* young fellah when he sta-arted out."

And then, without rhyme or reason, she looked at me defi-antly.

"He's a-alright *now*, I guess!" she said. "My! ca-an't a gen'leman jes' git hurt, I wa-ant to know . . . and ain't ut *mean* as he's there slavin' in tha-at drug de-partment when he's—"

She paused.

"Why, he's worth a-all of fifty dollars, Mr Johnston is," said she. "He certainly *is*. He's *fine*—tha-at bawss ain't in ut with

um. No, he ain't, tha-at bawss is on the bias. Every time. And
Mr Johnston's *straight*. He *is*. And," pursued Altabelle, "he
hates tha-at bawss. You ca-an't do nothin' with um, not sinst he
seen um try and kiss me once't . . . he jes' *hates* um. You should
hear um! Tha-at Mr Johnston ca-an speak up, I tell yer."

She stopped short and she sighed.

"Altabelle," I said, "when shall you go and work in the
Department Store?"

She started.

"I donno," she said. And then she said vaguely: "I s'pose
there's ladies workin' there a-alright—it's kinder more re-fined
p'ra-aps. . . ." And then she went away.

The last time but one that Altabelle came to see me she was
quite unlike herself. Most utterly unlike. She was absent-
minded—irritable. She looked "peaked," as she herself would
say. "Don't you feel *well*?" I said again.

"Oh, I'm a-alright," she said indifferently. After a bit she
added: "Well, p'ra-aps to-night I'm kind o' linty." And then she
relapsed into the most impenetrable silence.

"Tha-at Mr Johnston don't say nothin' now," she said
abruptly, emerging from the impenetrable silence. "He's kinder
stopped communication with the ladies."

She paused.

"I bumped myself against his leg as I wa-as pa-assin' him the
other day, and a-all he ha-ad to say wa-as, 'Will you please ex-
cuse *me*, lady?' "

She paused again; then, quite unnecessarily, she added: "I
could 'a' helped meself. I bumped aginst his leg a purpose."
And then, still more unnecessarily she remarked: "And I don't
care who hears me say ut neither!"

She paused.

"I can't ima-agine," she said irritably, "wha-at in thunder—"

She paused.

"*I* done nothin'. *I*'m not mean," she said. "It's up to him, I
guess."

And suddenly she sighed—she sighed . . . I've heard her sigh
and yet I never heard her sigh like that before.

"Say," she said, "ain't life *mean*? Ain't ut *ugly* on ye? Don't
ut play a low-down trick on ye a-alright? Ye ca-an't *do* nothin'."

She glanced downward.

"Why, I've wore this suit to ra-ags and bones," she said. "I feel a-all crumpled up. I'm kinder *tired*."

She stopped.

"How ca-an ye *help* . . ." she said, and stopped again.

"Oh, 'tain't *right*," she said with sudden passion, " 't'aint *work* fer ladies. Here I ga-at to climb and clean up there . . . and Mr Johnston sta-andin' there below. 'Tain't—'t'ain't *right!*" she said.

Her eyes were full of tears. Her face was scarlet.

"I don't *wa-ant*—I *tole* the bawss," she said; "he only sent me ca-ase he's gittin' ba-ack at me ca-ase I won't kiss um.

"An' I *won't*," she said. "So there! I hate tha-at bawss. He's ugly to me."

She sniffed and mopped her eyes.

"Oh, well, I s'pose," she said, "I got to quit. Tha-at's all about ut, an' I'm sick and tired. Them gen'lemen! *Ca-an't* they leave yer! I'm not sporty. I'm a straight, good girl, I am, and I been bra-aht up *good*. Ca-an't they see ut in yer—"

Her tears surged up again. She sniffed. She used her handkerchief.

"An' Mr Johnston sta-andin' there," she said. "Wha-at does *he* think, I wa-ant to know! He never ser much as—

"*Well—!*" she said.

She went away.

But the last time she came her eyes were shining. I never knew before that red-brown, velvety eyes can glow.

"Say," she said, with one foot inside the door on this occasion, "say, ef tha-at Mr Johnston ain't put up a marryin' pra-aposition!

"He wa-ants to marry me," said Altabelle.

"So ef tha-at certainly don't beat a-all," said she.

She stood there, with one foot inside the door, and gazed at me. Her eyes were shining—they were shining softly—happily. Life wasn't ugly any more to Altabelle—no, she was happy.

"Say," she said, "ain't ut *great!*"

She gazed beyond me.

"Come in," I said.

She came in, took a seat and sat there gazing at the far horizon.

"He'll stay right there in the de-partment where he is and keep his twen'y, Mr Johnston will," said Altabelle, "an' I'm goin' right straight in the De-partment Store. There's ladies there and Mr Johnston says as he'll feel easier when I'm with the ladies."

"Shall you work," I said, "after—"

"*Sure*," said Altabelle, most business-like. "I'm workin' s'rlong as Mr Johnston's gittin' twen'y. An' I kinder wa-ant to work."

She stopped.

"An' say," she said, "tha-at ma-anager there in the De-part-ment Store, he says he guesses as he'll fix me fer the model section. 'Say,' says he, 'you are a Slim-Jim pra-aposition. Why in hell don' you stout out?' he says. I guess," said Altabelle hopefully, "as I'll stout out some once't I'm a married woman p'ra-aps."

She looked at me.

"But say, he says he'll fix me fer the model section—ain't ut fine?" said she. "That-at's a-all of twelve. He says I ha-ave the regulation figger ef I'll jes' git fleshier. . . .

"Ain't ut swell?" she said.

She drew a breath.

"We've rented our apa-artment an' it ha-as two rooms," said Altabelle, "an' kitchenette and ba-ath-room awf ut. It's an elegant apa-artment an' it's on the down-town section too, so Mr Johnston ca-an git in and ha-ave his lunch served home and I ca-an run right round and fix ut ready for um. Ain't tha-at *good*? I tell um I ca-an run right home and fix his dinner ready fer um too . . . and when he gits home nights—"

She paused. She sat there busy with her castle-building.

"I guess I'll ha-ave a little lunch fer Mr Johnston when he gits home nights," said Altabelle, "fer when ye're tired it's *good* to have ut waitin' . . ." and she lifted up her face to me. "Say," she said, "ain't ut *great*? Ain't it a da-andy thing as Mr Johnston wa-ants to marry me?"

She paused. "It seems he always tha-aht I wa-as the dearest thing.

"He kinder loves to ha-ave me, Mr Johnston does," and suddenly her eyes filled up with tears. "*Oh*," she said, "ain't ut fine! Ain't Mr Johnston *gra-and*! Why, he's *i*-deal."

She stopped.

"I couldn't tell you ha-alf," she said, "wha-at Mr Johnston is. B'lieve me, he's some gen'leman. He's a *good* young fellah."

She sat lost in day-dreams.

"Altabelle," I said, "you're happy, aren't you?"

She started—her face lighted up.

"*Sure*," she said, "I'm happy. Why, he's *great*." And then a mischievous, dawning smile curled round and round the corners of her mouth. "Listen," she said, "you ain't forgot the time when Mr Johnston a-acted ugly to me?"

I shook my head.

"Well, say," she said, "I wa-ant to know ef you ca-an guess . . ." and she broke into laughter—the most delicious rippling laugh you ever heard. She laughed.

"Oh, *say*," she said as soon as she could speak. She laughed.

She put up both her hands and hid her face. The tears came oozing out between her fingers and she sat there rocking—wavering to and fro.

"Oh, *say*," she stammered out at last, "he . . . he . . . wa-as . . . ba-ashful!

"Tha-at certainly beats a-all!" said Altabelle.

She wiped her eyes.

"Oh, *my*!" she gasped.

She sat there looking at me with her hair all ruffled and her face all radiant—beaming—oh, so happy.

"Ain't tha-at rich?" she said, "ain't ut?" And then, quite suddenly, her eyes grew absent-minded. And her face grew grave.

"He's *fine* a-alright," she said. "I donno wha-at he sees in me. Oh, he's a *good* young—"

And once more her eyes grew absent-minded, and she sat there—looking through me into something that's eternal.

THE CHILD

SHE went about her work in the house and her heart was heavy within her. She swept her carpets and cleaned her kitchen stove, she cooked the dinner and washed the dishes, and all the time she was doing these things she was thinking—thinking bitterly. It was a good enough place she was in, the people were kind, as people go, the wages were average, the work was nothing to complain of, but she was very unhappy; and as day succeeded day she was more and more unhappy, till at last it seemed to her as if she couldn't bear what was coming upon her. For she was in trouble. She had got herself into trouble, as the saying is; and as she swept her carpets and cleaned the stove, as she went to bed tired at night and rose up unrefreshed in the morning, she knew that she carried within her—a child. Her child—hers and his, a child not wanted, a child that she thought of with terror and bitterness . . . and it was coming into the world very soon, and she was its mother.

She wasn't a bad girl. Not at all. She wasn't very much of anything—an easy-going, affectionate creature whose virtues had been the ruin of her. When—when it happened, she hadn't even thought of asking him if he meant to marry her. She had either taken for granted that things would go on all right, or perhaps she had never thought about anything at all. She had just yielded to the impulse of the moment and his entreaty—she had followed the line of least resistance, as she would have said if she had ever heard of the phrase—her good-nature had carried her away with it and she simply gave herself because it was the easiest thing to do—she liked him well enough not to want to refuse anything he asked her. So it was . . . and it had seemed simple enough, nothing specially right or wrong about it. His kisses had been warm and comforting and comfortable—she had liked to feel someone close like that—loving her; it had pleased her woman's nature that longed and craved to be loved, that would give all a lifetime of barren loneliness for—well, for that feeling of being able to *give* something someone wanted very much and to be thanked for the gift in kisses.

It seemed a long time ago, all that. And it seemed a lot to have to pay for a minute or two of warmth and contentment. For it hadn't been much more than that—she hadn't felt, she wasn't capable of feeling, perhaps, any of that passionate love, that desire, that joy, that losing of herself in something greater and stronger than she alone could ever be. No; she hadn't any of that to fall back on—not a scrap or a rag of any grand passion such as that. She had nothing to remember but that minute of warmth and the feeling of pleasantness that she had had something to give that someone liked very much to take—and now that didn't seem enough. It seemed to her sometimes as she wandered about the house, doing her work in a dream, that she had bartered away all she had to give for just nothing at all.

It had happened one night after a party. He had been seeing her home, with a big, round, golden moon overhead and a shimmering world all round them. It had seemed lonely, and they two had seemed alone and yet somehow at home together in the loneliness. She remembered how a whip-poor-will had cried somewhere away over the marsh, and she remembered the odd feeling that came over her all of a sudden that this was home—*this*, the outer air and the sweet smells of June, and the warm arm that had slipped itself round her body. She didn't love the man beside her, but she loved what he represented—the strength of man and his desire, and the home that man can provide, and all the other things that follow these things as a sort of matter of course.

So she had given herself. It might just as well have been another man—anyone would really have done in that moonlight, in that shimmering world—anyone who had a strong, warm arm, and a man's voice, and a man's desire—anyone who *wanted* her like that.

That was the beginning and the end of that part of the story. He had gone away after—to the War, perhaps, or to somewhere just as vague. She didn't know where to find him, and if she had known she wouldn't have known what to say to him to touch him—she didn't feel that he would care in the least for what she had to tell him. *This* wasn't what he was after, this weight that she bore inside her—this new strange thing that was growing day by day within her—this mysterious presence of which she could not rid herself, try as she might. All day long she thought of it, thought of it *behind* the other things, as it were. She could talk with the surface of her mind, take orders from her lady, carry them out, do her work respectably, eat her meals and digest them too, answer messages at the door and telephone; but *behind*, all the time that she was doing these things, something kept saying to her: "You will have a baby soon. A baby. A living child . . . it is growing and growing—and soon it will come to life." And then the voice within her seemed to say: "And what will you do?—what will you *do*?" And sometimes it said: "What *can* you do when that happens?"

There were times in the night when she would wake up terrified. She would lie there in the dark in the attic room that was reserved for the maid, and she would huddle herself together and lie quaking. She was terrified. What would she do! She would lie a while and think the same things over and over again and strain her eyes into the darkness, and then she would turn so as to try to go to sleep again, and in turning she would feel how heavy and unwieldy she was becoming . . . and she would be terrified again. "My God," she would think, "what am I to do; what can I *do*? . . ."

She hadn't any money except just what she earned month by month. Her home was in the country, where it happened—she couldn't tell her people there: hard-working, respectable, God-fearing folk, who would be furious with her. And in the city she knew no one that could help her. She wasn't a clever girl—she couldn't think of things—clever, original things—to do. . . . She simply didn't dare to tell a soul of her trouble, she just held her tongue. She knew that if she broke her silence to anyone—any human being in the world—that creature had a right to turn from her with disgust and horror—almost as if she were an unclean thing. Why, anyone had almost a right to lift his hand against her if she were to tell what had befallen her just as it happened . . . she knew that.

She knew it. She didn't question such things as that. She knew that for one moment she had stepped beyond the pale, and she knew that if you step beyond the pale and are a woman—you must stay there. You have to stay beyond the pale for ever and ever more. She didn't question a quite ordinary, everyday truth like that; but sometimes she felt as if she would go crazy if she couldn't tell someone the mess she was in and ask what she was to do—*what!*

As the weeks and months went on she took to counting over her money. She counted it over and over. The Hospital. That costs. And perhaps things might go wrong—they do sometimes—and she mightn't be able to work for a bit. *That* costs. And anyway, there would be ten days or so to pay for before she would be able to go to work again. . . . And if she couldn't *find* work for a bit—what then! And the baby. She never said that word but her heart leaped. The baby. It was unthinkable, but there would be a baby, a living, human creature soon—a new one. This thing that weighed heavier and heavier day by day, this thing that she vainly tried to hide by lacing it in more tightly as the days went by—this thing, in spite of her, would be another human being soon. And human beings cost money. She would have to *pay* to keep it alive.

She would calculate and calculate—and wonder, and sometimes she would feel her mouth dry with that haunting dread she had. Would she have to give it up to somewhere or something to bring up? Would she have to part from it—desert it? She hated it, she dreaded it, she feared it; it was the great distress of all her life, her shame and her disgrace . . . and yet, when she thought of parting from it, when she took to those everlasting calculations of hers, she would feel her mouth dry. Why? She wanted to be rid of it—and then when she took to thinking how she could be rid of it, her mouth went dry and her heart seemed to stop beating for a bit. It wasn't love, that—no. It was something else, something that seemed to rise, in spite of her, as it were, from some great depth in her. It was as if you drew something slowly up from a deep, deep well— truth, perhaps.

As the days went on she grew desperate. Once her mistress said to her: "Dolly, you look pale. Don't you feel well?" And it almost burst from her. It almost broke out of her—that long pent-up terror and anxiety. And then, as she looked at the calm face of her mistress, she forced it back. It wouldn't do—what could she say? Her mistress wouldn't, *couldn't* understand. She might drive her out of the house if she spoke. And then where would she go—what could she do alone in the streets? She was silent. "I'm all right, thank you, ma'am," she said.

Once—just once in the night-time—she had felt something else, something different from all this tumult of remorse and fear. She had felt revolt. Yes; she had felt that she hadn't deserved all this shame and misery. What had she done? Just a moment—a moment—and then these months of concealment and torture. Why? And obscurely another thing had stirred in her. Her child! Wasn't it as good as any other woman's child? Why not? Wasn't it alive—didn't she feel for it as any other woman feels—wasn't it a wonder and a miracle just like any other living, coming creature? . . . she dashed these thoughts down to where they came from—she threw herself on her pillow and she cried—she cried. She felt wicked—she felt wicked . . . not because of what she had done, but because she had ceased for a moment to think it wicked to have done it. No; her child was not like other children. She had brought it there when it shouldn't be there—if it could die at its birth so much the better for it and for her . . . and as she lay crying and thinking these things over and over in the darkness, suddenly her whole heart burst and blossomed into love for the child she was blaspheming. "I love it; I love it," she cried, and she sat upright and drove her clenched hands down into the mattress on either side of her. "It's mine—it's alive. It's a child," she said. And furiously into the darkness she kept repeating: "Oh, I love it, I love it—it's mine—it's mine!"

The next day, as she went about her work, when she felt her child bearing her down and impeding her and keeping her back and weighing heavier and heavier, as it seemed to her, with every minute, she loved the very hindrance of it. She adored this child that she had gained in pain and sorrow—she loved it with every fibre of her being—she would have died to give it a moment of life. . . .

And that night it was born dead in the hospital—and her way lay clear again before her. She was rid of her enemy and she felt that she had lost her salvation. She could drop her stained past behind her and step out bravely into the future . . . and she felt that God was cruel.

THE COCKTAIL

IT was a gleaming topaz. Brilliant. Alive. Jess Rivers sat on her shabby chair and leant her elbows on the table—and she looked at it.

A cocktail. It sounds nothing. Think how the men and women in the restaurants drink them off night after night and think nothing of them! A cocktail is a zest to appetite, a little extra stimulant to soul—a luxury; but to Jess Rivers a cocktail was something more than that. It was a treat—and a necessity. It meant economy—scraping. It meant personal self-denial. It was what she looked forward to from Saturday night to Saturday night; she tasted it a thousand times, though not with bodily lips, while she was working. Jess Rivers' cocktail was a sort of Mecca, to which she made her weekly pilgrimage.

Slowly it had come about, this habit, in the way habits do. May Henderson had first given her a cocktail to drink. May Henderson was "gay." Jess Rivers knew it—but she liked her. May Henderson had a ready tongue, bright eyes, red lips—she was full-breasted—she was full of life. Such come to trouble, and May Henderson in time had come to trouble . . . but before, when May was only loving, happy, gay, when she was ready to share her everything with anyone—then it was that she had given Jess the cocktail; and later she had shown her how to mix it. Jess never drank her cocktail now—after the years—but she thought of May. May's curls were topaz-colour—like the liquid. Her eyes had gleamed, just as the liquid gleamed when you looked into it. Jess Rivers sat and leant her elbows on the table and looked far down into the topaz-coloured glass. She sat there looking, without tasting. Just looking. Savouring beforehand.

For she knew that once she drank—the merest sip—she would be happy; and she liked to think of that. It is a great thing to be happy. She knew that just as soon as she had put that tiny glass against her lips she would feel—different. It was Saturday. Another week was behind her. She felt dragged, tired, drooping, sagged, dejected, but just let her drink!—the whole world would be changed. She knew that she would see a gleaming world.

"Once you drink that," May Henderson had said, "you'll not be
sorry you got born."

May! What had become of her? She was "gay." She wasn't
"straight." But for all that—you couldn't help yourself—you
loved her. She *wanted* to be straight; she hadn't gone to pieces
all on purpose. May was loving and she wanted to be loved.
That was the trouble. And she was pretty, *pretty*—that was the
trouble. How many of them went that way! Jess Rivers, old as
age goes in the business women's world, had seen so many of
them . . . drop. First they were bright, and reached out after
life—then they were feverishly happy for a bit—then they
couldn't believe that it was true—then they went all to pieces.
So many of them! It was to May and May's gen'leman friend
that Jess Rivers owed her cocktail.

Jess was a straight girl—straight as a die. She hadn't much
temptation to be otherwise. It wasn't only that she wasn't pretty,
wasn't taking, was pale and slight; no, it wasn't that—everyone
has a price. But her blood flowed slowly. She had no strong
desire of any kind. She merely asked to be allowed to get
along—to work away—to earn enough that she might eat and
drink and clothe herself; no more than that. It's easy to be
straight when you are bloodless.

Jess had been selling all her life. At twelve she sold tin tacks
and screws and dish-mops in the ten-cent store, sold all day
long, standing all day—at twelve years old. Sharp she had
learned to be, so that her eye was on her customers—if she took
her eye off they "pinched" her goods. She earned three dollars
in the week. That was her girlhood. It is not a way to grow.

Then came the store—a departmental store—drapery, first
one section, then another. Still standing every day and all day
long. Long days, long, interminable days with nothing to do but
try to please the customer who came your way. Sometimes you
pleased your customer, sometimes not. There were all kinds to
please—quick customers, slow ones, those who knew their
minds, those who didn't, those who hadn't any minds to know
. . . but they all wanted and demanded an efficient sales-girl.
You tried to please them all. You did your best, for that way
bread and butter lay. You earned your money waiting on them,
you knew that age was overtaking you—sometimes they com-
plained. . . .

Jess leant over, looking. What a tiny glass of beauty. Soon it would be time to take a sip. A sip! Exhilaration, that!

More than a quarter of a century she had sold things, waited on customers, done her best to get a living. It seemed to her there was but one thing she had left unsold—herself. All those years men's eyes had wandered past her in search of something prettier, more attractive, more alive—and she had let them pass. In consequence she had not risen, as those who manage love can do—nor had she fallen like the loving ones.

She was thirty-nine years old. Thirty-nine! Forty means— one doesn't think what forty means to one who is a sales-girl. Old! Queer to think one's old at thirty-nine. And people don't want old women selling in their stores—one knows that well. Jess thought of that woman in the smallwares section—grey-haired—lined—just waiting for dismissal. The least slip! . . . *She* goes to church at six o'clock, kneels, prays . . . and prays, and then comes on to work at eight. That's *her* cocktail. Will praying help her when they fire her! Customers like youth— rapidity—hustle. Forty is set. Old dogs learn no tricks.

Jess Rivers looked into her tiny glass. How it gleamed and shone! What a colour! Like May's curls, thick, natural curls that used to shake and quiver when she laughed—how they had laughed together when they drank their cocktails all those years ago! How May had laughed—what a merry laugh she had! And how she had wept that last night when they said good-bye— how she had wept, my God!

It's a long life—to sell for twenty-seven years on end. Three dollars. Five dollars. Then the maximum—seven. No more than seven dollars in the week unless—unless you're crooked. Impossible to make a penny more if you're just straight and ordinary. And such a lot of us are straight and ordinary—such a lot. And even—well, even if you try to sell old age, you can't. Who wants to buy?

There are cocktails. That's one thing. Two or three sips mean—not forgetfulness, but something better than forgetfulness. Two or three sips mean—nothing matters! The week-long round, the weariness, the boredom, the fatigue—the ever-haunting fear that one is getting old and showing it, and *that* means starvation when one hasn't laid by any money . . . well, drink your cocktail and it doesn't seem to matter, any of it.

This was the moment. For this Saturday night Jess lived all week long. The cocktail! The brewing, the sitting over it and looking at it, the gloating and the longing—the sip! The taste! The feeling! To be happy—just happy—isn't that the best thing that there is? If you can't get it any other way, can't you catch happiness for a second with a cocktail?

How can you lay by money? Seven dollars a week means a scrape to live. Your room, your car-fare, the decent clothes you have to have on pain of losing your job, your food! Oh, seven dollars means a scrape to live, an everlasting, never-ceasing scrape. Jess Rivers thought of the dinners in the store. She thought inconsequently of the great, bare, ugly dining-room the workers had, she saw the tables with their oil-cloth nailed to them, she saw the plentiful, coarse food carved at the centre table. So unappetising all of that, so—so *ugly*!

Of her own, Jess Rivers knew one beautiful thing, just one— this gleaming topaz drink. How she scraped to buy the ingredients for it! What dinners on the oil-clothed tables she forswore to keep these bottles by her—three: one white—one amber— and one red. Mix them, and you have your trinity—your shining, exquisite translucence. Jess Rivers sighed—and she looked deeper. Surely of such things is heaven made.

The store's a lonely life. The girls are mean. Yes, most of them are mean. They turn on you when you've grey hair, they talk behind your back, they say things just because you're old . . . that girl to-day, that tough, when Jess sat down beside her, why need she say, "Get out to hell—that's Miriam's place"? Why couldn't she ask her gently? How could one know that that was Miriam's place? But when you're old they turn on you.

Grey hairs! Jess Rivers drew herself together. When you're a woman—God, what a life it is! Grey hairs mean—

Well! Jess Rivers touched the tiny glass—and smiled. To-night she had it—and what a world of wonders in that topaz, gleaming beauty! What a world of life it held! What if one could live as one felt after drinking that—how wonderful if one could live like that! Contented—calmed—full of fellowship for everyone and everything. Yes, fellowship even for the girl who said, "Get out to hell—that's Miriam's place." What did it matter if she spoke like that? *That* was the way you felt when once you sipped—friendly!

Then—sleep. Deep sleep. Late sleep—Sunday means rest. No customers to worry you, ask questions, be discontented, complain of you, perhaps. No shopwalker to pass you over with his eyes for something younger, more attractive, no girls to spy your grey hairs out, note your lines and wrinkles—nudge one another—pass remarks. None of that. Nothing but peace— quietness—serenity.

Before you drink you have the knowledge that in that glass lies power. Something that fires you, something that travels to your nerve-tips, something that comforts—braces—soothes you. Something that takes away the sting of life. Balm in that glass—life's secret there, perhaps.

Jess Rivers bent down lower. She looked deep. The cares and apprehensions of her daily life passed from her. What do things matter? If one is sick and tired of life, isn't there a medicine?

Jess Rivers stretched her hand out. She took the glass. Her face was wistful as she raised the glass—she drank. The world grew luminous.

This was her moment.

THE WRESTLER

I WAS up at the hospital seeing a friend. I had had my talk and was coming away when I passed a face that held me fast. I stopped beside the bed simply because I couldn't get past it—I had no impulse beyond the purely egoistic one that I wanted to go on looking at the face upon the pillow. It was the face of a woman far through, very near the Great Acceptance, and she was a young woman to meet it with nothing in her expression save a calm and gentle patience. She was six or seven and twenty perhaps, not more. Pretty she had never been, I should think, unless you count kindliness as beauty; and now she was wasted, nothing left to her but those wide-open eyes and her smile. Such a smile! Sweetness itself.

I stood quietly beside her, and after a minute she seemed to notice I was there, and I saw she wanted to say something, so I bent down nearer her. She spoke with some difficulty already, because she wasn't very far from the end.

"I breathe bad," she said. "You'll have to excuse me. I can't help it . . . seems as if it got the better of me."

She looked at me with those wide-open eyes and smiled.

"I guess it makes a pretty poor impression," she said.

I waited a minute as you do wait beside those you feel can help you, and after a bit she spoke again. I don't suppose she thought very distinctly about who or what I was; she was just enough amongst us yet to realise that I was a human being like herself.

"They been good to me here all right," she said. "My, they been good . . . and me a stranger and all! It's been *quiet*. It's good to rest that way . . . and know you can rest. You get tired of bracing up to everla-asting."

We waited again.

"I couldn't go on," she said in that gentle, passionless voice of hers; "I couldn't do ut. The manager, he da-amned me . . . he said I had to . . . but I couldn't do ut. I lawst my job that way. . . . I tried! . . . But it seemed as if my strength was gawn some way."

The wide-open eyes looked, not so much at me as far past me; and she smiled.

"It was good to come here," she said. "My . . . it was good. And they been good to me too. They done everything they knoo to make me comfortable . . . and I been a lot of trouble. You are, when you're sick . . . you can't help it. And I imagine I was pretty sick when I had to give up.

"I lawst my job. It was worth twenty-three dollars a week. Good money too. I was the professional woman wrestler and boxer in the troupe . . . and they pay for that. There was five dollars had to go to mother . . . and five more to my boy. Every week. And that kind of makes a hole in the twenty-three. It's hard to save when you have to keep travelling . . . it's mighty hard at times to live on the thirteen that's left you. And keep your appearance up . . . the way you have to! And I been sick too. My, it's years sinst I been strong . . . what you can call *strong*.

"I don't know . . . I imagine that awperation in Noo York didn't do me the good I anticipated. The doctor was good too . . . but it didn't seem as if it succeeded the way I'd hoped. I haven't been strong sinst. It was pretty hard some nights to get on . . . and look the part. You have to keep smiling if you want to keep your job. But it's hard some way, when you feel kind of sick. . . ."

She was silent again. I thought of the look a horse has when it comes toiling up the hill with a great load behind it—a load too heavy for its willing strength. That was the way she looked.

"My," she said, "I make a noise. I'm a reg'lar noosance. You'll have to pardon me. I kind of hate to be a disturbance too.

"It's been a time! . . . There's been troubles. But I always got on when I could! . . . It's good and quiet here, I tell you. You can rest. Mother's going to miss that five dollars all right. Five dollars every week. And five more to the boy. He's four . . . my boy. I haven't been able to get to see him. I wanted to! . . . But I didn't ever have that much money. . . . With the fare and all . . . and the time awf. They tell me he's a fine boy. He's had the five dollars reg'lar. I sent that. . . . I never missed. If I was sick I made it up some kind of a way . . . but you get tired of that. There is but the one way . . . and you get tired of it. Men keeps on at you . . . and it's tiring. Men *is* tiring, it seems to me. But you have to keep in with them if you want to keep your job. That's what makes it hard for a woman in my line, I imagine."

She stopped again, and it was very peaceful.

"Mother'll miss the money all right," she began again. "I don't know whatever she's going to do. I don't see why I don't worry . . . but it seems some way as if I couldn't. No more. I done what I could . . . it's been tiring too. And now mother and the boy . . . well—"

I asked her if she would like me to write to them for her—to the mother to let her know where her daughter was.

"What's that you say?" she said, turning those wide-open eyes on to me. "What's that you say? Why, that's good of you. No, it don't matter. I got the doctor to take down the *ad*dress . . . he'll do what he should, I guess. He's been good too . . . the doctor. Sort of kind. He'll write. Poor mother . . . she'll miss it all right. I don't see what she'll do.

"That bag I brought in with me—there's money in that . . . lots to bury me. And some over for the boy. Could you ast them to send? . . . What kind of a way, did you say? The burying? It don't matter any . . . the easiest way. Get me out of the way . . . it don't seem to me as if it mattered any. . . ."

We were quiet again. Her head with its halo of hair seemed to have gone deeper down into the pillow—her poor, frazzled hair that she had peroxided and bleached and done God knows what to so as to make it worth her twenty-three dollars a week. Dyed and waved and curled it for the manager and the public— part of her work, that, and what she got her money for.

"I don't want them worried," she said. "I hate to be a noosance. And I don't have many that's near . . . so I don't care if no one knows. Mother and the boy . . . they'll have to know. But 'bout the rest . . . it don't matter. I'm tired. It's good to be here . . . quiet . . . and rest. . . ."

She lay quiet a minute, and then the blue eyes opened wide.

"My, the manager, he was mad all right!" she said. "He awften was. . . . I knoo in the end I had to lose my job. He got mad when I was sick. I felt badly to disappoint him too . . . it did seem too bad . . . it seemed kind of poor! But I didn't go back on him only when I didn't feel as if I could.

"He cursed and da-amned me good and hard. He said I was a bla-asted—! And I knoo I would lose my job . . . and the money! . . . I worried! . . . And I saw the manager was getting tired anyway . . . I couldn't seem to satisfy—

"But it's pa-ast. Oh, my . . . when you don't have to worry!
. . . It's good. I love ut . . . lying here. . . . "

Her voice dropped and I had to stoop low to catch what she said.

"It's over and done with," she whispered, "there's that. And I can rest! . . . When I'm gawn . . . put me out quick. For there's no one . . . and anyways it don't matter any. . . . "

The noisy breath grew noisier; the wide-open eyes closed. She lay there quite still, half smiling. Life had done its worst by her for seven-and-twenty years, and she lay worn and wasted, with her halo of dyed hair—tired . . . so tired! She looked as if she had outworn her sheath of life, as if it was dropping from her already as she lay there acquiescent—willing to accept.

I left her in the long, clean hospital ward waiting to welcome death and give it guesting.

BABY BUNTING

BABY BUNTING comes to clean my house. He is a darling and he does it—to admiration. I admit he brings a mother with him, just to help; but when I think of house-cleaning it is Baby Bunting that I think of. Placid, serene, smiling, busy—oh! very, very busy all day long.

He works, does Baby Bunting. Does his day's darg, and doesn't earn a sixpence for it. He brings some working tools along with him to start with—trifles—miscellanies: a book (advertisements from the drug store—" Have you that Tired Feeling?—Try Dr Jenkins' Ointment!), a bird that squeaks, a green plush case that once contained a jewel but doesn't now—things like that. Just regal trifles. And he sits and works with them—he works, he bends over them engrossed, intent, so busy!

When that palls, when he has thrown these treasures far and wide, then there are other things. There is a fascinating cupboard full of bottles—Apollinaris water, ginger ale, such harmless things. They are treasure trove. Baby Bunting makes on all fours for that cupboard, inserts a tiny—such a tiny!—hand, opens a crack, looks in, opens wider . . . disappears. And *then*— then are sounds with bottles, empty bottles roll—full ones clash. "Be careful, Baby. Take care, darling"—and a little head comes peering round the corner. "Be careful, Sonnie"—and he smiles. He smiles!

He is plump and pink and white. His head is round and large, thatched with fine straw-coloured hair, as soft as silk. His eyes are round as any owl's—blue as the sky. His cheeks are rounded. He is fearless.

Yes, he is fearless. As yet he has no knowledge of the world. He can't conceive the world could want to hurt him. When he sees you he stretches out two arms—two fearless, friendly arms. "Take me up!" they say, "show me the lovely world!" And you take him up and carry him to the window. "Look, Baby, see the tree . . . " "Da-da!" says Baby Bunting. He is a lesson how *not* to do with speech. What superfluous energy we waste in words! How far "Da-da!" goes! If you add "Um-m-m!" and "M-m-a!"

and "Bub-b . . ." you really are furnished. What more do you want? That is conversation.

"Bub-b . . ." has a story. It means two blisters on the tiny hand. Baby Bunting, not thinking that the world would hurt him, put a tiny hand on the hot stove. . . . Say to him: "Did Baby burn himself?" the rounded happiness is clouded. "Bub-b-b . . . " says he, and thrusts the little hand before you. When you say: "Naughty stove . . ." and kiss it, then he is appeased. "Bub-b-b . . ." he goes on saying. "Wicked stove to burn the Baby Bunting so."

When it is dinner-time he stops his work—I should rather say, perhaps, he intermits it. His eyes grow rounder at the sight of custard pudding. They gleam and glisten—his mouth smiles—and smiles—and smiles. Such a little thing there, seated at the table! So tiny, so intelligent, his mouth open like a bird's. Drop a worm in—I mean a bit of custard pudding—the lips close on it, the smile disappears. Earnestness. Concentration. "Is it good, Baby? Is it good, darling?" "Um-m-m . . ." says Baby Bunting.

After dinner there is the majesty of repletion. Not sleep—oh no. Just calm, and unreflecting majesty. But is it unreflecting? I wonder. He sits there on a cushion on the floor, his toys before him. And sometimes he bends, as babies do, straight from the middle—from the joint—and picks a bird up, makes it squeak, makes it squeak again—casts it from him, reaches for the book. Wonderful how custard pudding will infuse a majesty—a calmness!

When it is time to wash the floor his mother picks him up and fits him on a cushion in a chair turned seat to wall. It is an arm-chair, old-fashioned, with a high ribbed back. And there sits Baby Bunting, gazing through the ribs just as the monkeys at the Zoo gaze through the bars. "Goo-oo!" "Yes, darling, yes." His mother scrubs and washes. "Mother's darling!" "Goo-o-o!"

And then the blue, unwinking eyes grow heavy. The round head droops, the tiny hand grows lax. Down drops the bird—and for a second the round eyes open wide—gaze—and then they close again. "Sleepy, darling? Baby want a sleep?" And then mother rises from her scrubbing and takes her Baby Bunting in her arms and carries him into the bedroom—lays him on the bed. And there she takes the pink checked bloomers off and leaves the baby in his little shirt—such legs! Such grand, fat, dimpled legs—such skin, such delicate fineness! Smooth like a petal of a flower. Never again will Baby Bunting have a skin like that. Never again will he have that trusting innocence of soul. He turns a little—sighs. . . . "Sleep, darling. . . . Baby sleep. . . ." And even in his sleep his mother's voice can reach him. He smiles.

And the mother, in a sort of ecstasy of admiration, takes the tiny hand in hers—the little hand that she has put a ring on, a tiny, ridiculous ring—and kisses it—and kisses it.

She turns to you.

"Oh," she says—and in her voice is the assertion of a fact— "I am a lucky woman—I am a lucky woman."

She is poor. She knows the wear and tear of life. She has a husband sick—out of work—not likely to be ever very well again. She works her way from day to day, knows not from day to day what money she will have. She lives in some poor tenement, removed from everything desirable—removed from light and air as well as everything else; and she is far from home— for she is English—she has no friend to help her here in Canada. She has little—and she has everything. As she looks at you her eyes shine and glisten. There are almost tears in them—tears of pride and joy.

"I am," she says to you, "a lucky woman—oh! I am a lucky woman."

Baby Bunting's breath comes regular—deep—restful. He lies there relaxed, deep in some dreamland where we can't follow him. He is asleep.

We draw the coverlet over him. His face lies on the pillow infinitely serene—beautiful—majestic.

So Baby Bunting comes to clean my house.

LIVIN' UP TO IT

"I WANT 'im to be better nor wot we are, ma'am," my charlady said to me. She glanced down at the baby. "'E's 'is
mother's son, ma'am, ain't 'e?" she said fondly.

I reassured her on this point.

"I means to try to 'ave 'im be a doctor, ma'am," said she.

"Why in the world a doctor, Mrs Lynch?" said I.

"A doctor's 'elpful, ma'am," she said, "and 'e's a gen'lemen
at that, you can't deny it."

My charlady gave a gulp.

"I longs to 'ave my baby be a gen'leman, ma'am," said she,
"as good as any man! I 'as the cravin' for it. . . ."

"Oh!" I said. It wasn't altogether sympathetic, I'm afraid—
and yet I couldn't think of anything else to say.

"If 'e's a gen'leman," my charlady resumed, "I'll die 'appy."

She gulped again.

"I'll feel as it's wuth w'ile, ma'am, to 'ave lef' my 'ome and
England if my boy's a gen'leman once't 'e's growed," said she,
expanding.

"But, Mrs Lynch—" I said.

"Yer see," she went on, overriding my expostulation, "yer
see, ma'am, it's 'ard for to be allays over-trod. Yer tire o' that,
yer do. I've 'ad my turn of it, Gawd knows. I've allays been the
one to do with nothink all my life. So it's like this, ma'am, if I
'ad a son top-dawg, you take my word," my charlady said, "as
I'd die 'appy."

She paused, and when she had her thoughts collected she
went on.

"I want," she said, "to 'ave 'im do the orderin', so to say. I'd
like to 'ave a son wot's able for to 'ave the best o' thinks. I want
to 'ave 'im grow up strong, I does, and ready for to push 'is way
about."

I caught the glitter in my charlady's eye.

"If I could on'y know for sure," she said, "as my boy was a-
top of 'em I'd feel as it was wuth it, every bit I've 'ad to suffer."

We looked down at the baby on the floor. The future

practitioner had managed to upset a lot of paraffin all over himself. He smelt—he positively reeked.

"I thought," his mother said, "I'd start 'im with a name."

She stopped.

"What *is* his name?" I asked.

"It's Ernest Edward Asquith Lynch, 'is name is," said my charlady; her voice quivered as she spoke the sacred words. She added: "Jes' for short I calls 'im Ernie, ma'am."

She stooped and addressed herself to Ernest Edward Asquith.

" 'Ere," she said, "ain't yer name Ernest Edward Asquith, Sonnie? And don't yer mother call yer Ernie?"

Ernie made no response. He merely smelt of coal oil. Possibly it may have been the forerunner of some laboratory trick he had it in his head to play upon the world in later years. He answered not, at any rate—he merely smelt.

" 'E'll be a doctor, mark my word," his mother said. She paused to find a positive proof to bring me into line. "Give 'im a book," said she, " 'e'll sit there by the hower. Tear it 'e will and turn it hupside down. I never see a child ser fond o' books as 'im."

She seized a scouring-cloth.

" 'E'll be a doctor, mark my word," said she again.

She scoured the sink as if it was her bitterest enemy.

"But it's a worry livin' hup to it," she said.

"How?" said I. By this time I was reduced to permanent monosyllables.

"Well, ma'am," my charlady said, "it costs a bit to make a gen'leman."

"What costs?" said I.

"You take 'is food," my charlady said in an argumentative tone of voice. "Jes' look at it! Won't tech a bit o' porridge, Ernie won't. And won't 'ave milk, not if it 'asn't got a drop o' tea put in it for to take the taste away."

She paused.

" 'E'll eat a piece o' bacon, so 'e will," she said, "wot's eight-and-thirty cents the pound."

She paused again.

"*That's* eatin' money, that is," said my charlady. "Has to eggs, 'e'll 'ave 'em fried or none."

She screwed her nose up tight. She gulped again.

"Oh, '*e*'s a gen'leman all right," she said triumphantly. "So look at the expense 'e'll be to us!"

She shook her head despondently.

"Yer can't deny it takes a bit o' livin' hup to," said my charlady.

She glanced at Ernest Edward Asquith.

"But that don't matter," said the doctor's mother "not if I 'as a son a gen'leman, it don't."

Once more she turned her eyes to Æsculapius—and kept them there.

" 'Ere, Sonnie, don't yer love yer mother?" said my charlady. "She's come 'ere all the way from 'ome a purpose for to make a gen'leman of you . . . so don't yer love 'er?"

She paused for a reply. But Ernie merely smelt of coal oil. He answered not.

My charlady heaved a sigh.

" 'E 'as a look o' somethink rare, I allays thinks," she said. "Now, ain't 'e?"—and her tone was wistful. "Don't it strike yer, ma'am . . .?"

Ernie exhaled his aristocratic fragrance. He might have been a mine where we had just struck ile.

" 'Ere," said his mother, "you *say* somethink! Git a move on!"

"Ta-ta," said Ernie.

It was his contribution to the conversation.

UNION

ALISON JEFFREY sat thinking. She looked through the little window of her sitting-room, and through the window she saw the deep night sky. It was that deep blue that is almost black, and that is saved from being black by the sapphire tinge in it. Alison Jeffrey sat looking vaguely up into the blue-black and on the surface of her mind she thought how beautiful it was. But far beneath, deep down in her mind, she was not thinking of the sky. As she sat there the past eleven years of her life were slowly unrolling themselves—and she was watching the events of her life as they had come to her, unveiling themselves like a long, vivid, passing picture.

It was the eleventh anniversary of a great day. It was the eleventh anniversary of the day when Alison Jeffrey had joined her life with a man's—and when a woman comes to count up the days of her life there are two that count, and this is one of them. The other—well, of the other Alison Jeffrey had no anniversary to celebrate; and as she sat in her own little sitting-room that she had created and furnished, that she kept going day by day by her own efforts, she thought of this other anniversary that had no place in her life—and she regretted it.

For she had had no children. There had never been a time when she had had that first doubt—that wonder—that sort of stopping of everything in life because of—a possibility. Alison Jeffrey had never conceived. She had thought and thought about it and round about it, she had wondered what she would do with a child, and how it would fit into her life—and into that other life that hers was a part of; there had been times when she had longed for a child, had longed so for it that all else in the world had seemed worthless to her if she had not that. She had yearned to feel that she was carrying life about with her; she had passionately denied to herself that she was any good, that her life was worth living, that she was a woman at all, unless she could bring a child into the world.

It was a phase in her life. It was connected with the anniversary that she was celebrating all alone in her little flat to-night—

and the phase had passed as other phases do. Alison Jeffrey had recognised that life is many-sided, that there are infinite views and infinite possibilities in it—that a woman is a woman even if she is barren and childless . . . yes, she had even recognised, at moments, that life may be better so. For some women. The unreasoning craving—like that of a starving man for bread—had passed away from her, and days, weeks, even months sometimes, passed by her now without the child obtruding itself on her consciousness. And yet—sometimes as she would go along the road, to her daily work, or on pleasure bent, a child would come toddling across her path, or a boy would come swinging along in pursuit of his ball, or a little girl would look up at her from her seat on the doorstep—and smile . . . and the old pain would dart through her heart. There would be a pulling and a dragging as if the child she had longed for was somewhere and attached to her heart by a cord—and the cord had been jerked. And then Alison Jeffrey would hurry on with a sickening desire to get out of sight, so that the cord would stop jerking and she could be quiet again—and then she would forget. Till the next time the toddler ran across her path.

But as she sat looking out at the deep night sky it was not of the child—that was what she always called the little being who had never existed—that she was thinking at all. She wasn't thinking of the child or of any of her hopes or feelings or expectations or disillusionments regarding it. She was thinking of one thing and of one thing only—the man to whose life she had joined her own. The thought of him filled her heart and brain as the world is filled with sunlight on a glorious summer day. Alison Jeffrey sat quite quietly looking out, and as she sat there she felt the thought of the man she loved flooding her whole body and her heart and her soul. She felt no longer her own—she felt she was a part of another life, and so integral a part that even when that life was distant from her she was still a part of it and as much a part of it as if it were in the room beside her.

She realised that this feeling had not come quickly. She remembered the first days of their being joined together, and she remembered the discords and the jangles that the joining had caused in the souls of both of them. It was as if you took two totally different and unrelated things and sought to make them one by glueing them together. Alison had thought before her union that the two halves would meet—and join—and be one; it is the usual idea of the union of a man and a woman, and she had accepted it. Or, perhaps, rather she had imagined that she would be grafted on to the man as you graft a new piece into a tree, and that she would grow there and become part of the tree . . . as Nature manages these things. When she had first realised that there was no grafting of one self on to another self possible—when it had been brought home to her that two souls cannot be glued together and be one—it was as if a thunderbolt had fallen and destroyed something. Her cherished ideas had fallen to pieces, and for a bit after her union she had been at sea, and at sea in a storm too. All efforts at joining—so that the pieces should be not glued, but growing together—were useless and worse than useless. They were destructive. The two souls, each used to live its own life, had recoiled when their owners had tried to push them together. There were disagreements, there were quarrels, there were hard words—silences—bitterness—unworthy thoughts between them. Each had judged the other harshly—there had been moments of despair, when it seemed as if the world were not big enough to hold the two of them, or wide enough for them to be sufficiently apart from one another.

As Alison Jeffrey sat looking through her window, thinking of all these things, she smiled. And in her smile there was such an infinite contentment that it seemed to blend with the harmony of the outside night. She looked at the wintry night—and it seemed beautiful to her. She watched the deep snow everywhere, and the sparks on it that the frost made; she looked at the heavily laden branches of the trees, the twig tips bending deeply beneath their weight of white, powdery, fresh-fallen snow. And when she looked upward the deep hue of the sky seemed to her so infinitely lovely that she could imagine nothing lovelier. And she knew that without the great love that she had for that other life which was half her own she could not see the loveliness of the night like that—and that the freshly fallen snow would be just snow to her without that love, snow, and not the mantle of beauty that it was.

Eleven years had passed since that first night together. As Alison thought back, that night seemed yesterday—and it seemed to date back to another life. It was since that night that she had become aware of herself—and in becoming aware of herself she had become aware, too, of other people. It seemed to her, looking back, that until this joining of her life with another she had been asleep. She had seen the world through a glass darkly; and it was only with the coming of love that she had awaked and looked on reality—as it was. The clash of the two souls coming together had awaked her; and the difficulty they had had in growing together had roused her to definite consciousness. It was her repeated efforts and her repeated failures to attain that had brought her sharply to thought. "Why am I failing like this?" she had asked herself. "What prevents our striking root together—when we love one another so much?" For, queerly enough, even in their moments of disunion, even when they had quarrelled and thrown hard words at one another, even when they had deliberately sought out things to say that would pierce and hurt, Alison Jeffrey had never doubted for a moment that they loved. She knew that a streak of hatred ran across their love—first she dimly realised that, and then she definitely knew it; but she also both dimly realised and definitely knew that such a streak of hatred runs across all love—with passion in it; and that the working out of love is to eradicate this streak of hatred by—what? That was the thing that Alison Jeffrey had taken eleven years to work out and she hadn't worked it out yet—and as she sat looking out through her little window at the deep night sky she felt that she never would work it out in this life, that life was not long enough and that human understanding was not deep enough to reach the solution of this problem.

As she sat there she thought of all the problems that these eleven years had brought before her. Not problems remote and unimportant, not theories that are nice to dandle, not ideas that are amusing to toss from brain to brain—but problems the settling of which meant the ability to go on living. "How can I get round this?" Alison had said to herself—how often in those years! "How can I get round this—or through it—or across it . . . just so as to be able to go on at all!" There had been times when she had felt that she had come to a standstill. There had been times when she had felt that it was impossible to take a step further without wreckage. She had gone about the world—thinking. Hammering out her ideas as men hammer steel to bring it into shape. "People talk glibly of the union of two lives—have they tried it?" Alison Jeffrey used to ask herself; "have they tried it—or are they only talking?" She found that this fusion of two lives and two souls was something that took hold of her heart and of her brain and drained them of their powers—this necessity to solve the question how to fuse. And in striving to understand how it should be done she found sometimes with a start of surprise that she had been so lost in trying to understand the attitude of the other soul that she had forgotten her own; and then the fusion had gone on—quietly—deeply—inevitably. She had loved. That was her master-key. She had loved the man with whose life her own had been joined—she had loved him passionately—tenderly too. She seemed to herself sometimes to love him with every kind of love there is—he was her son and her child, something to pet and protect and indulge; and at the same time he was what she looked up to, what she admired and listened to—and adored. These two moods alternated in her. Sometimes she felt immensely grown-up beside the big man who was her very own—and sometimes she felt like a child beside him . . . and she revelled in both feelings and welcomed each as it came. And sometimes she felt herself his mate and equal—and then were the moments for the streaks of hatred to fall across her love. And sometimes she felt herself his counter-part—his other half—he was the thing she needed, and she was what he required; and these times were the best of all.

Eleven years had gone by. There had been flaws in them, big flaws—there had been rents and fissures in them. But all the time something—Alison Jeffrey felt it almost touch her some-times—had been drawing them together. As she sat quite by herself thinking, as women will, of all the intimate events of her life, she realised that without those flaws, without the rents in their love, it never could have grown to be the thing it was. She thought of the great winds that tear down trees and go whirling on to more destruction; she thought of the storms at sea and the great waves—and she realised that, just as storms burst on the world—as the winds come tearing along, destroying as they go—so too there must come the great winds of passion, destroy-ing—and clearing the sky. She realised, sitting all alone in her little room, that without those disagreements, without those pas-sionate angers at one another, she and the man she loved could not have been drawn so close together to-day. "It needs all kinds of things to make love," she said to herself. "It needs sorrow to make gladness, it needs loss to make gain. If I had not misunderstood I could not have understood as I understand to-day. If I had not suffered, how could I be so happy? If I had not missed the child how could I—?"

Her thought died away and she left the sentence unfinished in her mind. She felt, sitting there, a great wave of happiness pass over her. She looked out at the night and it seemed wonderfully beautiful to her; but even as she gazed up into the blue-black sky what she saw in it was the thought of the man whose life was half her own. He was inextricably connected with every event in life and with everything in nature. She could not see a patch of blue sky without longing to point it out to him. She could not watch the big grey squirrels go chasing each other along the branches outside her window without seeing him in their gambols. As she sat looking out she realised that she had got—nowhere. In the journey that she was taking there is no end. As you reach one turn in the road you see the next turn before you: and when you have clambered on to that—you see the next. Life is too short and too shallow for the solution of anything at all. Alison Jeffrey knew, as she sat looking out, that she would never know why she felt as she felt about the child. She knew that she would never be able to explain what that cord was or where it was tied about her heart or who tied it there—or what the other end was attached to. She knew that she would never be able to explain that streak of hatred that ran across her love and fouled it. She knew that least of all would she ever be able to explain why she loved—where her love began—or if it would ever end. And all her thinking and hammering of ideas had ended in this—that she loved. And what does that mean? It means that you are only interested in yourself—that you only value or care for yourself—as a part of something else. If this life is all, then there is no such thing as the love Alison Jeffrey sat watching in the sapphire sky outside her window. But Alison Jeffrey, as she sat there celebrating all alone the eleventh anniversary of the greatest day in her life, knew very well that this life is not all. This love of hers had taught her, year by year, that existence is the unfolding of love—and that here we only prepare the soil. "Our quarrels, our misunderstandings were the digging and the hoeing of the earth," she said to herself; "that was the dirty work by which we made ready for the planting." And as she sat looking out, her heart said to her: "We have planted our seed—it is growing in us now."

She felt an absolute contentment with life—as it is. Its difficulties, its drawbacks, even its cruelties and its terrors seemed to her to be just necessary steps. To what?—to the furthering of love.

Alison Jeffrey rose and went to her window and stood looking out. There were houses all round her, with their roofs piled high with snow. And the great tree outside her window stretched out its branches, and in the twilight that the snow makes Alison Jeffrey could distinguish the tracery of its tips and twigs. She stood looking out and a great happiness flooded her soul. She felt that she embraced the world—that everything in it was dear and precious to her. And she felt that she could pack the whole world into her love and make it a part of it—that her love was so big that it could hold everything, even what is base and defiled. She felt that she had slipped out of the narrowness of self and become a part of life.

She leaned her head against the wooden window-frame and she stood looking out. Night is lovely—and suddenly Alison Jeffrey longed to share the loveliness with that other soul that was her own—and yet not her own. And the longing to be united with it by the means of the flesh sent a sharp pain through her body, and she seemed to feel her soul throb in her. "Will the time ever come," she cried out to herself, "when we shall be one—free from the flesh and indissoluble? Is that what they mean by Eternal Life?"

And she stood looking up into the night sky as if she expected to see the answer written across it.

THE LAST HOPE

"IT'S our only chance."
     She heard this dimly, as if the words came through a
     veil of something. She listened intently and she heard the
words again.

"It's our only chance."

She lay very still. And a third time the same words came
through to her—through that veil of—what? It seemed to her as
if a veil had suddenly fallen between her and life, as if she were
held off somewhere, segregated, alone, while life went on as
usual at the other side of the veil.

She lay quite still in her bed, and she kept her eyes shut. And
then she heard her husband saying: "Does she hear, do you
think? Can we make her understand?"

She heard him quite plainly, as she had heard the doctor—
across that something. And it seemed to her as she lay there that
it was impossible for her to reach these men that stood close to
her bedside, bending over her; she felt that even if she were to
make that superhuman effort to speak, her words would never
get to them. The veil that divided her from them seemed to her
to be more impenetrable on her side than on theirs. They could
reach her—dimly; but she was held off from them, kept away—
it was impossible for her ever to get near them again.

She lay very still for what seemed to her a long time, and
then she heard another voice coming through the veil—a small
voice with a frightened tremor in it.

"Mamsie," it said. "Mamsie! . . ."

And it trembled away again behind the veil.

Mona Derrill made that great effort that she had felt it was
impossible for her to make. She reached up out of that place
apart where she had been put, she tried to lean over so that she
might get near the veil and poise her voice so that it might go
through those close, almost impenetrable meshes.

"Yes, darling," she said.

And then she heard her husband's voice again—far away
from her—ever so far away—beyond all getting at. "She hears

you, Anna," her husband's voice said; "speak again."

"Mamsie," said the voice again, and this time it was at her ear, "Mamsie, can you hear me?"

She made another of those superhuman efforts and tried to reach for the little hand that she knew could not be far off.

"Mamsie, darling," the little voice said, and into her hand there slipped a tiny clinging hand. "Mamsie, they want to take you away. But you'll come back when you're better. Can you hear me, Mamsie?"

She pressed the little hand in hers—and then suddenly she opened her eyes wide.

"Must I leave them?" she said.

And they asked Anna what she had said and Anna repeated it word for word—and she heard her do it.

She lay still a moment and then she made another of those superhuman efforts.

"And the baby?" she said. "Anna, ask them if I may have the—"

And then the veil fell between her and them and she heard their voices on the other side of it but she could distinguish no words that they said.

They took her into the city, her and the baby together. The doctor went to take care of them, and the husband went—to suffer; and Anna stayed in the house with the little brother that came between herself and the baby—to mother him. There was the ride to the station first, through the pitiless cold of the Canadian night. The sky above was a deep blue and there were cold, frosty stars set here and there; and the trees hung heavy with rime and snow, and the ground rang like steel beneath the runners of the sleigh. She opened her eyes and she looked upward into the night sky—and it looked threatening to her, and cruel.

"Have I to leave my children?" she thought dimly to herself; "must I leave them and go out naked into this pitiless night? . . ."

And her eyes closed again and the veil came down between her and the things that we can touch and handle round about us.

Then came the station—the car . . . and she lay in the bed made up for her there. The tiny—the infinitesimal—bundle of wraps they had carried with them out of the house and into the sleigh was handed to her now, and she felt the life that she had carried within her till a few hours before move at her side. This child that she had thought of for nine long months, this precious third in her household of delights, this boy that she had longed for and yearned over and felt an infinite tenderness for, was alive. She had carried him triumphantly into life. He had crossed the threshold of her womb and he had come into the world to go his way in it. She had brought forth a man-child— as she had hoped she would do; and she was going out of the world as he came into it. Her life for his. She had brought him here, and now she was leaving him to fight his way without her through the quick-set tangle of life. She was not one of the ignorant, closely sheltered women. She had lived and known how difficult it is to live; and now, just as she was able to show the way a little bit to those coming after her, she had to go. She had to go out into that deep, impenetrable darkness of which we know nothing and be separated from life by something we cannot pierce.

The train sped through the night and nearer and nearer it came to the city. She lay there inert, motionless, and close at her side there lay the little bit of life that was giving all her life for.

"I shall die," she kept saying to herself. "I shall die—and the children will have to do as they can."

And when the bitterness of that thought became too great for her to bear—the veil fell between her and it, and she passed away into that dim, muffled region where nothing but love can reach us. She thought of Anna and she thought of her little sturdy Jackie at home—and she thought of the little unnamed creature at her side that she had meant to call Frank—and she lay there loving them.

"Shall I have to forget them when I go?" she asked herself dimly; and all her being cried out in her that she would never forget them—she had carried them into life and to forget them would not be asked of her.

She was in the hospital, that great, bleak, beneficent place that is full of healing and death. She lay there in her bed—and with an effort that seemed to wrench the very soul out of her she moved an arm.

"She wants the baby," she heard someone say. "Give her the baby."

And she felt the little piece of life laid at her side.

She had to die so that this might live. This thing had come into life to try its luck, and her turn was over. She had ceased to think connectedly, but she felt the warmth at her side, and she felt that if that warmth were taken from her she would die.

"But I shall die," she said to herself. "I shall die even with it there."

And suddenly her brain flickered into life and burned with a momentary, steady, brilliant flame.

"I am dying," she said to herself, "I am dying. This thing that we all think we think about and never do think about has come to me. I am going out of life—out of all the sweetness and the bitterness of it—I am leaving the beautiful things that we see all round us, I shall never hear again those lovely things that my ears have delighted in. Spring will come—and the budding trees will break into leaf—the birch in the garden will clothe itself with radiance . . . and I shan't be there to see it."

It all passed before her like a wonderful picture. She saw the garden as she had so often seen it—she smelt the fragrance of the newly cut grass—she heard the whistling of the birds.

"I sha'n't see it," she said to herself. "It is for other people, that—my turn is over."

And as she saw the garden she seemed to see Anna racing along the lawn of it with her hair flying and the colour in her cheeks, and she heard her laugh ring out into the spring sunshine—and make it more lovely.

"I have to leave Anna, my God!" she said to herself. "How will she get on? What kind of a turn will *she* get?"

And suddenly, for the first time in her life, she knew what prayer means.

"Shelter her, my God," she said, "shelter her. Keep her from those sharp pains that women suffer. Teach her patience gently. Do not let her be rent with sorrow and learn patience so. Deal gently with her—be kind—help her!"

She felt as if her whole soul was going out in prayer. She felt that if ill-luck came to Anna she would come back through those unimaginable obstacles that separate death from life—and rescue her child.

Her husband? She thought of him with an extraordinary tenderness. He was in her thought unceasingly. She felt the rent there would be in their love when she could no longer come close to him—she thought of the days and nights she had spent with him—she thought of quite little unimportant things that he had said to her . . . and she felt her heart grow big in her with tears.

"Wrap yourself up well!" "Take good care of yourself." "Don't worry, my dear. Go to sleep now."

As she thought of her husband these were the sort of things she thought of—just the little human kindnesses that had passed from him to her day by day and night by night. She thought of a thousand little things that he had done—quite little things that anyone might have done; yes, but everyone would not have done them as he had done them for her—for he loved her. The thought of her husband was the undercurrent of her thoughts. He was always there just as he had always been there through their life together. She loved him—she loved him dearly: she knew that he loved her. But she also knew that he could take care of himself. He would be desolate without her—for a time anyway; but he could go on with life. His life was modelled and he could continue it. Somehow, however much he missed her, he would go on. He was having his turn. He was in the very midst of it, and her staying or going couldn't hinder that turn from being played out.

But the children! Their turn was scarcely begun. She and the man that she loved had brought them there. These children were a bit of their love that had taken shape and had come into the world alive. When she thought of leaving her children—it seemed to her impossible that it could be asked of her. How could she leave them—leave Anna, that tender little thing, to find her way through this difficult, difficult world? She thought how she had watched Anna and planned how she could help her, how she would guard her and shelter her and keep her from harm and from danger of life. She thought of her little sturdy boy—and she thought of this morsel of flesh and blood tucked in at her side. As she thought of him all the rest seemed to fade away from her.

"My baby, my baby," she cried to herself. "Why must I leave you? Why did I have you if I had to die and leave you here alone?"

And it seemed to her that she hated God.

And then, in the very middle of her hatred, she felt something else. "Their turn has come," she said to herself. "We all have our turns—and our griefs and our happiness and our sorrow. We are here to learn. Perhaps if I had stayed with them I should have hindered them from learning."

The steady flame flickered and went out. And as it went out her whole being seemed to be irradiated with love. She no longer knew the difference between her husband and her children—and God. She knew in one divine flash that to die is happiness. And she was dead. . . .

THE DAMNED OLD MAID

"HE said I was a damned Old Maid," said Miss M'Guire. " 'A damned Old Maid,' says he, 'that's what ye are, so chew the cud on that,' says he."

Miss M'Guire's conversation was apt to be like the chaos that the world was before God began to make it, so that when she had a lucid interval I made the most of it.

"Who said such a thing as that?" said I.

"It was Charlie MacBryan said it," said she, "and I like um too. He wanted to marry me when I was young, only I wouldn't look at um. And then his wife come along with her beautiful face and nothin' in ut, and she grabbed hold of um and married um to herself. 'A damned Old Maid,' says he to me last night. 'That's what ye are, Mary M'Guire,' says he."

"Never mind, Miss M'Guire," I said. "It doesn't matter."

"It wouldn't matter," said Miss M'Guire, "if it wasn't true, but it is. It's just what I am, God help me! And him to be tellin' me that!"

She paused and seemed to swallow down something with difficulty; and she sewed at my gown with an unnecessary energy.

"There was him last night," said she, "soused through and through in me cousin's house. He sat there talkin' to me with one foot in his boot and the other naked in his golosh and he . . ."

Miss M'Guire seemed to swallow something more.

"Believe *me*," she said after a pause, during which she wrestled with something, "it's the barebones truth ye'll hear from a man when he's soused through and through. 'Ye're a damned Old Maid,' said he."

She went on sewing with unnecessary energy.

" 'Why didn't ye have me when ye could, Mary M'Guire?' says he. 'Why wouldn't ye take me when I asked ye to marry me? I liked ye, Mary, I wanted ye. The wife I've got got me, but I never wanted her the way I've wanted you, Mary M'Guire.' "

Miss M'Guire swallowed something more.

" 'It's a bad eye ye had in your youth, Mary M'Guire,' says he. 'It beckoned the fellahs and made them come after ut. And it's the light foot ye had,' says he, 'and the white hand. . . . ' "

Miss M'Guire glanced downwards and something shining fell.

" 'Couldn't ye have turned to the fellah that wanted ye, Mary M'Guire?' says he. 'Wouldn't ye have been the proud girl with me son in your arms? I'd have loved ye, Mary,' he says, 'I'd have made ye care. I've never cared for the woman that got me. She's me wife,' says Charlie MacBryan, 'she's the mother of me sons. But I never cared for her, Mary M'Guire. It's you I cared for,' says he, 'and it's you I care for this day.' "

Miss M'Guire went on sewing with unnecessary energy, and something more that was bright and shining fell on the stuff of my gown.

" 'Mary,' he says, 'ye're changed. Ye're the Old Maid now,' says he. 'Ye've the bad eye yet, but your lightsome foot's gone past ye and the colour's died out of your cheeks and your hair's streaked with grey and there's no fellah after ye.' "

Miss M'Guire sewed and three tears fell on the stuff of my gown.

" 'Where's the sense of ut all?' says he. 'Here's me lovin' ye yet and what do I love? Ye're homely,' says he, 'this day. Ye're grown old and ye're bent at the neck and ye're wilted and trod down in the dirt. But I love ye,' says he."

Miss M'Guire reached for her pocket-handkerchief.

" 'Mary,' he says, 'it's the want of the drink's been your ruin. If ye'd cared for the bottle,' says he, 'it's married we'd be and children between us.' "

Miss M'Guire hid her face in her handkerchief and her remarks came out of it inconsecutively, and sometimes I heard them and sometimes I didn't.

" 'Water!' says he. 'The damned dry stuff! And you, Mary M'Guire, you'd see a man with his tongue hangin' half a yard out of his mouth and you'd offer um water to drink!' "

Miss M'Guire sobbed.

" 'Hell, Mary M'Guire!' says Charlie MacBryan, 'ye should have danced when I piped. Ye should have come when I wanted ye. I'm a drunk,' says Charlie MacBryan to me, 'but, woman dear, ye were wrong.' "

Miss M'Guire wiped her eyes with a good deal of elaboration, and once more she concentrated her attention upon my gown.

"It's true words Charlie MacBryan was speakin' last night," said she. "If I'd married um long ago it's a wife I'd have been. It's a wife I'd have been this day, and it's children I'd have had be my side. I'd have known what it is to nurse the child at the breast. I'd have known the sorrows of marriage."

She sewed. She sewed as if her life depended on her getting to the end of her seam before the hour was out.

"It's right he is," said she. "A woman's not a woman if she's had no man. I'm no woman to-day. I'm a damned Old Maid sittin' here, knowin' nothin' of life save be hearsay. And what's hearsay," said Miss M'Guire, "when ye want to *know*?"

She sewed.

"I had as gay a foot and as light a heart," said she, "as any woman, and I had as many fellahs after me as any woman ever had. And I turned them down. Why did I?—my dear, I was dry meself and it's half-frightened I was at the men and half waitin' I was on somethin' that never did come. I should have married Charlie MacBryan," said Miss M'Guire, "he's right. What if he did get soused? What if he did turn and beat me as they say he beats his wife this day? Isn't it better to be sore and live with a man than to live safe and sound with yer past behind ye and no future to come? What's life? . . ." said Miss M'Guire.

She sewed.

"There's times, God forgive me," she said, "when I've envied the bad women. They've known!"

She sewed.

"Who's me to be left all alone," said she, "who's me to be left knowin' nothin'—never havin' tasted life at all?"

She was silent. There was a considerable pause.

"Ye mustn't mind me, what I'm sayin' this day," said Miss M'Guire, breaking all of a sudden into the pause—and her voice was as the voice of Miss M'Guire once more—"it's meetin' with Charlie MacBryan that's makin' me talk. It's not that I care for um," she continued explanatorily, 'it's just that no woman wants to hear a man call her an Old Maid—and a damned one at that. It's true," said Miss M'Guire, "and it's just because it's true that Charlie MacBryan shouldn't have said ut."

She sewed.

"He was soused," said she in a philosophical tone after the lapse of a minute, "he was soused through and through and we mustn't forget ut. Ye must take what ye get when ye talk with a drunk."

There was a long silence that was somehow full of conflict.

"D'ye think, me dear," said Miss M'Guire at last, "if I'd been less dry meself it's happier I might have been? 'It's water, the damned dry stuff's been your ruin, Mary M'Guire,' says Charlie MacBryan to me."

Silence encircled us.

"She ran after um and she got um," said Miss M'Guire, cutting the silence in two with a trenchant tone of voice, "and it's comfort to know that she got her troubles with um."

She sewed.

"But she got um," said Miss M'Guire, "she's lived if she got her troubles. And here's me a damned Old Maid. . . ."

She sewed.

A PAGE FROM LIFE

TIM DONNELLY had won the raffle. He had put in two tickets, not because he wanted the pony—he didn't, though he had the Irishman's love of ponies and all that appertains to ponies in his blood. He didn't want the pony, because he had nowhere to put it; and even if he made somewhere to put it, he had no one to ride it. What is the use of a pony hardly bigger than a Newfoundland dog to one who is childless? What good is all the prettiness of a toy like that if you have nothing to play with it? That was the question Tim Donnelly kept asking himself as his wife bothered and bothered him to put in his ticket for the raffle that the Mother House was giving for the benefit of one of the best of causes, you may be sure.

"But what is the good of ut, Katie?" said Tim. "What good is a pony to us that has nothin' to ride on its back?"

"Sure, Tim, aren't ye the spoil-sport!" said his wife. "Isn't there a driveway right up to our Apartment House? And can't ye lodge the beast in the yardway at the back when ye've built a house for ut there? And what is the good of all that money ye're makin' if we can't have somethin' to show for ut? Away with ye," said Katie, making an end of it, "away with ye to the Mother House and take yer tickut like a man!"

Tim Donnelly had gone like a man—but a man with a stone at his heart—to take his ticket at the Mother House, as Katie told him to do. Tim Donnelly was one of those big men that do do what their Katies tell them. And Katie was one of those small, masterful women that order about their Tims. He went to the Mother House, and when he got there he found that it was Father M'Shane who was the seller of the tickets; and so he went to Father M'Shane and stated his case.

"Sure, ye're in the right," said Father M'Shane. "The money's needed, and the pony's been sent to get us the money. And if ye'll all take tickuts the thing's as good as won. Wouldn't ye take *two* tickuts, Tim Donnelly?" said Father M'Shane.

So Tim Donnelly took two tickets, and just as he had his hand in his pocket, reaching for his purse, what should come into the room but a gold-haired angel, holding in its hand a three-cornered notelet which the Mother Superior was sending to Father M'Shane on a matter of business.

Tim Donnelly stopped short, with his hand in his pocket and his mouth open and his eyes as big as saucers, gazing at the angel. He stood like a stone, gazing with all his soul in his eyes. The angel was three years old. It had legs—stout, chubby ones—and arms—they were covered with the sleeves of a blue blouse—and little dimpled hands coming out at the ends of the sleeves. It had large, blue eyes as round as an owl's. It had a little formless nose, and pink cheeks, and a great mop of curly, shining, glistening hair. It had feet on it on which it stood firmly. It had a smile on it that seemed to shed a radiance round it as it stood. It was all complete but for the wings—and it looked as if it had left those on the mat outside with its rubbers, and would pick them up and put them on when it was ready to go out again on to the snowy path which divided the Mother House from the place where Father M'Shane reigned supreme.

"Us that a letter?" said Father M'Shane.

The angel spake not. It merely advanced its dimpled, angelic hand and held the letter out. And it smiled.

"Sure, Tim Donnelly," said Father M'Shane, catching Tim Donnelly's eye, "it's a pity ye've no children of your own. Don't ye want a boy to bring up and dedicate to the Blessed Church?"

At this point Father M'Shane caught something further in Tim Donnelly's eye.

"Here's one of our boys wantin' a home," said Father M'Shane. "Why wouldn't ye take um an' put the Mother House free of the expense of his keep? He's an orphan all but for his mother, and she'll be dead in a couple of weeks from now. She's in the Hospital for Incurables, God help her! and her boy's comin' on us for his upkeep if there's no Christian heart that'll bring a blessin' on itself by takin' him off the hands of the Sisters."

Tim stood looking. He said nothing at all because his heart was so full that he couldn't speak. But he looked and he looked and the image of the child seemed to come pouring into him as he looked—till whatever it was inside him that it poured into was full and brimming over with—what? Love and longing and the desire to reach out and take the angel into his big arms and never part with it any more. . . .

Tim Donnelly paid down the money for the raffle and he took the two tickets and he went away. And as he walked along the road vague ideas came surging up in him, and as they surged they turned to definite desires—and the desires turned to practical thoughts of—Why not? Why shouldn't I?

"Sure, it's a child we want in the home," said Tim Donnelly to himself as he walked along. "It's a child and the noise a child makes, and the sound of the little voice, that's needed between Katie and me!"

And as he walked all sorts of thoughts that he had kept down in himself till then came breaking in on his consciousness as waves break on a seashore.

"It's a child I've wanted," he said to himself; "that's what's been lackin' to ye, Tim Donnelly. If ye had a child—"

He paused and stood still in the roadway a minute.

"If ye had a child," he cried to himself, "ye'd be another man. Ye'd have somethin'—somethin' *outside* of yerself to work for."

And then the angry toot of an automobile horn sounded right into the very midst of his thoughts and Tim Donnelly had only just time to save them from utter annihilation on the spot by sprinting for the sidewalk and thinking of nothing at all for a bit but the mercy of God that had kept him from being killed. As to the driver of the automobile, *his* language was of Hell and the Folly of Mankind—two subjects that are more closely allied than we sometimes think.

A fortnight passed and then Tim Donnelly got word that he had won the pony.

"Ye'll have to start an' build," said Katie gleefully; "it's the luck we've run into. Tim Donnelly, we're on a streak of good fortune, glory be to God! an' we'll have to live up to ut."

Tim stared at her. He wasn't thinking of the pony.

"Ye've the face of a jelly-fish on ye," said Katie, with all the breezy freedom of marital speech on her. "Git a move on! Brace up, Tim Donnelly. It's ponies for ours!"

Tim Donnelly made his arrangements with a neighbour to house the pony till he could get something thrown up of his own that he could keep it in; and once more he took the road to Father

M'Shane's, and as he passed by the Mother House his heart went to the angel inside and he wondered what it was doing.

"Sure an' ye're the lucky man," said Father M'Shane. "It's God's blessin's on you, Tim Donnelly. Will ye take the pony back with ye now, for it's a drain on the Mother House keepin' ut alive with all that it eats?"

Tim Donnelly was so busy thinking that he hardly heard what Father M'Shane had to say. But he managed to stammer out that he would take the beast away with um—and Father M'Shane rang the bell.

"It's a fine pony, Tim Donnelly," said Father M'Shane while they were waiting for the bell to be answered. "Sure, it's the pity ye've no child to ride on the back of the beast."

He was silent a moment.

"Ye should take a child, Tim Donnelly," said Father M'Shane, "ye should take a boy and train um up to the glory of God."

And just then the old housekeeper came in answer to the bell and Father M'Shane went across the room and spoke to her in a low tone, and she nodded her head and went away again.

"It's the poor house that has no child's voice ringin' through ut," said the priest. "It's a sore heart your wife has, Tim Donnelly, though she'll keep a quiet mouth on ut."

And Father M'Shane went on talking and Tim sat, half listening to him and half far away in some other world. He was away in the world of desire with something tugging at his heartstrings . . . and somewhere in the half of him that was listening to Father M'Shane there was the thought of Katie.

Would Katie care for a child?—Katie, that never had said one word in all the barren years of any longing for such a thing as that? Would Katie care for an angel? Wouldn't she think it a trouble, she that was always talking of trouble, to care for its shining hair, to tend its little angelic body, to cover up its iridescent wings from the dust and the dirt of the everyday world? What would Katie say?

And then the door opened slowly and softly and into the room came the angel. It was smiling shyly and it carried nothing in its little hands this time. It just stood by the door with a flush on its rounded cheeks and its shy smile on its lips and all its little angelic soul looking through its clear and shining eyes.

And, as Tim Donnelly looked at it, the things that had been
surging and surging up in him broke—the wave came into the
shore and broke triumphantly at its goal.

"I'll take um, Father," said Tim Donnelly, "and by the
blessin' of God I'll train um to be a man."

Father M'Shane went up to the angel and took it by the hand
and led it up to Tim and put its little hand in his.

"That's your father now," said Father M'Shane to the angel.
"You'll go home with him and you'll do what he tells you.
You'll obey him and love him and you'll be a son to him. And,
Tim Donnelly," said Father M'Shane, "as you do by this child,
may God do to you."

Father M'Shane turned and went back to his place by the
black oaken table.

"It's takin' a great burden off the Mother House ye are, Tim
Donnelly," said Father M'Shane with a sigh. "May God reward
ye and give ye increase on the money ye're savin' His Blessed
Church!"

Tim Donnelly and the pony and the angel all went home
together. The angel had a hat on over its angelic hair, and it had
a little coat buttoned over its blue blouse. It didn't speak at all.
It seemed a little overwhelmed by the newness of the situation—but it didn't cry. It just walked along very solemnly by
Tim Donnelly's side, and when an automobile gave an extra
loud toot Tim felt the little hand close more firmly on his own.

"Sure an' I'll buy um a 'coon coat to umself," thought Tim to
*him*self. "It'll keep um warm in the bitter weather."

And he clasped the little fingers tighter in his own—and
when he felt the pressure of the little hand against his own
something seemed to run up his arm and down his body till it
got to his heart—and there it was at home. He wanted to lift the
child and carry him. He wanted to feel it close to him—close till
it was a bit of himself. All the passionate longing of the childless years of marriage seemed to come from all the different
directions of Tim Donnelly's soul, and when they had concentrated on the little figure that walked so seriously by his side
they changed into love—and the barrenness blossomed out into
joy and plenty.

First of all they took the pony to the neighbour's and saw it
lodged there. The angel kept its eyes on the pony; and when

they left it the angel's eyes kept turning back and back to see the last of it. It almost seemed as if there was a link between the little shaggy beast and the angel. They seemed to understand one another. Perhaps they had come from the same place, and they had neither of them quite forgotten what it looked like there.

"Ye'll see um again," said Tim consolingly, as he saw the angel's eyes turning back and back to where they had left the pony. "Ye'll see um sure."

The angel looked up at Tim. It hadn't spoken yet. It looked up with its wide, blue eyes—and was silent.

When they came in sight of home Tim's heart, for the first time, began to jump. He had never taken any advantage of Katie, that small, masterful creature who managed his flat for him. He had always consulted her and deferred to her, and if she had said a thing wasn't to be, then it wasn't. And now, here was he, bringing an angel unawares, and not just for temporary hospitality either. He was bringing it home to Katie's apartment house for good—and goodness only knew what the angel meant to turn into in the end . . . and possibly Katie wouldn't want it even if it would consent to stay an angel all its life. Katie had never said a syllable—except just to shut Tim up if he so much as mentioned the word child.

They got to the door and Tim drew out his latchkey and turned the key quietly in the lock. He opened the door, he stooped and lifted the angel over the step and he set it down softly on the clean linoleum, with which Katie elected to cover her hallway.

"Is that you, Tim?" cried Katie from the kitchen. Well she knew it was Tim, but she cried out at him to ask if it was he just in the way we all do when our husbands turn their latchkeys in the door and come home to us.

And then, as she got no response, no reply at all, Katie Donnelly came out of her kitchen and into her linoleum-covered hall, and she saw the angel standing timidly on the clean floor where it had been put. It stood there with its cap over its shining curls, and the flush in its cheeks had faded from nervousness, so that it was a little pale, and its great eyes looked and looked in front of it—and its lip quivered.

"For-the-love-of-Mike!" said Katie Donnelly, and her voice trembled into silence.

She stood there with her arms at her sides, facing the angel; and the angel stood on the mat looking at her with all its eyes. And then suddenly the angel—for the first time—spoke. "Mother," it said. "Mother, is that you?"

Katie Donnelly's arms went out in the front of her. She stood for one second like that. And then—I don't know which of them it was that began to run, or if it was both of them at once—all I know is that half-way down the passage Katie Donnelly was in a heap on the floor and the angel was in her arms and on her lap and inside her heart.

"My child, my child," said Katie, and she cried and cried, "have ye come to me, have ye come at last? . . ."

And she rocked to and fro in the old, old way. She might have been her grandmother in Ireland with a child in her arms. She rocked the child on her heart. And all the unspoken misery of the barren years faded away from her too and her whole being radiated out joy and plenty.

"Sure," said Katie, "the child's fastin'. He's hungry and thirsty, God bless um! and here we're just wastin' our breaths."

With the child in her arms she hurried to the kitchen and she warmed milk in her little pot and crumbled bread into a bowl.

"Bread-an'-milk ull do um now," said she, "but, believe me, he'll have a great supper with cream to ut!"

Tim stood by. His mouth was stretched from ear to ear almost. He smiled and he licked his lips with satisfaction. And the angel ate.

"Tim," said Katie, slipping her arm through his, "where's the mother of um?"

"She's in the Hospital for Incurables," said Tim, "God help her! And it's fourteen days that the Father said she was due to die in a couple of weeks from then."

Katie was silent. She kept her arm where it was. The two, with no child of their own, stood and watched the child of this other unknown, nameless woman as he ate his bread-and-milk. In Katie's heart there was a struggle and a strife. She was silent for a space—and away down at the bottom of his bowl the angel saw the end of all things coming.

"Tim," said Katie at last, "it's Friday to-day. We'll take the pony Sunday, and we'll loan some kind of a rig from Grogan & Sons and we'll drive away to the Incurables and we'll show the child to his mother. If I was dyin'," said Katie Donnelly, "I'd die easier if my child had a home. So we'll show um to her," she said, "an' then when she's dead we'll say nothin' more about her. He'll be ours when she's dead," said Katie, "yours an' mine, Tim—an' we'll *have* um. . . ."

The angel finished the last spoonful. He laid his spoon carefully in his bowl, as they had taught him to do in the Mother House. And then he turned his head to where Katie and Tim were standing together—and he smiled.

Katie Donnelly took her hand from her husband's and she held out her arms.

"Come, darlin'," she said.

The angel came running.

A WOMAN OF BUSINESS

MADAME SLOYOVSKA gave me her story in snatches under the glare of the electric light. We were standing together in the hallway, with only a minute or two to spare, and something unlocked her tongue. Usually she kept it with the key turned on it, and when you parted from her you knew no more than when you met her. But as we stood together there something made her speak. It may have been one of those sudden desires to tell someone else something that we are all acquainted with, or it may have been that she was on the eve of leaving the life I knew her in, and when we are entering on a different chapter of our books of life—we talk. Reserved as we may be while the thing is going on, we speak just as we are taking leave of it for ever; and then all that we have hidden for years with such care and pains bursts out of us in a torrent. We all know something of this—and if we are women we know it only too well. A woman is as good a secret-keeper as a man—till the strain is over; and then she talks and talks and it isn't a secret any more. So it was with Madame Sloyovska as we stood together last night under the glare of the electric light in the hallway.

As she spoke the light fell on her face. It fell cruelly there, as electric light does fall on us. It touched her face with age. Every fold and wrinkle stood out in the soft skin. The eyes looked tired, the mouth looked drawn, and in the plentiful black hair the grey strands and streaks were pitilessly shown up. Never before had I thought of Madame Sloyovska's age; but as we stood together there I saw that she was what we, in our modern slang, call "an old woman." We mean by that, not age, but that a woman is past her definitely womanly cycle of existence. Madame Sloyovska was just passing into the epoch when she would be a woman no longer—but just a human creature. And she knew it.

She knew it—and she didn't care. For, by hook or by crook, she had pulled out of the maelstrom of life. She had managed to do what so few women of business do manage to do—she had made money. And now, with her money solidly invested and bringing her in good interest, she was *re*-tiring, as she said. She was leaving all the bustle and worry and eternal strain of money-making and she was going to desert the rest of us and live somewhere happily on the proceeds of her industry.

"For zees haf I streeven," said Madame Sloyovska. She spoke rapidly in her fluent, execrable English—and a little breathlessly. "For zees haf I worked. For zees haf I—"

She stopped.

"Look you," she said, "I haf a daughter. She ees mine. For her I vorked."

When Madame Sloyovska spoke of her daughter she changed. All the hardness died out of her face, her eyes beamed with a very beautiful light, her mouth softened into a smile.

"Look you, I lofe zees daughter," she said simply. "I lofe her. She ees beautiful."

And then Madame Sloyovska began to tell me how she had made the money, on which this daughter was to live—and *that* was the unexpected part of the story. For, though I had always suspected that Madame Sloyovska had—shall we say seen life?—I never had suspected that she had seen it to the extent she had. She had seen it with a vengeance. She had had not one Past, but many Pasts. She had gone right down into the deeps and let them all go over her—and the odd thing was that she didn't seem much the worse. If ever I were in a tight place I don't know anyone I would rather have with me than Madame Sloyovska. She gives me the feeling of a straight woman—and yet her life has been crooked enough if we judge it by our customary standards.

First of all she told me of her first "gen'leman friend," as she called him. He had given her a house.

"My own," she said. "He gif it me. Zat vos ze beginning."

Then we came on to the next "gen'leman friend," and he had given her certificates of stock.

"Zat," said Madame, nodding sapiently, "vos goot. Ze stock go up."

The third gen'leman friend had run to diamonds.

Another had planked the money down.

"And von goot friend I haf," Madame Sloyovska said, "for keeps. He gifs me vords how I shall put my mooney in."

There was no confusion in Madame's variety of Pasts. She had had many lovers and she had made them all pay—according to their means; and I dare say she had given them honest value for their money.

"I done my duty by zem," she remarked. "I vork goot for all ze mooney vot I haf."

And that was not all she told me.

Madame Sloyovska has led what we call a bad life. She is thoroughly disreputable from head to heel. She has walked in the shadiest paths, and there are few dirty tricks that her hands haven't dabbled in. The snatches of her life, as she gave them to me hurriedly in the glare of that unprotected light, sounded like something you might read in a dime novelette. They were bald and bad and low and mean and unspeakably sordid—they were the life of a loose woman from her own lips. Madame Sloyovska had had lovers galore, and when she had had one lover's money she had gone on to the next one and she had had his money. Could there be anything more definitely against the moral code? And yet—explain it how you will—I felt no rancour against Madame Sloyovska as she told me—things. I felt even that no special blame attached to her.

"I most haf mooney," she said simply. "How, if I haf not mooney, can I keep my daughter pure?"

She used queer words—words that we do not usually employ.

"How can I keep my daughter pure," she kept on asking me, "eef I haf not mooney for to gif her?

"I *had* to haf my mooney," Madame Sloyovska said. "I vorked always viz my daughter in my heart. Ven my friend he gif me money, I say, 'Zat ees for Dilli!' Dilli ees my daughter's name."

When she spoke of Dilli, Madame Sloyovska's eyes shone. A lovely maternity settled on her. One could see that now she had money she would fetch Dilli out of the convent she had put her in for safety, and that she would guard her and keep her unspotted from the world, as only one whom the world has splashed can do.

"Dilli," Madame Sloyovska said, "ees beautiful. She is dark, she has shining eyes. And she ees young."

Madame Sloyovska looked at me, and even in the electric glare her face was—may I call it beautiful?

"Dilli ees young," she said. "Look you, I find a man. I marry Dilli. She knows nozing."

Madame Sloyovska paused.

"For zees I vorked," she said.

It is odd to me to think that I don't really know anything about Madame Sloyovska. I haven't the slightest idea of her nationality, beyond the fact that she comes from what we in Canada vaguely call "Eastern Europe." I don't know her religion or if she has any. I can't form the slightest conception of her childhood or how she was brought up or what her father and mother were like. We are separated by almost all the things that do separate us human beings. We can't even say much to each other, for a lack of language comes between us. And, besides that, all sorts of other things come between us. We know different sides of life. Madame Sloyovska doesn't read, she doesn't think—not consciously, at any rate—she isn't interested in any of the things that I am interested in. Yet last night for the few moments that we stood beneath the electric light together these differences were wiped out as if they had never been. We understood each other to the very deeps. I knew why Madame had worked or sinned or whatever name you like to put to it. She wanted to keep the thing dearest to her out of the mire—and how could she keep it definitely and surely out of the mire unless she made money for it to pay its way through life? If Madame had led what we call an honest life, earning a sparse livelihood, say with her needle, then Dilli would have had but a poor chance of virtue. She would have been the scapegoat instead of her mother and there would have been all the difference. As it was—Madame had sold over and over again the only thing she had to sell—her body. And while she was busy selling and putting the proceeds out at interest, Dilli was in her convent learning gentle manners from the nuns.

"Ven Dilli comes," Madame Sloyovska said to me, "I most be irreproachable. She knows nozing—never. I go from here. And I begin again. I find a hosband. Dilli shall be goot. . . ."

I said that Madame Sloyovska's life sounded like a dime novelette. But no dime novelette ever sounded quite like the way she told about it. There was no sentimentality about Madame Sloyovska. If she sinned she knew she sinned, and she knew why she sinned too. And when she gets to the next world I think she will find a place prepared for her—but which of us shall say where?

THE SOCIAL PROBLEM

I CAN'T imagine what made me fond of Donna. She embodied all the things that I most dislike. She was smart—in her clothes, in her thought, in her speech. She affected all kinds of abominations just to show that she was "in it," a bit of the passing show, a crumb of the world's pie-crust. She wasn't good for anything much—except to look at; and to look at she was "elegant," as she herself would have said. From the gloss of her exquisitely arranged hair to the shine of her perfectly fitting footgear she was—adorable. Thought had gone to make the outward observance of her, and it was thought not thrown away. As an elaborated bit of prose stands out in the memory, so Donna stood out as you thought about her. She was so poised, so balanced in her appearance, there was such a sense of artistic fitness in her clothes, that your eye rested on her—yes, it rested in spite of you—with pleasure. I don't mean to say that Donna was beautiful as to her clothes. Oh no! Far from it. If you looked at Donna's clothes a year or so after they were made—if you looked at them immediately they were discarded by her—why, then, your eye deceived you no longer and you saw that they were very bad. They were bad in every way. They were idle and soulless, or at least they represented idle and soulless states of mind; and they were provocative. They made you look at them—and as you looked they forced out of you an unwilling admiration. We have all seen clothes like that. We have all seen people more or less like Donna in them. We have most of us disapproved—we have most of us envied—we have most of us admired . . . and a year or two later we have almost all of us seen that they were bad.

Why did I like Donna? How can I tell? Do any of us know why we like or dislike other people? Can one of us state with precision the whys and the wherefores of our affections—and hatreds? I disapproved of Donna, root and branch, as I have said. I thought her way of life silly, and her views past speaking of, and the way she passed her time unhealthful; and yet, in spite of all this, in spite of her speech and the way she told risky stories, not for the wit of them, but just in order to be "smart," I liked her. There was something back of her eyes, to use once more her own way of speech, that made one pause. If she had had her chance—if she hadn't had all that time to misuse and all that money to spend and all those useless clothes to play with, she might have been a nice thing enough. But what is the good of thinking what people would be if they weren't what they are!

Donna had a lot of time to misuse, and she had too much money to spend, and far, far too many clothes and jewels to play with, and so she hadn't a chance at all. The masseuse who came regularly to keep her skin smooth and unwrinkled, the scalp specialist who worked at her hair, the manicurist who sat patiently over her nails—the very scrubwoman who came on Saturdays to get down on her knees and scrub the basement into which Donna never went at all—these women had more chances than Donna had ever had. They all worked for their living and they knew how hard it is to earn money and how easy—how fatally easy—it is to go wrong; and they knew the consequences of going wrong, and how unpleasant they are. If the scrublady took so much as a bit of butter that didn't belong to her, it was as much as her place was worth; and if the manicurist—who was young and pretty—stopped and answered the young gentlemen who approached her as she walked home at night, why, that was as much as her life was worth. These hard-working women who contributed each her mite towards keeping Donna exquisite, they all had their chance. They knew something at least of life. They realised—each one of them—what temptation means, and what yielding to it entails. They had their chance—for, after all, isn't life just the bringing home of knowledge?

But Donna hadn't much of a chance to learn anything. She lay in bed late and thought the morning a terrible time of day. If it hadn't been for those satellites who circled round her at their appointed times, and for her "friends," as she called them, and for the telephone which stood by the side of her bed, connecting her with the outer world whenever she took the receiver off, she would have been in a sad plight. Donna never read anything—except, perhaps, the newspaper, and not much of that. She never did anything, except try on gowns and hats and shoes and stockings and gloves and coils of hair and things of that kind. Her day was all taken up in preparing. For what? To show off these things that she had been trying on all day. She went to restaurants to show them off, she went to theatres and operas and cabarets and lunches and teas and dinners, or she walked a little way in the street perhaps—the right street—or she "received" in her own home. Whatever she did, or wherever she was, the thought of these adjuncts to herself never left her. She was never just unconscious. She never lost herself entirely in anything. The nearest approach she had to losing herself was when she was just deciding to buy a new—something—anything. She loved clothes and jewels and things, and when she lighted on a thoroughly successful anything, she did perhaps lose herself in it for a minute. But she soon found herself again. Just as soon as she purchased the thing and got it home and put it on, then the unconsciousness—the losing of herself in it—vanished.

As soon as the gown or the jewel was "on," Donna regarded it no longer as a thing by itself. The question in her mind then was, "Does it suit *me*?" And she would look anxiously in the mirror, and turn and peer and gaze from every angle, with hand-glasses and without them, twisting and craning so as to get every possible view . . . and then, when afterwards she would wear it, the thought of it was inextricably entangled with herself. "Am I *right*?" she would say to herself, gazing earnestly at her reflection; and then, later, wherever it was that she and it were going, "Look!" her air would say to all the world, "look at this I am wearing and watch the way to wear it." And you would look, and against your better judgment, as I have said, you would admire. For Donna—with her piled-up dark hair and her luminous eyes and her unlined skin that had the sheen of a rose-petal, and her round, smooth neck and her supple body and her arched foot—was a lovely creation. She was the acme of—of what civilisation can do for a woman. Donna in a print gown, bending over a wash-tub—only I can't imagine it!—would have escaped both comment and criticism, I dare say. She would have been a good-looking girl enough, with scores and scores more like her on every side. But massaged and manicured, clothed by artists with the feeling for "cut" and "style," arranged and polished, turned out by efficiency in the shape of a maid, and always, always with the perfectly harmonious setting behind her . . . well, she was Donna. She was a thing that your eye followed and clung to. You let her pass out of your sight unwillingly. "What an exquisite creature!" you said to whoever happened to be with you; and whoever that was, whether man or woman, it answered you, "Yes, isn't she perfect!" And its eyes followed Donna too—and drank her in.

I think I may say that I was in Donna's confidence. I mean by that that I was a good deal with her for a time and she liked to talk to me. She happened to be in a muddle while Fate threw us together, and she had the feminine propensity for liking to go over the muddle with anybody who would listen, and go over it, not once, but five hundred thousand times. I never bore Donna any malice for doing this. All women like to do it—I like to do it myself; and this is, I suppose, the reason why one woman never takes it ill when another woman goes on repeating—to nausea!—the same thing over and over and over again. We all like to do it. It seems to us the only thing to do when we are in trouble. Donna would go over to me the history of her brief married life—with all the most intimate details superadded— and how that married life had been dissolved and why it was necessary to dissolve it and whether she missed the intimate details or was glad to be rid of them . . . all this for as long as I would consent to listen. She would talk and talk and repeat over and over again the very same words, and all the time she would adjust her clothes to herself with rapid, skilful movements of her manicured hands. She would touch and lightly fluff the hair that her maid had so carefully arranged for her—she would powder and dab and burnish and pencil—and into her eyes there would come the rapt, earnest expression of the devotee . . . and all the time she would talk and explain what never can be explained—and everything would come pouring out of her mind as water comes pouring out of a jug.

"Say, don't ut seem a pity," she would say, "that Jim and me had to pa-art! He was good. I liked him. But he got kind of on the loose. If it had been one woman he kept I wouldn't have said one word. I wouldn't have minded a particle. But it was *girls*. . . ."

She took a fresh pinch of cotton batting between her finger and thumb and dipped it in the powder bowl.

"You can't stand *girls*," said she; "you've your health to think about, eh?"

She powdered lightly and scanned the result narrowly in the glass.

"Eh?" she said again, and she took up the chamois and began lightly polishing her cheek with it and stretching the skin—like a strap—against the muscles of her eyes and chin. "Eh, ain't ut so? A man has to stawp awf somewhere, I guess. You can't afford to get yourself all tangled up with truck." She leaned forward and gazed. "Some going, eh?" said she, and she reached for something for her lips. "I liked Jim, make no mistake! He was great. I'd have stayed on with him right along, believe me, if he'd kept in reason. But he got on the loose, Jim did, and I got kinder scared. So we had to pa-art."

She bent backwards, with her eyes always on the mirror and she took hold of the hat that lay ready on the bed and lightly she held it poised above her head. "Stunning, eh?" she said. "Ain't ut a dandy production, say?"

She lowered it gently—and as she gazed at her own reflection there was a steady look in her eyes. She might have been an artist setting a model. She might have been a helmsman guiding a ship. She might have been God with His hand on the wheel of life.

"How's tha-at!" she said.

She sent her hat-pin through—and it was done . . . and she stopped looking at herself in the mirror and looked downwards at the rug.

She sat there a moment, half turned from the mirror, with her arm on the back of her chair and her cheek on her hand. She sat motionless and she looked at the rug. She looked at it, but she looked as if she were looking, not at it, but through it—to hell perhaps, for the expression of her face was restless and mournful.

"Listen," she said, and she lifted her eyes to mine without moving her head or her hand, "do you ever feel . . .?"

She sighed—and the sigh seemed to find its way up from somewhere deep down in her.

"There's times," she said, "when I feel as if dying was too good to be true—and this is one of the times."

She looked away from me. Her eyes went restlessly round the room and found nothing to settle on.

"What's it all *for*," she said; "that's what I want to know. I have *the* time. I got all I want. I'm rid of Jim and I'm goin' to be married to a man that's 'way beyond lovely. But there's times——"

She stopped.

"There's times," she said, "I feel like I'd go ravin' mad. And to-night's one."

She sat in her Louis Seize chair. She was dressed, all but her frock, and as she sat there in her miraculously fine petticoat, in the delicate lace of her slip-waist, in her wonderful stockings and her Cinderella shoes—in the stunning hat—with the earrings hanging from her tiny ears and flashing with every movement of her shapely head—she looked infinitely finished; she looked more finished somehow than when she was fully finished and dressed. There was a look of gilt and brocade about her as there was about the chair she sat on. All round about her was the frippery and elaboration of her toilet-table. She sat there, with one foot over the other, thrown back in her chair, with one arm over the back of it and her face in her hand, and she gave one that impression of mournfulness that something beautiful and yet out of place gives you. She looked as I have seen a beautiful tropical bird look—in its cage. And one felt that the fresh air and God's blue sky and the wind and the rain and the driving beauty of a winter day and the tender loveliness of a spring morning had all been kept from her. She was the product of electric light and the elaborate bathroom and the telephone and the limousine, with its heater and its vase for flowers—and all the other things that we make to stand between ourselves and life.

"Say," she said, and she turned her dark eyes on me again, "say, what's the good of ut all? I keep goin'. And I'm goin' to keep goin'. And if this man don't suit I'm goin' to have the next one—and that's goin' some, believe me! But it's"—she sighed, and this time the sigh seemed to come from her very soul—"it's tirin'," she said.

She kept her eyes fixed on me. They looked straight at me and it seemed to me that there was something mournful looking out at me through them.

"Say," she said, "are you fond of children!"

She did not put it in the form of a question. It was just a bit of her thoughts that was forming itself by a sort of instinct into words—so I didn't answer her.

She sat there, with her small teeth on her lip. Under the stunning hat she somehow looked incongruous—and curiously old.

And the mournful thing behind her dark and luminous eyes continued to look out at me.

"If I had a baby," she said, "I'd want ut to be an elegant one, you bet your life. But you can't . . ." She stopped.

"Well," she said after a minute, "you can't. You're all in if you have a baby. It plays merry hell with you."

She continued to look at me—and the thing behind her eyes gazed out steadily on life.

"And so I guess you'd best leave well alone," she said.

She turned back to the mirror and looked into it. The thing behind her eyes sank back—and back. . . . It was like watching something go down through clear water to fathomless depths to sit looking over her shoulder at the reflection the glass gave back.

"Say," said she, glancing at her wrist-watch, "would you ca-all Berth to come and fix me in my gear. For it's goin' to be some show to-night and," she said, "I'll have to get a move on if I want to be on time."

I called, and Berthe, crisp and adequate, rustled in.

"Keep your eye on the gown," cried Donna, waving a festive arm. "It's a God-sent mercy. I want you to understand it's corkin'—ain't ut, Berth?"

"Mais oui, Madame," said Berthe, "c'est magnifique. Une robe superbe!"

She knelt to fasten it.

"Stunning, eh?" said Donna. " 'Way past elegant!"

When Berthe stood off from her she paused a second before the mirror, posing, appraising the rippling beauty of her gown—and she looked like Venus just risen from the infernal regions.

She waved a glove at us. "So long!" she said—and she was off.

A CIRCULAR TOUR

"EH," said she, taking a look around her, "but ye've a grand place here! Grand!" said she. "Fine!" said she. She cast her eyes up to the ceiling piously. "Great is the power o' Mammon yet!" she said.

I cast *my* eyes around.

"Not much of Mammon here," said I; "it's small enough."

"It's that," said Miss M'Gruther, "but it's a grand Apartment!"

There was no gainsaying her. I let her call my tiny flat a grand Apartment—such is the power of unadulterated Scottishness.

"Ye suld see mine," said Miss M'Gruther.

She gave a pious sniff. All Miss M'Gruther's sniffs were pious. *She* was pious. Her very bonnet-strings had a Pharisee's touch about the tie of them. Down to her stocking-feet she was ecclesiastical.

"It's a puir thing, mine," said she, "to ca' a hame." She sniffed again. "Money," she said, "money's a power." Then, with a touch of comfort: "Yet maun we no forget, mem, that it's man's destruction!"

With that she closed the door, upon whose peg she had just hung her bonnet by its pious bonnet-string. She tied her apron on with righteousness, she came and took her place in the best chair she could see, in the best light my grand Apartment had to give. She smoothed the creases in her lap.

"What's your wull?" said she.

Once she had my wull and had set to at it she began again.

"Eh," said she, "ye're weel seetuate here! As I was comin' through yer entrance ha' this mornin', mem, just to mysel' I passed a wee remark. 'It's wonderfu',' said I (just to mysel', ye understan'), 'the w'y things comes to pass. Here's her,' said I, 'sae weel installed. And here is me wi' my puir hame and naethin'' (in a manner, mem, o' speakin') 'ye could ca' my ain. Why,' said I, 'is that? And whercforc?' "

Miss M'Gruther sniffed.

"Yon," said she, "was the remark I passit wi' mysel' as I was comin' through yer entrance ha' this mornin', mem."

She paused. Righteousness pervaded her.

"God's w'ys mysterious are!" said she.

I felt now was my chance to rise or never.

"Some things," said I, "we have to take on trust."

I felt I had done not so badly. Miss M'Gruther sniffed.

"It's a grand entrance ha' ye have," said she, "sae light and clean! There's dirt on mine," she said, "and waur than dirt . . .!

"It's the Lord's wull," said Miss M'Gruther.

There was a pause.

"Next door to me," said Miss M'Gruther, when the time was ripe for her to speak again, "next room to mine ahint a wa' that's holes in it—"

Around the lath and plaster of my holeless walls did Miss M'Gruther cast her eagle eye.

"A-ha!" she said. "Dear me! Weel, weel!" She paused.

"—ahint the wa' that's holes in it," said Miss M'Gruther, "mem, there stays a man."

She paused again.

"A man that's lost in sinfu'ness," said she.

"What kind of sinfulness?" said I.

"Drink, mem, drink," said Miss M'Gruther.

She sat a while and shook her head.

"Eh," said she at last, "to think, mem, that there's men-bodies'll pit inside theirsels the de'il and a' his warks!" She paused a moment, then she added: "No to speak o' spendin' money on it!

"Tch, tch, tch!" said Miss M'Gruther.

We sat a while and thought about it.

"Straucht forninst me," Miss M'Gruther said, "there stays a hussy."

"What kind of one?" said I.

Then for a period Miss M'Gruther sat and bridled with her ancient head.

"A hussy that is ower aquent wi' life, mem," Miss M'Gruther said.

She shook her head and shook and shook it.

"If ye'll excuse me, mem," said she, "I'll say nae mair."

She said nae mair. We sat.

"Eh me, the sinfu'ness o' life," said Miss M'Gruther, bursting out. "The ungodliness!"

She hitched her nose.

"Hm-ah," said she. "Eh dearie me!"

Again we took a pause for meditation.

"You that's wi' law and order at your back," said Miss M'Gruther, when the pause was over, "you that has money to your hand, it's hard for you to guess at what the likes o' me has to endure!"

She shook her head. I felt apologetic.

"It's the Lord's wull," said Miss M'Gruther.

"Toots!" said she.

So did she punctuate our conversation.

"Her that's forninst me," Miss M'Gruther said when it was meet for her to speak once more, "her, Annie Matheson she ca's hersel', *she* has an eye to catchin' him that's lost to sinfu'ness i' drink."

"Dear, dear!" said I.

"Ye weel may say," said Miss M'Gruther. "Her wi' an eye to him! (He answers to the name o' Jock MacBayne.) It's ondecent, mem. It's fair past speakin' o'."

She fixed me with a stony eye.

"Eh, mem," said she, "but spinsterhood's a grand possession!"

Faintly I answered yes.

"A grand possession, mem," said Miss M'Gruther; "integrity's a precious gift!"

She sniffed. A righteous sniff.

"I doubt," said she, "but mebbe Annie Matheson has slippit her time for learnin' that!"

She sniffed.

We took a little time to think it over. There was lots for us to think about. Spinsterhood—the lack of it—Jock MacBayne—drink—indecency—righteous sniffs. When Miss M'Gruther spoke again her tone was almost blithe.

"There's ane thing, mem," she said, "I dinna think she'll get him."

"No?" said I.

"Na," said Miss M'Gruther. "Na. I dinna think it's likely."

She almost closed one eye and slowly shook her head from side to side. The whole of her was fraught with infinite meaning.

"Na," said she again. "So far as I can see she'll ha'e her wark for naethin'."

She leaned a little forward. Her voice dropped to confidence. "Jock's promised to anither woman, mem," said she. "A widow woman—wi' house plenishin's. And napery. And feather beds."

She smiled, did Miss M'Gruther.

"Little does Annie ken," said she.

She hitched her nose.

"Gin she had sneb she micht jalouse," said Miss M'Gruther, taking a cleansing bath of Scotch.

"Couldn't you tell her?" I suggested.

Miss M'Gruther sniffed. She made no verbal answer—she just sniffed. Whole worlds were in that sniff.

"We maun a' dree our weirds," said Miss M'Gruther, apropos of nothing.

After a bit she fidgeted in her chair. She hummed and ha'd.

"Whiles when I'm at my word o' prayer," said she, "I'll hear the hussy, mem, ahint the wall. 'Tak' yer gless, Jock,' she'll say, 'tak' it and drink it up and say you'll hae me.'"

Miss M'Gruther coughed.

"I'll no can sleep," said she, "for hearin' her. 'I've no' been whit I suld be, Jock,' says she. 'Fine I ken that. But, Jock . . . Jock, tak' me. I'll be true to ye. Oh, Jock,' I'll hear her say, 'I lo'e ye, Jock. I lo'e ye, man. I'd cut my han's aff, Jock, to pleasure ye. Tak' me, tak' me, Jock!'"

Miss M'Gruther groaned.

"Her tellin' him she lo'es him, shameless besom. Me hearin' that. *Me* that's a member o' the Presbyterian Church!

"It's awfu', it's just awfu'," Miss M'Gruther said.

Speech failed her. As it seemed the end I rose to leave her— and her speech came back again.

"As I was comin' out the morn," said she, "Jock cried at me. At *me* . . .! 'Lassie,' cries he, 'a gless whusky, lassie, here.' 'Na,' says I. 'A gless Kuyper, lassie, then,' cries he. 'It's fine ye ken,' says I, 'that I've nae drink on me to bring. Learn Christian w'ys,' says I. 'Weel, darlin',' cries Jock at me then, 'if ye've nae drink I'll tak' a pinch o' snuff if you'll obleege me!'"

Miss M'Gruther groaned. She groaned.

"Snuff," said she, "to me! Sic' ribaldry!"

We sat a while in meditation.

"Decency," Miss M'Gruther said at length—it was a sort of proclamation—" yon's what money buys ye, mem.

"Ay!" said she.

Again she meditated for a space. And then she smiled.

"There'll be a skirl," said she, "when Annie kens."

Once more she smiled.

"I hope," she said, "I'm in my room to hear."

So do the Harpies smile while they are sharpening their claws.

"So yon, mem," Miss M'Gruther said, steering her way for where she started from, "*yon* was the reason why I felt it laid on me to say that you was grandly seetuate here."

She glanced about her.

"Eh dear me," said she; "dear me!"

She sniffed.

"It's grand," she said. "It's fine. Money's a power."

And then did Miss M'Gruther spy her sprig of balm of Gilead—and pluck it.

"Ay, it's a power; it's a' that, mem," said she. "Yet maun we haud i' mind that money is the root o' evil!"

"The *love* of money is, you mean," said I, correcting her.

"That's what I say," said Miss M'Gruther. "Money's the root o' evil, mem. A' evil!"

She glanced about her.

"Tch, tch, tch," said she. "Ou ay! Dear, dear!"

She sniffed.

So are our conversations sometimes circular in form.

ART

THERE is nothing so wearisome in all the wearisome possibilities of this world as to be talked to about Art. I dislike to be talked to about anything beginning with a capital letter—Love, Art, Vice—anything of that sort. The more people talk about such things the less do they do them; and unless you do a thing what can you possibly have to say that is worth listening to about it? I haven't known many criminals—to give them their technical name—but I'll be bound that if I did know them they wouldn't talk to me about Vice. They might spin me a yarn about housebreaking, perhaps, and very diverting it would be, but they wouldn't call it by the name of Vice. They would call it—whatever the slang for burglary may be. As to lovers—none that I have known ever talked of Love—while artists are generally too busy to be talking much at all. Art, indeed, may be described as a thing to be done and not talked about. I daresay the War will help it on its way—so far, at least, as not talking about it is concerned. But why, as Mr Granville Barker says, worry with it at all? If it is there you can't miss it, and if it isn't there no talking about it will produce it. Let it take its chance with love—which is much in the same box.

This was not the point of view of Charlie Ralston when he came out to Canada—five or six years ago, before the War. How well I remember his advent among us—Charlie, pleasant-voiced, intensely and passionately interested in all sorts of things that didn't seem to the Canadians to matter, unpractical, artified to a degree, and with a way of saying: "Quite a charming person!" or "What a delicious little bit!" that set the Dominion's teeth on edge and made it writhe. Canada didn't like him. Oh, not at all; it didn't.

I am sorry to say he talked about Art. I hate to say or even to hint anything about my countrymen and countrywomen—of whom I am and want to be so proud: but when they come to Canada a demon seems to enter into them, and too often not one demon but seven demons; and nothing seems able to cast them out again. I mean the demons. Long ago in Paris, before we were at all popular there, it used to be pointed out to me that all Englishwomen had rabbit mouths, with teeth sticking out in front where no teeth should be. This I indignantly denied. But when the Parisians of those far-off days took me walking on the boulevards, lo! all the English we met *had* rabbit mouths with teeth sticking out in front. I can't explain it—so it was. And reluctantly I had to admit the fact. In Canada it isn't teeth that stick out of the English; it is opinions. Canadians (before the War, also when we were not so popular as we are to-day) used to point out to me the angularity and the Himalayan superiority of the English once they crossed the ocean. This, in the face of anecdote and even of proof, I indignantly denied. But when the Canadians took me walking on their wharves, lo! all the English, as they disembarked, *had* opinions sticking out all over them where no opinions should be—chiefly opinions inimical to Canada and the Canadians. And these opinions they—the English—did not desist from mentioning until they reached the wharves to go away again. They were Pauline in their power of mentioning things in season and out of season. And the Canadians didn't—and don't now—like it at all.

Charlie Ralston was no exception to the rule. Once more I do not attempt any explanation. I merely mention. He went on talk-ing about Art and why it wasn't in Canada and why it should be and what was the way to bring it there instanter, until the Canadians, if they weren't the most long-suffering people on earth, would have tarred and feathered him and sent him home with the freight unpaid. Being, as they are, *the* long-suffering people *par excellence*, they listened. They had lots of opportu-nity. When they asked Charlie to dinner he talked about Art. What Futurist music is and isn't. What is the reason of the Canadian being unable to understand it. Why he—and still more she—probably never will. And the pity of it. He talked. He did talk. Oh my, he talked a lot!

Once I remember sitting next to him at lunch. First he told me silly, would-be-funny stories of his landlady—"such a charming person!" And then he told me all the "little bits" he had been "jotting down." And then he told me things I couldn't understand—and wouldn't let me talk to anyone else. All in the name of Art. (What is it?) After lunch was over it was worse. He drew—yes, he did—from his pocket a slim book full of—

imagine what! Aphorisms. Yes, aphorisms, as I'm a woman.
And he read them. He read them all, and as they were pretty
Futurist he had to act the meaning in a sort of drawing-room
lecture. We sat round. Yes, we did. We sat there listening with a
cerebral indigestion growing on the lot of us—don't tell me,
after that, Canadians aren't a long-suffering race. He read them
every one . . . he exhibited them internally, as doctors say.

℞
    La Rochefoucauld ꭑi
    Aq.   Fill the bottle.
    To be taken as directed after food.

That was the prescription.

Another time it was a play he read, one that "a manager" said
was excellent. The first Act, said the manager, was something
fine. Ditto the second. He didn't happen to be in want of plays
just then, otherwise he would have—Charlie read it to us. Well,
we won't say anything more about it. It was a play. *Requiescat
in pace*, and please not *resurgat*!

So Charlie Ralston was a bore, as will be seen. A bore of the
first water. And yet Canada put up with him. He talked at it, he
openly corrected it, he criticised its way of dress, its ways of
speech, its ways of life—and Canada went on asking him to
dinner. Canadians are a funny folk. Instead of turning on the
English when they come and grow their rabbit teeth across the
ocean, Canadians bear with them. The English criticise, find
fault, put the Canadians in the corner; Canadians grumble, they
don't like the drubbing—but they bear it. Whether the War
will—But that's not what I have to say. It's Charlie.

After a bit Charlie took up with a Canadian girl. She was
pretty, not unkindly, practical, with hands on her and no ideas to
speak of. Good ground to clear and plough. I don't know what
she saw in Charlie, unless it was his violet eyes, which should
have been a girl's. Anyway, they were together as often as they
could be—and people looked at them and said to one another:
"Is there anything *in* it? Freda Wanham's gone on *him*!" She
was. I met them on their way to somewhere once. She was fresh
in her white frock, walking beside him as if he was the King.
Why can a woman never hide her feelings if she loves a man—

not from another woman anyway? Do men read men like that? There was in Freda's face that morning the look you can't mistake, that look of something that's not far from adoration—her eyes were brimming, her cheeks were flushed, her body swayed towards his. And her little happy laugh rang out, that happy little laugh—not humorous at all—a woman has when she is walking with the man she loves. Freda was very sweet that morning. She didn't even see me as I passed them—her eyes were seeking his.

Charlie didn't see me either. He was settled down with Charlie Ralston. He liked the pretty girl beside him, but his thoughts and aspirations were firmly on himself. He looked nice, good-looking, well-set-up. His tie was suitable. Under his arm, poor boy, was a Shelley or some such thing—I fancy he meant to read to her when their secluded spot was reached. Well, she could look at him as he was reading. I daresay she was happy.

That came to nothing. Freda's brother said that Charlie was "the God-damnedest fool . . .!" That was his calm opinion—and the family more or less agreed. I don't know whether that influenced Freda or whether Charlie stuck to Shelley and didn't "handle" poetry as a matrimonial theme, but, anyway, Freda married someone else—a practical man who talked of Mergers, not of Art. I daresay Freda's safer with him than she would have been with Charlie. Marriages are ticklish things at any time, and international marriages are—well, they are difficult. England and Canada are separated by more than water. They are relations, and relations, we all know, are apt to differ. I think Charlie and Freda, on the whole, are best apart. "Will the love that you're so rich in light a fire in the kitchen?" I'm sure that Charlie when he came to Canada couldn't have lit a fire with all the love he had at his command. Since then the War has taught him things.

What made me think of him to-night was that I read a letter from him. It was to Mrs Wanham, Freda's mother. Charlie wrote to tell her that her son, Lieutenant Wanham—the very one who said that Charlie was the God-damnedest fool!—had died in France. And Charlie Ralston used no aphorisms in writing. He told quite simply all he could. He put down every little fact he thought might lighten grief. He thought of everything, all the details; he wrote as if he were beside the mother, talking, consoling, watching the changes on her face and comforting her with every tiny thing she wished to know. Charlie writing that way! It was a revelation of him. And then I remembered how one day Charlie had come to see me, and how suddenly, unexpectedly, as happens sometimes when you talk alone with someone, affectation had dropped away from him. He had talked simply, told me of "home," talked of his mother, told me foolish little tender jokes about her—"the old lady!" that was what he called her. We had talked all afternoon that day and never mentioned Art. There was no improvement—we discussed nothing. We just sat and talked of England, of the spring there—the starry primroses—the English birds—their song—the perfume of the English flowers. Perhaps that *was* Art—I never thought of it till now.

Anyway, when Charlie went away that day I thought: "What a pity!" Here was a nice boy growing rabbit teeth just out of cussedness—and partly out of shyness too, perhaps. Why do English people come out to Canada and antagonise the whole Dominion? Why? Why can't they be the natural, kindly people that we mostly are at home—and let Art take its chance? As I said before, after the War, perhaps, things will be different. We shall be *doing* then, please God, not talking quite so much. There's lots to do. . . .

As I finished reading Charlie's letter I stopped to think what I should say—it's hard to think of things at times like that—and as I paused I glanced at Freda. Freda's a married woman now, as I have said. She has another love, a little one that *is* Art, but can't talk about it. She's happy. But as I glanced at her I saw her eyes fixed on the letter in my hand . . . and in her eyes was something—something that was there the day I met them on the hill. She's quite happy. But women, when they've cared for someone, keep a feeling—they don't forget. They can't. I fancy if you said to Freda: "Who is your favourite poet?" she would answer: "Shelley." The present Mr Freda never heard of Percy Bysshe and doesn't want to.

When I began I thought there was a story, but it seems there isn't. The thing I really had to say was—what a pity English people do themselves injustice when they come out here! How often have I blushed for English men and women in the past ten years! How often! When I've heard them puffing, blowing, boasting—or, on the other tack, freezing, extinguishing, well, I've suffered. They come out here and set us right on every possible point . . . it's hard to bear—it really is. I can't help hoping that the day will come when they'll be less superior, and when I can feel truly proud of all the opinions that stick out of them. English like that there are at home. Why can't they stay like that when they come out to Canada?

Charlie is learning, anyway—that letter shows it. I hope he has the best of luck and comes back here after the War to show us what an Englishman can be! I use Canadian phraseology and the present tense just to encourage him in—Art!

ROSE OF SHARON

WHEN you want a maid in Canada you are much in the case of the elderly Scotch spinster of the last generation who began by saying: "Wha'll I tak'?" and ended by saying "Wha'll tak' me?" The justness of this parallel I realised on the day when Rosie called in answer to my advertisement.

Rosie came, as I say, and she was the only one who did—and that was exactly where the rub came in, as Shakespeare says. If there had been anything to choose amongst, you may be very sure I wouldn't have chosen Rosie. But there wasn't. There was just Rosie. Like the late lamented Scotch spinster I had to take what was sent and do my best to be thankful.

The trouble with Rosie was not that she was bad. Oh no! Don't think it. The trouble was that she was so awfully good. She was painfully good. She was fearfully good. She was horribly good. She was so good that, taken as a daily food, she gave you a perennial indigestion.

With no solicitation on my part, and just at the very beginning of that first interview, Rosie informed me that she was a Christian. And when I insinuated that we most of us called ourselves by such a name as that and acted nevertheless as ill as anyone else, Rosie said that was not the kind of Christian *she* was. She was, she said, a Very Early Christian—the same kind of Christian as St Paul. Now this, I confess, staggered me. I yield to no man, or woman either, in my admiration for St Paul, but there is a place for everything and everything has its place, and I cannot but feel that St Paul, sweeping carpets and doing up the kitchen stove of a Saturday afternoon, is not in *his* place at all. Also it flashed across me as Rosie spoke that he would be a good deal to live up to, especially first thing in the morning— not to speak of the question of his correspondence. Why, if he got to that straight after lunch, it is a question in my mind whether he would be through by supper-time.

I therefore put it to Rosie whether she couldn't sink her Christianity, and St Paul into the bargain, while she stayed with

me; and she rather softened me by answering that, although a
Very Early Christian, I mustn't expect too much of her. She
could only do, as she said, "her best." It was this speech
(together with the fact of there being no pagan sister handy) that
settled it. Rosie brought herself and her trunk and her Very
Early Christianity and I paid twenty dollars a month for the lot.

There were days when I was fond of Rosie. I can't deny it.
She was a pretty little thing, not at all like St Paul to look at—not
that I mean any disrespect to him; but Rosie was more like a
sparrow than anything else and I never heard it evened yet that
St Paul was of *that* feather. She had soft, glossy hair, had Rosie,
just the fawny-brown shade at the tip of a sparrow's wing. And
she had bright dark eyes, with just a sparrow's intelligence at the
back of them, and she had a way of standing looking at you with
her head on one side as if she were perched on a bough and you
were on the ground beneath. I like sparrows. And if only Rosie
would have consented just to *be* a sparrow and to cease being so
overwhelmingly interested in the health of my soul, I would
have liked Rosie. Nothing would have pleased me better than to
strew crumbs for Rosie's breakfast and scatter shreds of silk for
the building of her nest—but you can't strew crumbs in front of
a Revival Meeting or shreds of silk in the maw of a hymn. And
Rosie was a walking Revival in the house all day long, alas, and
the concentrated tabloid of a hymn all the evening. There was
nothing for it but to put fondness on one side and make the best
of it. And for a long time a bad best it was.

The first objection I had to make was an objection to Prayer.
After the coming of Rosie, all day long at intervals I was pursued by a voice. A loud voice. An insistent voice. A noisy voice.
Now, I am not above confessing that I don't like promiscuous
voices in the house. Perhaps I have nerves. Perhaps I haven't.
Anyway, it is my house and I won't have voices in it. So one
day, when the voice was at its very loudest, and I felt I couldn't
stand it a minute longer, I sent for Rosie. And Rosie came, looking more like a sparrow than ever.

"Rosie," said I, "who *are* you talking to?"

"No one, ma'am," said Rosie.

"But you *are*," I said, with the emphasis born of the long
exercise of a deadly patience. "I often hear you talking to someone. Who is it?"

Rosie's face changed. The sparrow disappeared. The Revival Meeting took its place.

"Oh!" said Rosie.

"Well?" said I.

"Oh, *that*," said Rosie, and she lowered her voice. "That's God, ma'am."

"Oh!" said I.

I must say I was taken aback. I had started with St Paul and now here I was invited to come a step up higher. I paused.

"You mean you're praying, I suppose," said I at last.

"Yes, ma'am," said Rosie.

The Revival Meeting was by this time in such force that I felt the only right thing for me to do would be to call out "Hallelujah!" But I didn't. There was another pause.

"Can't you pray inside yourself?" I asked, after a bit.

Rosie settled herself for testimony. She clasped her hands in front of her.

"Well, ma'am," she said, "there's the two kinds of prayer. There's Audible. And there's Inaudible."

"Well," said I, "all right. You try the Inaudible kind and see what that feels like."

Rosie hesitated.

"*That's* for nights," said she, and the look of the Martyr on its way to the Lion overspread her face. I felt the time had come to strike a blow.

"Rosie," I said, "while you stay here you've got to take to inaudible Prayer for day-time. When you go to bed at night you can shut the door tight and have the Audible. See? That's the way of it while you stay here."

Rosie's head went to one side. I saw the distant sparrow coming back again.

"It's not the way we're told to," she remarked.

"Well," I said, "I can't help it. It's the way it's got to be."

Rosie considered. Then suddenly the sparrow fluttered down, close beside me.

"Very well, ma'am," said she. "That's my Cross, I guess. I'll bear it!"

And, bearing its Cross, the sparrow went to dish the dinner.

Dinner was another of those bridges that somehow we had to get across. Rosie, the sparrow, was quite a teachable little cook.

But Rosie, the Revival Meeting, was no cook at all. She scorned it. Her meals were stony-hearted and settled down inside of you to do their worst by you, and generally succeeded. Your dinner, therefore, was in the nature of a surprise packet. Sometimes you would like it, and sometimes you wouldn't. And when, as happened on one occasion, you got your soup after your meat (in consequence, I suppose, of Prayer), you *didn't* like it. And said so.

The great stumbling-block in the way of dinner (and lunch and breakfast too) was Rosie's Bible, and this, during Rosie's stay with me, was a constant ornament to the kitchen. It was of immense size; and, as it lay open upon the dresser (as if it had been a cook-book) all day long, it gave you every opportunity of noticing its appearance. It lay open in this way so as to be ready for constant reference. If Rosie were making a pancake, say, and she had just got to the psychological moment of "tossing" it, then, exactly then, at that very particular second, she always had an immense, an inordinate, a not-to-be-gainsaid desire to verify some text. So she would leave the pancake and run to the Bible on the dresser. And there she would stand, feverishly turning the pages back and forth (for one of her sparrow-like propensities was that she never could find the place), seeking first the salvation of her own soul, while the pancake was losing its only chance of ever getting one in the frying-pan on the fire. We gave up pancakes and took to stews at last as the safer choice. And then we got on better.

This was our weekday, workaday existence. But the highday and holiday of Rosie's life was "Meeting." To It (It occurred three evenings in the week and twice on Sunday) she would go forth, with her big Bible under one arm and a Prayer Book under the other, thus clad, as I may say, in shining armour. For her Meetings were held at street-corners and they all (Rosie, too, I daresay) addressed the passing world; and if the passing world insisted on going on passing without listening to what was being said to it, someone attacked it with ecclesiastical argument and tried to *make* it stop. And when it still wouldn't it was prayed for—audibly. If there had been fewer of these debauches I think we should have got on better. For just at the farthest remove between the Meetings the sparrow always showed itself strongest and our dinners came up quite nice and tidy and eatable. But just before or just after a Meeting the atmosphere became thick and murky, and our dinners were but flies in the ointment and we weren't comfortable at all. Also, as the direct offshoot of a Meeting, I sometimes became aware of a tendency to Audible Prayer, with a suspicious substratum of entreaty for myself. Such guinea-pigs as this were sternly suppressed by me.

Rosie's money affairs were another problem—they were more like the National Debt than anything else. Twenty dollars a month went into her, so to say, but the puzzle was that nothing ever seemed able to come out again. She never had a cent. She was always asking me for an "advance," and for a bit I "advanced" as requested. But, being by nature of an interfering disposition, the time came when I said to Rosie: "Rosie, what do you *do* with all your money? You never seem to have any."

Rosie blushed and flushed and said nothing.

"You don't spend it on clothes," said I, glancing at her.

"Oh no, ma'am," said Rosie, finding her tongue. "That would be sinful."

I didn't feel it my duty—or "laid upon me," as Rosie would have said—to go into this, so I merely reiterated: "Well, what do you *do* with it then?"

Rosie began to explain her pecuniary life.

It appeared that in the first instance she had come out to Canada in the hope of regenerating it—as a self-appointed missionary, in fact; for it was on the other side of the water that she had first taken to being a Very Early Christian. Arriving in Canada, with the expectation of finding it peopled with the Heathen, something of a surprise had been in store for her; and she had felt that, before attacking the Dominion as a whole, some preparation was needed. She had therefore made arrangements with a "Correspondence Class," and had corresponded with zeal and energy, and two of the subjects she had corresponded about were Architecture and Politics. I admit that the Dominion is badly in need of instruction on both these subjects, but I doubt if Rosie and her Correspondence Class will be the means of its regeneration. However, I now saw why my kitchen—what with ink-pots and foolscap—had so often presented such a Pauline appearance. On this correspondence, with its class fees, preliminary and otherwise, its books, with their necessary and unnecessary instruction for the various courses, etc., Rosie had already spent ninety dollars, in instalments of five dollars apiece. Twenty dollars still remained to pay.

"Do you think you have profited much by your studies?" said I, after a pause for assimilation.

"Oh yes, ma'am," said Rosie.

"Where are the books?" said I.

"Upstairs, ma'am, in my room," said Rosie. The sparrow looked out at me with a dawning hope of sympathy. "Would you like to see 'em, ma'am?" it said. "I'm sure I'd be glad to show 'em you."

Rosie paused.

"They're a lovely set o' books!" she said.

"Have you read them?" said I.

"Not yet, ma'am," said Rosie. "They're too many of 'em to *read*."

She paused again and thought it over.

"But it's nice to know you have 'em," she remarked.

It strikes me that it will take Rosie a lot of Prayer, both Audible and Inaudible, before she gets even with the inventors of the Correspondence Scheme!

(I may say here that, later on, I looked at Rosie's ninety dollars' worth of books, and, as Meredith says of Morris's poem, I looked away again. Rosie was right. They were not for reading.)

Not content with having established a National Debt of her own, what must Rosie do next but present a banner to her Sorority, or whatever the name of it might be—for the "Meeting" was composed entirely of "Sisters." She thought a banner would add to their appearance as they marched through the streets. She also thought it might seduce the souls of the worldlings. A banner, said Rosie, is perhaps the thing to bring 'em in! And, as a last argument, when the banner had come home and was waiting to be paid on delivery and she was begging me for an advance to pay for it, "Besides, ma'am," said she, "they've been so *good* to me!" "They" being the Sisters. The banner cost ten dollars, and the first time Rosie took to waving it audibly she broke the kitchen window with it.

"Rosie," said I, "if you want to do such things as that, why don't you save up money of your own to buy them?"

The sparrow disappeared. Nothing but the Revival was to the fore.

"We are told," said the Revival, "that it's wrong to put by for the morrow!"

"Yes," said I, "but if *I* didn't put by for the morrow, where would *you* be to-day? If I didn't put by something sometimes you wouldn't be able to have banners to break my kitchen windows with!"

I saw the sparrow take a squint through the eyes of the Revival.

"Where *would* you be if I didn't lay up riches?" said I again.

"I'm sure I couldn't tell you, ma'am," said Rosie.

"No, perhaps not," said I, "but *I* could tell *you!*"

The sparrow looked a trifle disconcerted for the moment, but just as it was going out at the door the Revival turned its face to me a moment. "I'll pray for enlightenment, ma'am," said the Revival, "and then I'll let you know about it."

"Thank you," said I.

The last and final crash of Rosie's finance was, I think, on the occasion of her entering the literary career—by what we may call a side-door. One day when I strolled into the kitchen to see about the health of my next meal, Rosie, with shining face and glistening eyes, ran to meet me. She might, from the look of her, have been a mother with her firstborn on her arm to show me, or a poet with his first sonnet on the tip of his tongue all ready to recite.

"Oh, *look*, ma'am," said Rosie, and she thrust a leaflet in my hand. When I glanced down at it I saw that *Outward Adorning* was its name. And this was how a verse or two of it ran:

> O think of God's beloved daughters
> Here on earth a little while,
> Spending all their precious moments,
> After fashion, dress and style.
>
> See how like the world they're getting,
> Only look upon their head—
> See what should be in the garden,
> Fixed up to adorn their pride.
>
> See the little wings and feathers
> On their hats and bonnets worn;
> These are only second-handed,
> Worn by the birds before.

> Nice to see them on the birdies,
> God Himself did put them there;
> None would care for wings and feathers
> On their head instead of hair.

Then came a verse or two of a more specialised and technical character. I shall not trouble to quote them:

> Gather all your flimsy decking,
> Lay them down beside His blood,

and that kind of thing; and the poem ended with the same simplicity as it began—with this verse:

> God would have His daughters tidy,
> All they wear both good and plain,
> Wearing nought to be ashamed of
> At His coming back again.

I read it all through twice—to get my breath, as it were—and then I said:

"Rosie, where *did* you get it?"

She didn't answer. She was perfectly quiet. I glanced at her.

She was trembling with eagerness. Her face was full of colour and her eyes were full of tears. The poem had gone in at one side of her and come out at the other; she was penetrated through and through with it. It *spoke* to her. It touched something in her that she couldn't express in words. She tried to speak and at first she could only stammer and stutter. She was drunk with her own feelings. Shakespeare or Shelley could have done no more for a poet in the making than *Outward Adorning* had done for Rosie.

"Oh," said she at last, "oh, isn't it *lovely*, ma'am!" And she stopped from sheer emotion.

"Rosie," I said, "you didn't *write* it?"

"Oh *no*, ma'am," said Rosie. "I saw it in a paper. The Lord must have led me to it, ma'am. For just as soon as I read it I knew that *that* was the thing to bring 'em in. And so I've had it printed, ma'am, in leaflets, and at the next Meeting we'll hand it round."

She paused, trying to get hold of her voice to speak with.

"And they'll *come* in," said she. And she looked at me mistily through her tears.

My own speech was taken away. I just stood and looked at her, while my dinner that I had come in to see to went dry in the pot.

"*Rosie!*" I said at last. And stopped.

For Rosie was gazing out of the window, leagues and leagues away. She had forgotten me and my dinner and every other earthly consideration. We had all faded completely out of her mind.

"They'll *come* in!" said she to herself—or was it, perhaps, to God?

And then, just in a whisper.

"Think of *that!*" said she.

"Rosie," said I, when we had recovered a little bit, "how many leaflets did you have printed?"

"Two thousand, ma'am," said Rosie.

I gave it up.

I suppose, when we don't quite know what to do with something, the impulse of all of us is to shuffle it somewhere out of sight. That, at any rate, was the principle I followed out with Rosie. The best way out of the National Debt and all its complications was, it seemed to me, to send the Prodigal Daughter home again—I mean, to send Rosie back to England. In England she had a mother, another Very Early Christian. She also had a father somewhere, but he had run away, it seemed, at the first dawning of Very Early Christianity, and he hadn't been heard from since. An immense amount of Prayer, both Audible and Inaudible, had been employed on his behalf, but so far it had proved ineffectual in discovering his whereabouts. He remained sequestered—in other words, he just lay low and no one but himself knew where he was. I may say that I can't help feeling a certain sympathy with Rosie's father. I know so exactly how he felt. He couldn't persuade Mahomet—I should say St Paul—to go away, so he just took heart of grace and up and went himself. I have lived with Rosie and I know about it. Even a mountain will uproot itself if you give it sufficient cause.

Meanwhile Rosie's mother was alone—and ill; and it seemed to me that Rosie might as well be looking after her as converting the Dominion. I therefore suggested to the sparrow that there is lots to be done yet about converting England; and when that is all finished it will be time enough to begin to think about Canada. I also suggested that I might pay her passage home and that she might go back to her mother—and stay there.

The sparrow looked at me. Its eyes filled with the ready tears—for it was an affectionate piece of goods and fond of its mother, as it would have been fond of anything that was just a little bit decent and kind to it. It looked at me very solemnly. "Well, ma'am," said the sparrow, "God willing, I'll *go* home, ma'am, and stay with my mother." God apparently was willing. For it went. And the very last I saw of it was perched on the deck of the home-going steamer, with its head a little to one side.

I hope and trust that some day soon my sparrow will meet another sparrow, strong-minded and of heathen ancestry, and that together they'll make shift to build themselves a nest and occupy their minds with—eggs.

THE CHARLADY

I KEPT no servant for my little flat—in the transatlantic vernacular, I "did my own work." But as we none of us, or few of us, are holy enough to like to do the roughest parts of our work ourselves, I had a woman once a week to do the cleaning. I ought to have done it myself, I know, but I didn't. I paid someone else a dollar a day, her meals and her car-fare, to do what I should by rights have been doing myself. And she bore me no malice.

Her name was Mrs Chaffey, and she said her given name was Hannah. She hailed from Scotland, but by the time I came across her, ten years or so in Canada had turned her into Scotch-Canadian—a very different matter from Scotch pure and simple, and one of those cross breeds that are difficult to place.

I liked Mrs Chaffey—I may even go so far as to say that I was fond of her; and I certainly never knew a woman more grateful with less apparently to be grateful for. For a long while, however, my views of her were mostly guesswork, for she confided nothing at all to me about herself or her way of living; not from reticence exactly, I think, but simply because it didn't occur to her to enter on any life history. She was not introspective in the least; indeed, she was one of those rare people who appear to be superlatively interested in the present—the Everlasting Now. Whatever she found to do she did with all her might, and the past and the future were, for the time being, nonexistent for her. She lived emphatically in the present, and she loved it.

She was not beautiful. In her palmiest days she can hardly have been that, I should imagine. She was a small woman, spare by nature and scraggy by force of circumstances. She had lost her teeth and she never had had money enough to buy herself any more. Her hair was fine and scanty, and it had a trick of going into wisps—rats'-tails, as the children call them. Her bones made altogether too much of themselves, and her knuckles were twisted awry with overheavy work and rheumatism. Take her for what she was, she looked much as you would expect a woman to look who, for all the years of her life, has spent her days, and part of her nights too, probably, scrubbing and lifting, and washing and ironing, with patching and mending for the holiday moments of life. Housework in moderation is good for any woman, but too much housework is just as bad for her. And Mrs Chaffey had been systematically over-houseworked all her life long, so that she hardly knew what it felt like to live normally and healthily, with just a little scrap of leisure every day in the week for her very own.

One beauty, however, her round of everlasting work had still left her—her large and candid eyes. Such nice eyes! You hadn't to look far down into them to find the humanity. It shone out of them, and when she smiled and showed her toothless gums she and her brown eyes positively radiated. Her smile lit up herself and you and anything that happened to be near, and as for you, you forgot everything except that it was good to be near her and looking on at such unforced contentment. For she *was* a happy creature—there was no mistake about that. She loved life. It positively intoxicated her just to be alive—no more than that; though, of course, if you had put it to her in just that way she wouldn't have known what you were talking about. Sunlight and a cloudless day made her glow all over; rain made her think of the gerse growin' and the wee things comin' up; the sough of the wind took her to the water and a never-to-be-forgotten day when friends had taken her a trip to Loch Lomond. And the snow—the white, thick, soft, fluffy Canadian snow—why, that took her thoughts quite naturally and just as happily to her winding-sheet, and how peaceful she would be one day resting, deep down wi' God's greenery a-top of her. Her mind turned naturally to growing. She loved everything alive—puppies, kittens, nestlings, bulbs shooting green through the brown earth, the bursting of the buds in spring, the coming of children—she loved them all, coming and come; and she loved to take hold of such things and tend them with those gnarled and broken-nailed fingers of hers. She loved her dinner too. And what I would have to eat on those days when she came to clean was a source of the deepest interest and speculation. She wondered about it beforehand, she looked forward to it with zest, she adored it while she was eating it, and even in retrospect it seemed to taste as sweet. "Yon was a grand piece o' meat ye had last Wednesday

was a week," she would say. "I ha'e thocht o't mony's the time!
. . . Grand meat the like o' what you ha'e, mem, is a treat
alright. Gentlefolks has fare fit for kings is what I say, and it's
right they suld, too. Eh, it's nae wonder the grand things they
get after wi' food the like o' that!" I always forbore to ask just
what grand things the fine folks did get after, for Mrs Chaffey's
belief in the power and uprightness of gentlefolks was so genuine and hearty that it seemed a shame to disturb it.

I used to wonder sometimes what could have brought her out
to Canada. She was past the age when any woman ought to
think of emigrating—she was fifty anyway, and thirty is the last
limit of age for the emigrant. But Mrs Chaffey was an exception
to many rules—perhaps because the rule she lived by was the
rule of life—so I never asked her any questions. There was lots
for us to talk about while we were working away together, I
doing all the nice light jobs, she the heavy work, and each of us
sure that all was just as it should be. She would talk away by the
hour as she worked, and I loved to listen to her, and if by chance
subjects of conversation ran dry—and it wasn't often that they
did—she would croon away to herself some old song or hymn,
with no possible tune to it and nothing to make it pleasant but a
certain natural lilt that was her very own in everything she did.
Her prime favourite was *Lead, kindly Light*, and I thought she
and it fitted one another very nicely.

One day we were having a grand turn-out. It was spring-
cleaning time—one of those dread moments dear to the hearts
of so many women when a house looks as if it never, never
could be itself again. We had all the china of the house collected
on the kitchen floor, and Mrs Chaffey was washing and I was
drying, and things looked generally as if we were there for some
time to come. I am not one of those creatures who like such
operations, but I will go so far as to admit that there is an awful
fascination about them. You feel through all the discomfort that
you really *are* doing something—making a tiny spot of cleanli-
ness in a somewhat grimy world, if no more than that; and so,
even if you are not a born housewife, I defy you not to enjoy
yourself in an inverted sort of fashion. Doing my light share of
the work, then, that afternoon I was in this half-hearted frame of
mind; while as for Mrs Chaffey, with her lion's share of the
work on her hands, she was up to her eyes in a wholehearted

enjoyment of everything that was going on. It was a light afternoon's work for her, it didn't call for her undivided attention,
and she could hold forth as the spirit moved her. So it was as we
sat there on the floor together that she began to tell me about
herself, and how she came to be there with me on that sunny
spring afternoon.

"Seems kind o' queer too," she began suddenly, "that I suld
be here in Canada like. Little did I plan to come i' days long
past, but the ways o' God, mem, is His ain. Him it was that
brocht me safe ayont the mighty ocean . . . and fine has He
tended me sin syne.

"I cam' awa' frae Scotland tae forget. For sorrow had I seen
there . . . weary waitin' on sorrow. Time's been, mem, when I
thocht that a' was past for me. Seemed someway as if I couldna
get happy-like again . . . as if a' was ower and dune so far's I
was concerned. But God's hand led me through . . . and Him it
was landed me here i' the midst o' plenty."

She looked up at me with that wonderful toothless smile of
hers, so sweet, so trusting, so absolutely happy: that smile of
hers that always made me feel uncertain whether to smile back
at her—or cry.

"Oh, Mrs Chaffey," said I, "I think you can't have had such a
very easy time out here, have you? Didn't you, just at the first
sometimes, wish you hadn't ever come?"

"Na, na, mem," said she. "Whaur wad we land if we was
regrettin'? When a thing's dune—it's dune. E'en mak' the best
o' your mistake . . . and whiles it'll turn a blessing upo' your
hands—when you've learned the way tae wait like."

We washed and dried for a bit, and I let her take her own
time to speak or be silent, as the fancy took her.

"I was out at a lecture yestreen," she said at last. "I saw the
adver*tise*ment o't . . . a leddy tae speak in ane o' thae big churches
like. Sae when I saw it was free tae get in I took a mind I wad
gae doun and hear what it was she was for sayin'. I niver had
my chanst o' an eddication, mem, sae it's grand for me whiles
tae listen tae the eddicated. It kind o' enlightens you, the eddicated word does; it gi'es ye something like tae work your mind
upo' . . . whilk is healthy like. Sae I cleaned mysell and doun
went I tae Emmanuel Church. She was a wee body that was for
speakin', wi' a plain bit gown on her . . . and up got she and

began the way it might be a conversation betwixt the twa o' us here . . . you and me like. But ance she was intae the swing o't she spoke out good and strong. She tell't us how that there wasna ane o' us there that wasna o' importance, and no in God's sicht alane, says she, but here . . . right here . . . in the warld we live in. Eh, it's fine tae hear the like o' that! It gars ye feel as if your heid was lifted up like the everlasting gates of old. She said we could a' help . . . that there was poorer than us, everyone o' us there . . . and that, never mind how weak we was, there was ay a hand we could outstretch. It's that kind o' talk that raises the ambition i' the heart, mem."

She stopped washing a moment and looked up at me wistfully with her large brown eyes.

"I doubt ye'll hardly be for believing it," said she, " but when I was young I was ambitious alright, mem. That was afore I got married on Chaffey. I tell't mysell then that maybe God had laid out His wark for me . . . for I ay wanted tae dae, ye ken . . . I ay wanted tae help . . .! No just tae spend my life waitin' upo' naethin' the way some folks does. And yestreen a' that seemed tae rise up fresh i' me as I listened. Ye'll ken the feel o't, mem, when the strength o' the Lord arises i' the heart and learns ye what life is . . . and oh, if ye but kent the way tae mak' it clear tae a' the rest! For it's a grand thing just tae be alive . . . and feel . . . and ken what happiness is! But it's haird someway tae express the like o' that, and ye'll no be for understanding my way o' pitting things maybe."

"Yes, I do, Mrs Chaffey," I said. "I understand all right. But you *do* help other people, you know. You are helping me at this minute."

She looked at me and smiled again.

"Eh," said she, "that's a freend's way o' speaking . . . askin' yer pardon, mem, for makin' that free. Help! I'se daein' my work. But it's a' for the best, never fear. We've been led, mem, and never doubt it. And good it is tae be here . . . wi' the sun shinin' doun on us . . . and the trees comin' intae leaf! And it'll be the same sun, mind you, that'll shine doun on us when we're awa! Restin' there . . . wi' the growin' green atop!"

"What made you think of Canada, Mrs Chaffey?" I said. It seemed natural to ask her, for she seemed in the mood to talk about it. But her face clouded at the question.

"I was i' trouble," said she. "It was sair grief and trouble that I was in, mem. I dinna cast back at it that often, for it'll rax the heart tae dwell on sic-like sorrow, and ye're safer maybe just livin' yer life day by day. But there's comfort i' tellin' . . . and if ye wad listen, mem! It wad be a relief maybe tae gae back and win through wi' it ance mair."

She took up an old Japanese vase and began carefully washing the dust from the delicate leaves and flowers and birds some Oriental hand had traced on it.

"There's been times I've wondered," she went on, after a minute, "if I've had what ye might ca' luck. I been happy alright . . . but things has gane cross wi' me whiles. It was for the best . . . dinna doubt it! But it seemed as if they went back on me some.

"I was a foundling, mem, that never kent feyther nor mither. My mither pit me doun on a stoop, puir body that she must ha' been, and left her bairnie there. I doubt she was at her wits' end, puir lassie, tae loss her wean that like way. That was how I got upo' the parish. . . . I hadna freends o' my ain, as ye might say.

"I hadna sae muckle as my name," she went on, after a moment. "Naethin' did I bring tae life wi' me but my minnie's wae."

She paused.

"There's been times when ye've felt as if it wad be nice maybe tae ha'e *something* o' yer ain!" she said. And sighed.

She laid away the Japanese vase, washed and wiped, and took in its stead a tiny Tanagra figure, poised dancing, one foot lifted—serene and exquisite.

"They kept me upo' the parish till I could wark," she said. "And then it was a lodging-house they landed me in. I was nae mair than a bairn, mem, and it wasna that easy for a bairn maybe. But oh, ye win through wi' a willin' heart. And whiles there was a man that was kindly tae . . . there's ay a heart tae pity, choose whaur ye'll gae. God sends His ain tae comfort maybe.

"I wasna bonny. I was a plain-looking lassie . . . wi' nae siller for claes. I was lucky tae get sae muckle as the offer o' Chaffey wi' the face I had on me . . . and him a fine-built fellow! I jaloused for a bittie that I wasna tae get my hands on ony man, and that's a shame for a lassie tae ha'e tae bear. A woman canna bide tae hear it evened tae her that there wasna the man that wad tak' her at the gift!"

Here I said, with more truth than tact, perhaps, that I didn't think it mattered much. But Mrs Chaffey shook her head.

"Na, na, mem," she said, more positively than usual, "a lassie needs man and weans, and if she canna get her hands upo' the man . . . that's a bitter pill for her tae ha'e tae swallow. I kent weel that Chaffey had his fau'ts, that he drank, ay, and that he had a heavy han' wi' him. He didna wark . . . he hadna the habit o't . . . a' that I kent fine at the asking, though I didna ken a' that wad come o't. But I needed a man and I hadna the chanst o' mair than him. A lassie disna ken the taste o' a bairn till she gets it . . . and she disna ken the right taste o' a man till she's sampled him. It was Chaffey or naethin' for me. But it was haird years that I had tae win through . . . me and the bairns wi' me."

"So you have children, Mrs Chaffey?" said I. "Well, thank goodness for that, anyway."

"I had them, mem," she said. "I had them."

She was silent for a moment.

"Ay," she said, "I had them. But I buried the twa o' them . . . far awa' i' Scotland. It was them that brocht me awa' ower the sea. I cam' awa' heartsick, mem, when the twa o' them was pit awa' . . . and it was here, i' Canada, that God led me back tae rest and peace ance mair."

I left her to herself and we washed away. I knew she would go on if I didn't bother.

"There was Jesse," she said, after a bit, "and he was my first-born. He was a fine wean, mem . . . sic grand legs as he had on him . . . and the smile that weans seems tae bring wi' them. Ye ken that kind o' an unearthly smile that the wee things has? And then there cam' Elspeth. A wee lassie, no wi' the strength o' her brither, but a sweet-like wean, and a sweet face o' her ain. She was ay ailin', was Elspeth, the bit lassie, and her feyther got put past her, for a man seems tae tak' a grudge someway at an ailin' wean . . . it was ay me that had tae get in betwixt her and him. Puir lassie, mony's the time I've feared she wouldna win through tae her womanhood. But she lived tae be a lassie, and whiles I think it's wae's me that she did.

"When Chaffey was ta'en awa', mem, it was like God's ain mercy come hame tae me. Never a hand's turn did he, and it's haird for a woman when she's carrying if the man's han' is heavy on her, and she no that able tae pit through a' that she's willing for, maybe. And he kept us poor, drinking the bairns' very bite and sup the way he'd used tae.

"But he was ca'ed awa', and left us tae our peace. The bairns had their blacks, for it was but seemly they suld mourn their feyther. Sae they had their blacks at the funeral, the twa o' them, and I thankit God wi' a' my heart that He had seen fit tae tak' Chaffey tae Himsell."

She bustled about to get fresh water, and when she was settled down again to more washing she looked hard at me as if she had something in her mind to say that she didn't just know how I might take.

"I've wondered sin syne," said she, "whiles . . . if maybe Chaffey can get anither turn. He wasna what he suld be, it's true. He didna dae what was right maybe. But if he was to get anither turn! . . . Maybe, mem, he wad ha'e learned hissel' . . . he could wark wi' his hands . . . and wark out some o' what's past?"

I shook my head at her and smiled.

"Who knows!" said I.

And she seemed quite satisfied with that.

"Sae when Chaffey was ta'en awa'," she went on, "it seemed as if we could be happy-like thegither . . . the three o' us there. The bairns could get their eddications. And I could spend my siller the way I fancied. I got wark . . . lots o't . . . and the bairns grew . . . and I kept a hame ower their heads. I was that happy!

"Jesse got tae be a fine stirring laddie, wi' a' the meat I had for him . . . and then he grew tae be a man. Tae think o't . . . my boy a man! . . . And sic a fine-like man tae look at, mem. Big and strong-like Jesse was . . . big and strong, the set o' his feyther—the very look o' his feyther was in that blue e'e o' his. It fair brocht the heart tae my mouth whiles, mem, the way Jesse looked, for his feyther wasna a guid man and I wanted my Jesse tae come tae nae harm. I hopit, mem—I ay hopit. But he took tae bad ways for a' I could dae . . . naebody could stop him . . . and then I just hopit against hope. When ye love your bairn, seems someway as if he couldna ha'e the heart tae bring hissel' and you tae shame . . . and I took that pride in my boy, mem. He was a grand wean . . . wi' a smile, ye ken! . . . And when it's the bairn you've carried . . . and fed . . . and washed . . . and watched him grow a man . . . ye canna bring yoursel' tae believe his heart isna whaur it suld be. But wi' a' that I could dae . . . he went wrang. He went far astray . . . he drank the way his feyther did afore him . . . and then he took money that wasna his, the puir, misguided lamb! . . . And me keeping him till Elspeth and me didna ken the way we was tae win through. So when he took the money they shut him up, mem—they took him out o' God's light and shut him awa'. And he couldna thole it. . . . He wasna that strong for a' he lookit sae fine and big and braw, my boy! . . . They shut him up, and God took my bairn . . . the bairn I'd carried and nursed and loved like my ain flesh."

The afternoon sun came glinting in on us sideways as we worked. We were silent for a little, and then Mrs Chaffey began piling the washed plates one on top of the other, so that she could carry them back in piles to the china closet. Moving to and fro, with piles of plates in her careful hands, she took up her tale again.

"There was Elspeth left tae me," she said. "She wasna Jesse, but I had her onyway. She was ay a weak-like lassie, Elspeth . . . and she favoured me, mem, so she wasna that bonnie—I could see it, for a' that I lookit on her wi' a mither's e'e. She had what I could gi'e her, for she was a' that I had left me when Jesse went. But she couldna be content wi' a' that I could dae for her, puir lass.

"She went wi' a lad . . . and she fell intae trouble . . . and the lad wouldna haud tae his word. And I couldna comfort her, mem, for her heart was his. She wanted her lad; and her wean, when it came, wasna eneuch—puir, wailing bit thing that it was! And in the end, when she saw that he wasna for comin' back . . . she e'en went out ae nicht wi' the wean, mem, and she took its life and her ain! . . . She couldna face tae live her life wi' nae man that she lo'ed by her side . . . and she couldna ha'e her lad.

"It was after Elspeth went, mem, that I turned sae I didna rightly ken mysel'. It wasna that I was impatient . . . but I felt as if I had had eneuch o' life—God forgi'e me the thocht! It was a' dark. . . . God turned His face frae me . . . seemed as if I couldna win through. I couldna sae muckle as ca' tae mind what it was tae be happy, I was that black cast doun wi' sorrow. And it wasna till God pit the thocht o' Canada intae my heart that I seemed tae get a glint like o' my nainsell ance mair. He pit it intae my heart tae wonder if I couldna try a new life far ayont the sea . . . and me an auld clout o' a body! . . . For they tell't me in Canada a' was new and wonderfu' tae see . . . siller for the picking up . . . happiness in the very air ye breathed! . . . And it was the hearing o' the like o' that that seemed tae bring me back . . . as if I could leave a' that sorrow maybe and see the way tae a new life upo' God's earth! . . . Sae I warked wi' a will till I got the money pit past for my fare . . . and I took train and boat . . . me that had never been out o' the city in a' my life! . . . And tae Canada cam' I!"

"You were brave to come," I said.

"When your need is sair," said she, "ye stop tae count nae cost. Here I cam' . . . ayont the sea . . . no that young . . . but wi' the twa willing hands I brocht along. And wark I found . . . wark for every day in the week, and siller tae mak' my room intae a wee hame for mysel'. I wasna that happy at the first maybe, no just the way I'd hopit, but I could ay get awa' hame to my room nights, and ken that a' was at peace there . . . nae drink . . . nae grief . . . nae repining at God's wull! . . . A' at peace . . . and me wi' my burying money lying ready tae my han'! . . . And, as the years passit by—I couldna help but dae it, mem—I got happy-like. . . . No happy the way I'd used tae be wi' my boy, maybe . . . but contented-like in my day's wark . . . and ready for my meat . . . and my sleep o' nichts. . . ."

"And have you friends now that you can have a chat with?" I asked. "You aren't lonesome yet, are you, Mrs Chaffey?"

"No just what ye might ca' friends, maybe," said Mrs Chaffey. "I was sair borne doun wi' grief and sorrow, and no that young, mind you, when first I cam'. And new friends is no' for the auld and heavy-laden. But if I havena' friends . . ." she hesitated—"if I havena friends," she went on, "whiles there's folks you can be wi' for a' you're neither young nor bonny. The leddy i' the kirk spoke God's truth there, mem. There's been lassies here I feared was ganging the way o' my Elspeth—and laddies no' that awfu' far frae my boy. And it's the likes o' them my heart gaes out tae.

"Eh, mem," said she, and she seemed to look into my very soul with those woman's eyes of hers, "eh, mem, if ye've kent what it is tae carry and bear . . . ye canna just stand and see anither woman's child gang the way o' your ain. The heart's trouble is what learns ye . . . when ye've suffered yersel' and ken what it is tae suffer . . . ye canna bear it, mem, tae watch ither folks suffer your ain bitter wae if your hand can haud them up. Sae when I see a laddie wi' a thirst upo' him . . . or a lassie wi' the love glint i' her e'e . . . I canna rest till I slip my hand in theirs, mem, and gang along a piece o' their road. For it's a haird road, mem, for the boy that drinks and disna wark—and a haird road for the mither that bore him—and a haird road for the lassie that's gi'en her heart intill his keeping. It's them that's my friends, mem—the lost lads and the lassies that's ower fond o' them . . . and it's my ain bairns that seems born again in ilka ane o' them."

The work was done. The china was washed and dried and all put tidily away. It was tea-time. I filled the kettle and lighted the gas-ring under it, and then, as I turned to answer Mrs Chaffey, I saw that she was standing quietly looking over my little verandah to the tree-clad hill beyond the city. The last brilliant gleams of the setting sun played over her worn face and bent and shabby figure, and lighted up her radiant eyes and her living smile.

"Eh, the sun!" said she. "The sun and the green hill far awa'! Canada isna what they tell't me it wad be, mem, but if ye dinna find the siller ye hope ye may—no, nor just the happiness maybe—ye find the sunshine here ayont the sea. Eh, just tae think o't . . . the grand way things is! The winter days wi' the sun upo' the dazzling snaw . . . and the lang unending summer days wi' the sun upo' the rustling trees! . . . And God's blue sky abune wer heads, mem, a' the months o' His year. It's a grand warld, mem, when a's said and dune. A grand warld it is! Ye can ask nae mair surely than tae be here awhile and mak' a pairt o't."

Her eager eyes looked out into the sunset beauty—past it, perhaps.

"And when ye've tell't your tale o' days," she said, "and can get intill the guid ground . . . weel, there's life ahint ye ony-way—there's naebody can tak' yer life awa' frae ye, try how they may. Ye've lived . . . nae matter through what tears and wae . . . ye've lived. And ye ken—ay, if ye havena chick nor child tae leave—ye ken that God's life stretches out ahint ye and afore ye tae. Ye ken a' that, and maybe mair tae it, by the time ye're safe planted in His guid earth . . . ay, mem, dig ye doun deep as they may. God's life is atop o' you, and you sleepin' . . . and ye ken that new life is added tae it day by day!"

The sun went down behind the hill. The sky was ablaze with glory. It seemed to answer Mrs Chaffey better than I could, so I said nothing at all. Just then the kettle boiled. I masked the fragrant tea-leaves, lifted the teapot over the steaming kettle to infuse and set out our tea-table with all the good things my little larder could provide.

"And now, Mrs Chaffey," I said, when all was ready, "now that you've said our grace before meat . . . come, my dear, and let's have tea!"

She turned to smile at me with eyes and mouth.

"Grace?" said she. "I've said nae grace. But, wi' the Lord's wull, mem, I'll drink a cup o' tea wi' you gladly. And maybe twa. And thank you and Him for it!"

POLLY

ER name was Polly, and she went out cleaning by the day, when she could get any cleaning to do. When she couldn't she stayed at home in her garret room and philosophised over life. She was not young. I may say she was old. But she resented age, and fought it tooth and nail, and stayed as young as she possibly could. Her hair she dyed, and the dye she chose to conceal the ravages of time was a brilliant purple. The purple was complete in the front, but at the back (where the dye had given out and she hadn't had money to buy any more, I suppose) it was incomplete. And all the new little hairs that were growing in were the purest white, so it was a purple surface with a silver fringe. The general impression was, as Polly herself would have said, "not too bad!"

In her youth Polly had been pretty—very, very pretty indeed. Perhaps when you first set eyes on her it would seem to you ridiculous that anyone should say she was pretty—this poor, bent, old thing of shreds and patches, who edged herself in at your door early of a morning, with a pair of worn boots in a newspaper parcel under one arm—"to change." But if you took your mind off the present and fixed it on the past, you could see that the skin was still of a wonderful texture—fine, fine—with a delicate colour just underneath, that came and went almost with her every breath. And if you looked at the eyes you could see that they were big and gentle and violet-blue, and that not even the fine network of wrinkles and little criss-cross lines all about them could dim their bright intelligence. She was only a tiny bit of a creature anyway, this little old woman, and the day had been, most likely, when she was a fairy thing, light as a fleck of down, slender and trim, full of laughs and ready answers, in love with life, and every boy in love with her.

On the third finger of her right hand she wore a plain gold ring, and in all her chat and talk she never mentioned it. It never left her finger.

"Might you be one of the clean ones, or one of the dirty ones, or one of them in the middle sort, might I ask?" said she, as she sat on the kitchen chair changing her boots that first morning.

I explained that I was neither a sheep nor a goat, but probably a something midway or so in between the two.

"Well, God be praised for that!" said Polly thankfully. "For it's God's truth I'm telling you when I say I'm not caring for those who'll go to extremes with their houses. I've one lady, if you'll believe me, and she's that clean she'd root up the very flagstones, so she would, to see if there's dirt underneath."

I said that I also regarded that as going to extremes.

"I believe you!" said Polly, squinting up sideways as she went buttoning on at her broken boot. "And what's more, she'll have the paint washed with the pure soap, and that's the truth, and nothing between you and the dirt but the strength of your trunk. And digging in between the boards of the floor with the hairpins out of your head to root out the good dirt once it's got home! What I say is, it's sinful, so it is, to go interfering with God's dust that road. 'Let it be,' I'll say to herself—'and offer up thanks you're here at all to be living the life!' And you think, I suppose, that she'll stop to hear me!"

She stooped to her boot again.

"Well, but, Polly," said I, remembering that, after all, it was cleaning she had come to spend the day with me for, "Polly, there *is* a lot of dust, you know, and you can't let it all be. Where would *we* be if you did? I can't imagine where it all comes from, the dust . . . but it's there!"

"Faith," said Polly, buttoning away, "faith, aren't we told we're made of the dust? And won't it be ourselves scattering bits as we go that'll make the trouble yourself is speaking of? We're one with the dust, glory be to God! and we can't get away with that, try as we will!"

This seemed to close the subject. Polly finished buttoning. And then, true to her name, she put the kettle on.

"Is is English you are?" said she.

I said I was Scotch.

"There's a difference between the two of them," said she emphatically, "and it's thankful you may be if it's Scotch you are at the least—for if you're English there'll be no nobility in you, and that's what I say. Look," said Polly, rinsing out her teapot with warm water, "look at Annie Bullen for a queen, and *there's* a queen for you! And look at Henry himself! Did ever you see a king the like of that . . . with wifes on every side of him? If it was Irish he'd been there'd have been no wifes all at the one time for him, for if he'd taken them to himself the priest would have been after him and taken them all off him again— and right would he have been! And," said Polly, with yet deeper meaning as she spooned in the tea, "there's kings in England nearer us than Henry himself that had the wifes all round him and no one saying the word! So what I say," said Polly, falling back on the main issue, "is thank God you're Scotch the way I'm Irish. For Scotch isn't the like of English anyway," said she, pouring the boiling water on to the tea-leaves. "And if it's English you'd been you'd suffer for it in the life that's coming and that's one thing sure, and . . ." she paused and looked at me earnestly, "and if it wasn't Scotch you say you are, I'd like to see you suffering in this very life we're in now, so I would!"

She set her teapot on the top of the steaming kettle to infuse.

"It's a way they build the houses," said she, dismissing the question of nationalities and taking a rapid glance round my little kitchen, "and it's easy to see it's the men that's had the hand in it. For it's nothing but the men that'll turn to with their hands and build themselves a dust-trap to live in. You look at your stove," said she, "and the dust running under it while we talk and making its home there and no one saying a word to it! It's a hard thing," said Polly, "when a woman has to fight her way after what men has done before her, getting her fingers in where there's no room left for fingers to go, and rooting out the dust and the dirt out of their cracks and their crevices. All a man thinks of is how it'll look when he leaves it at the first . . . and then the woman comes in at the door and battles with it all the rest of her life."

Polly sat down at the breakfast-table and began to butter her toast.

"Sure," said she, "you had no need to boil the egg. It's little I touch, and if I get my cup of tea of a morning it's all I'm ask-ing—and eggs here not the way they are in Ireland anyway. It's good eggs you get there, and good butter too, with the cows thinking of the kind green grass they've eaten all the time they're giving their milk. And it's good bacon you'll get in Ireland, glory be to God! and if I was to meet an Irish pig in the streets of Montreal I'd put my arms round its neck and I'd kiss it, so I would, for the sake of the days when I was happy."

"Don't you ever want to go back again?" said I.

"And what would I do when I went?" said she. "When your father and your mother is dead the rest of the crowd looks another way when they see you coming. Sure, I'd like to smell the smell of peat again, and see the Irish sun rising over the hills of Clonmel—but it'd be the sun that'd be the only thing that wouldn't turn its back on me if I was there. For I've no money nor nothing, and the sight of my eyes is going fast, and what would my brothers and sisters with children of their own in their arms want with a sightless woman and she begging in their midst!"

"But is it true that you're losing the sight of your eyes?" said I.

"It is that," said she, "and the man at the Hospital no more use to me than a bird on the branch and him not able to sing. He said it was scars on my eyes and that was what it was, and take them off was what he couldn't do. So I paid him a couple of dollars and I wished I had kept them in my pocket and left what he had to say in his mouth, for that's all the doctors can do when there's trouble."

"What did he say you had done to your eyes?" said I.

"Sure," said Polly, munching her toast and washing it down with great gulps of tea, "sure, he said it was the fine work I'd be doing for the nuns and me but a slip of a girl. And I'd do it," said Polly, suspending her breakfast operations and with a ring of pride penetrating through the toast, "I'd do it and I'd work the fine way you couldn't see when I'd finished it was anything at all . . . and I'd go out and I'd copy the leaves and the flowers, and I'd work the very branches of the trees on my stuff till they'd wonder at me, so they would, and wonder the way I'd do it at all."

"And how did you do it?" I asked.

"Faith, I couldn't tell you," said Polly, cutting herself another slice of bread. "You look at the things God made to please Himself and you try to copy them the way you'll be a friend of His . . . and you sit and stitch the livelong day and when the night comes you've a flower made the way Himself would know it for a copy of His own."

"And that made you happy, Polly?" said I.

"If it's happiness you'll get in this world at all," said Polly, "that's the way you'll surely get it. And," she went on, "you couldn't tell the way you're happy either, for you sit there with the needle in your hand and you so busy thinking how you'll do it you're never thinking at all . . . and when it's done you look, and no one will wonder like yourself at what you'll see."

She paused a moment with her slice of bread in her hand. She looked up at me with her shining eyes.

"And they'd sell everything I could sew," said she, and there was the ring of pride in her voice again; "they'd sell it . . . and they'd get money too!"

She sighed.

"And if my eyes hadn't gone back on me," said she, "I'd have been sewing at God's flowers to-day."

"Don't you sew any more?" I asked.

"It's how to thread the needle would puzzle me now," said she, "me that could make my fine stitchery crouched down in the firelight of a winter's night!" She sighed again. "So I'm turned a scrubwoman. But if I had my eyes, God help me!" said she, beginning to clear away the crumbs and remains of the breakfast, "I'd be in a factory all the day long earning my twelve dollars a week, and in the evenings I'd come home, so I would, and I'd sew the flowers of God, and the little birds on the trees, and the clouds that sail in the sky . . ." she paused and drew a long breath, "and I'd be happy," said she.

She cluttered all the cups and saucers and knives and forks into the sink together and she turned the tap on them.

"That'll give them a rinse," said she, "and there they'll sit with never a word to anyone and, glory be to God! we'll get them clean by dinner-time."

She tied her apron-strings in one emphatic knot.

"So what's your pleasure to begin on?" said she. "I'm no ex*pert*, but I'm ready to turn my hand to anything yourself can suggest, and if I get it done some way we'll give thanks to God after."

Later on—after Polly was gone—I pondered over this statement. But I gave no thanks to God.

The next thing I knew was a confused sense of my flat being turned upside down and inside out and outside in, and then Polly was skating up and down the long waxed corridor with soft polishing-cloths tied round her broken boots.

"It's the way we'd polish the floors for the nuns, with our

feet in bags and we but young things at the school," said she, "and it's a fine way."

She turned a radiant old face back at me as she waddled past.

"And I was always good at the dancing, God help me!" said she, "and I'd sing when I was dancing, so I would, and they'd think it was a thrush upon the tree."

At that she paused in her skating. And then she bent down and she untied the cloths and she took them off her broken boots.

"I'm forgetting," said she, and she went down on the floor on her hands and knees with her cloths in her hands, "I'm forgetting . . . I'm old now. I'm past the dancing, and my voice is cracked the way an owl's is. I'm old . . . and soon now I'll be losing the sight of my eyes."

She rubbed for a moment in silence, and she crawled slowly along on her old knees—rubbing.

"There's times I'll wake up," she said, "and I'll think 'I'll be old soon . . . and blind. And I'll not see God's trees any more and the sun on them . . . and His shining stars in the night.'"

She rubbed again.

"I'll be in the dark soon, God help me!" she said. "I'll be losing the sight of my eyes. And I suppose there'll be no one minding but just meself . . . for I'm far away here . . . and I'm lonely. . . ."

She went on rubbing.

THE BACHELOR GIRL

A BACHELOR girl! What visions of cigarettes and latch-keys—and liberty! Yes. But if it be a professional bachelor girl the liberty is restricted by the necessity to go on earning money to be free with. Be a professional woman and stop earning money—and where are you? In a hole.

The bachelor girl that I have in mind was a professional one. She earned by the labour of her hands the wherewithal to be a bachelor. She worked—worked hard. She had her professional life and she had her little den—her two rooms and a bath-room—her home where she passed her nights and Sundays. Latch-keys were hers—at least, one latch-key was. If she went out without it there was nothing for it when the time came to go inside again but to be hoisted up in the back elevator where the groceries come up, or have the janitor break the lock of her front door. Of course she was at liberty to forget her latch-key if she wanted to. No one would interfere. Such are the joys of freedom.

Modern and latch-keyed as she was, Old Maid is what they would have called her fifty years ago or so. The same thing—no difference. What's in a name? She was—and is—neat as a pin. Throw her from any housetop and she would fall right side up. You simply couldn't imagine her untidy. As soon find rents in the self-possession of our friend the cat as holes in any stockings that she wore. Morning, noon, and I am sure at night, my bachelor girl is perfectly clean and neat and tidy. She is self-respecting in her dress. Immaculate. Moulded to her clothes.

Tryphena Harris is her name. The first part of it—from which I gather that her parents were well up in their New Testament—suits her. It suits her down to the place where her neat footwear rubs the ground. She is Tryphena to the life. St Paul, if he came along, would, I am sure, approve of her. And she, so far as she could tolerate a man at all, would like St Paul.

But men are nothing to her. Even St Paul she can do very well without. She has never really known a man. Her father died before her birth, her mother died just after it; and as Tryphena

was the first baby of two young and inexperienced things she
has no brother. She was brought up by some maiden relative
somewhere—not a bachelor girl, but just a good, old-fashioned
maiden lady—who likewise had no men-trash about the house;
and in the Convent where the maiden relative sent her to get her
education, priests were the only wear in men. Today Tryphena's
patients are all women. She lives in a manless world. If, since
she has lived in her own bachelor domain, she has spoken to the
janitor about bringing up the ice, it is as close as she has come
to any man.

Men for Tryphena really don't exist. She does not so much
dislike them—she simply feels an absolute indifference for and
about them. They don't exist for her. She walks along the street
in her trim suit and her eyes go here and there—they glance at
the shop windows, at the passing women, at the hats, they take
in the richness of a fur, they appraise a pair of walking boots . . .
men they glide over. The eye sees only what it brings the power
to see. Tryphena's eyes don't bring the power to see a man. Men
don't exist for her. She is indifferent—and this indifference in
her is as clear as the hoar-frost on an autumn flower in the early
morning.

This liberty to look past men she buys with work—hard,
honest work. Her work is, as she says herself, "just rubbing
arms and legs." She is a masseuse, and arms and legs she rubs
sometimes from seven-thirty in the morning on till midnight.
She knows her work—and she is popular. Women like her quiet
ways, her calmness, her self-possession, her neatness, her little
flow of peaceful talk. And they admire her too—Tryphena is
emphatically a woman's woman. Her slight figure, her fair skin,
her delicate features, and her thick, fine hair—so pale that it
sometimes looks like silver in the sunlight—all this in her
appeals to other women. "Isn't she *sweet!*" they say of her to
one another. And without a trace of jealousy they look at her
frail beauty and admire it.

Not that she is frail. Far from it. Under her appearance of
fragility she hides a steely strength. And she takes care of herself—quiet, indefatigable care. Once in her tiny bachelor home
she suits life to herself and not herself to life, as many of her
wealthier sisters—her patients—have to do. She considers all
things. She tends herself just as she tends her clothes. What she

shall eat, what she shall wear, such things as these are of supreme importance to her; how to get the best bread—the freshest eggs—where to run to earth the most tender chicken. "I had a lovely chicken yesterday," she will say to you on Monday sometimes. Then with an infinite tender interest in her voice, "Do *you* like chicken fricasseed?" she asks you. And she will await your answer almost breathlessly . . . and sigh. *"Nessun maggior dolore . . . "* as Dante says.

I, like all other women, like to see her. An aroma of the Convent seems to come into my room as she enters it—something restrained—something a little far-away—something with a quiet beauty of its own. Tryphena loved the nuns, and evidently they loved her. They would. And she has learned from them all sorts of things—even the trick of pinning her neckwear accurately. All the ten years that I have known her the pins that keep her neckwear in its place have lain the same—one to the right, one to the left—criss-cross—just as the Sisters pin their headwear. Such perfect accuracy has a beauty of its own. Tryphena's fricaseed chicken would taste good, I think. It would be accurately planned and cooked.

But the last time Tryphena came all this was changed. Her pale face was flushed—her eyes gleamed—the words rushed out of her. Never had I seen her that way. I was alarmed . . . as she bent to start her work I saw her hands were trembling.

"Is something wrong?" I asked her.

"No," she said; and then, 'Oh *no*."

She stopped. She offered no further explanation.

"What is it?" I said; "tell me—has something happened?"

"Yes," she said, "something's happened."

She ceased her rubbing and she straightened up and looked at me. Her eyes were large and shining.

"Oh," she said, "guess what I've done. Guess!"

The years dropped off. Suddenly she was young—a girl—a child.

"Not," I said, then hesitated for a second. "Not . . . surely—"

Instinctively she guessed. Into her cheeks there surged a wave of colour.

"Oh *no*," she said. "Not that."

She looked at me reproachfully.

"How *could* you think," she said, "I'd ever marry!"

I felt a positive criminal. And from that moment marriage and giving in marriage vanished as completely from my mind as if I had been one angel talking to another.

"Well, then," said I, "what is it?"

Her breath came quick.

"Guess what I've done," she said again.

"How can I guess?" I said—and then I laughed. "Buying a chicken, perhaps—"

"*No*," said she, "buying a . . ."

She stopped again just on the brink. Again she straightened up and looked at me. The light fell on her moonlight hair, tinged at the temples now with delicate grey.

"Buying a *what*?" said I.

And then Tryphena said, "A baby!"

"A baby?" I said to her, thinking my ears had told me wrong.

"Yes," Tryphena said, "I've bought a baby. Think of it! A real—live—Baby! I've been saving up for years and years," she said, "and now I've got it."

"A baby!" I repeated. "What for?"

"To keep," Tryphena said. "Oh," she said, "I love babies so. I love them. . . . Long, long ago I said I'd have one—save up and buy it. Now I've got it!"

She clasped her hands and looked at me. Her face was full of delicate colour.

"Yesterday," she said, "I bought my baby!"

I took a breath.

"Where did you buy it?" I said; "at the market?"

"No," she said, gravely innocent; "the Sisters got it for me. Long ago I told the Sisters. I asked them to look out."

She looked me in the eye.

"Listen," she said. "I been saving. Oh, I wouldn't take a baby," said Tryphena, "not if I hadn't money so I could keep it comfortable—start it. I done well. I've made my little pile. I've worked all right—I got my pension coming on."

She drew a deep, deep breath.

"And when you got your pension at your back," said she, "*that* makes the difference. You can afford to look at any woman. You can get old all right. And"—she caught her breath—"see what my money's done for me. I got my baby for it. It's my own—to keep!"

I took another breath. All the ten years that I had known Tryphena we had talked of housework: how to wash paint— where to buy chickens—how to cook them; we had been calm, self-respecting human creatures, just conversing. And now here was another woman—not calm—hardly self-respecting—lost to everything—triumphant—another Tryphena altogether. A thing I didn't know existed had burst its sheath and was in flower before me.

"You never talked," I said at last, "of babies."

"Talked!" said Tryphena. "Where was the good of *talking!*"

"But I mean I didn't know," I said, "that you were even fond of them."

"Fond," she said—"*fond* of them!"

She gave a sort of gasp.

"Why," she said, after a little bit, "that's all that's kept me going—just the thought I'd have one."

She paused.

"You can't help it," she said, "if you're lonesome. What are you to do?"

"You never said," I said to her, "that you were lonesome."

And there Tryphena interrupted me—a thing she had never done before.

"Oh, where's the *use?*" she said again. "Lonesome! You're sick with lonesomeness. But now!"

She laughed. Tryphena actually laughed. In the ten years that I had known her I had never heard her laugh before.

"Last week," she said, "listen—Thursday it was—the Sisters sent me word they had a baby. Healthy. Just the right one. Come at last. I didn't know the way to wait for Sunday."

She drew a deep, long breath.

"Yesterday," she said, "I went.

"Oh!" she said.

Her hands — her useful working hands — went fluttering towards each other.

"*Oh!*" she said again.

"Is it a boy?" said I.

That revived her.

"A boy?" Tryphena said. "A *boy!* No, sir! What do you take me for, I want to know? Why, it's a *girl*. A baby girl. The loveliest thing—tiny—all crumpled up."

"Is it as new as that?" I said.

"Yes, *sir*," she cried, "it's new! It's new all right. It's brand new, for it only came last Wednesday."

She laughed again. Happiness came effervescing out of her.

"It's mine!" she said.

"But where will you put a baby in your tiny flat?" said I. "Who will take care of it while you are out?"

Tryphena's face fell just a trifle.

"The nuns will keep her for me till I—till I have the money for her," said Tryphena. "There's money yet to earn. I can't have her yet—to keep."

She paused a second.

"But," she said, "when I've earned the money—then I'll have her."

She paused another second.

"It's not long to wait, I guess," she said; "time passes."

She rubbed.

"Sundays I'll have her out," she said; "the Sisters say I can. Sundays I'll fetch her good and early."

Tryphena smiled at me. I thought a little.

"How long have you thought of this?" I asked at last.

Tryphena sobered down a trifle.

"Years and years," she said. "I'm crazy about babies—I just *love* 'em. Why, these years past I've cut the babies out of every magazine."

She smiled.

"I got the loveliest collection."

Again her hands fluttered.

"Oh," she said, "there's one—I had it framed so I can see it always! And there's another—in its tiny shirt—the little thing!"

Her voice trembled.

"Now," she said, "I got a real one."

"Where," I said, "is your baby's mother?"

Tryphena clouded over. Something dark and threatening seemed to emanate from her.

"She's dead," she said. "The baby's mine."

She rubbed a little while—kneading with two strong thumbs—in silence. When she looked up her face was wistful.

"She'll grow. . . ." Tryphena said.

Her voice was tender.

"Think—only think," she said, "a tiny, crumpled thing like that can grow a woman!"

Tryphena's clear, pale eyes met mine.

"And I can share my pension with her—when I'm old," Tryphena said. "I'll have Tryphosa."

"Who?" said I.

I never would have asked a silly thing like that but that my wits had gone wool-gathering. I was thinking—thinking.

Tryphena rubbed. Her tone was matter-of-fact intensely.

"Oh," she said, "didn't I tell you? That's my baby's name . . . Tryphosa."

I wonder if the dead mother heard Tryphena say it—and if she felt a pang.

DIVORCED

SHE was free. That was her main and abiding thought. After eight years she had shaken off the shackles of something—disgraceful. She was free again. That was the way she viewed her marriage—as something disgraceful, one of those things you put behind you and don't think of any more. Not, at least, if you can help it. But there was the difficulty; put her marriage behind her as she would, cast it out of her thoughts wholesale as she did, she couldn't get away from it altogether. In a queer way it still enveloped her life, this marriage of hers. Divorced as she was, free of husband and all a husband's claims, she was still a married woman. And a married woman she would go to her grave.

Her marriage had been a definite and ghastly failure. One of those failures that are so absolutely failures that they almost make the circuit and come round to being successes again—they are so positive. For isn't the mark of a failure the being negative—the not having succeeded in getting where you wanted to get—the not having succeeded in getting anywhere at all? But Ella Hume's marriage had been definite enough. It had been an out-and-out mistake. Thousands of times while she had been married Ella Hume had cursed the day she ever saw her husband. She had hated him at moments—she had wished for singleness for weeks at a time—she had prayed for deliverance night after night. Her married life had been one long agony of failure, each day bringing with it some new item of disaster to add to the interminable list. Eight years!—they seemed to her, looking back, like eight centuries. It seemed to her as if she had lived in that degradation and misery for untold eras. Beyond that married life, looking backwards, she could see herself dimly as a girl . . . but, oddly enough, she felt no fellow-feeling with that girl. It seemed to Ella Hume as if her life had only begun when she entered into the failure of her married life.

Her husband had done everything that a husband should not do. He had been mean and dishonourable; he had been cruel. Ella Hume remembered him as she saw him first, handsome and

full of life and overpowering; the very thing to carry a woman
off her feet and swing her into matrimony. She remembered his
tricks of speech, how they fascinated her, and the little movements of his large hands—and the way she loved and admired
him . . . and how he had loved her. Then!

And now she had been a whole year free. A year. When the
marriage had been first dissolved she couldn't bear even to
think about it. When she had heard of her freedom she had said
to herself: "That ends it. God willing, I'll never think of him
again." But God wasn't willing, apparently; for she had thought
and thought—of her husband, of the days immediately preced-
ing her marriage, of the days immediately coming after it: of the
way he had first taken her to his arms, of her deep surprises at
matrimony—of her willing trust. All these things kept coming
back and coming back and breaking on the shore of her mind
like waves. She had heard the roar of the sea of matrimony as
you hear the roar of the ocean in the shell you hold to your ear.
She had thought of old, half-forgotten things; she had gone over
old conversations between herself and her husband; she had said
things to him in her thoughts that she never had said to him
in reality—and she had wondered whether they would have
touched him if she had said them. Night after night she had
dreamed of him. And night after night she had waked up in her
bed of freedom, and turned, and sighed, and tried—tried, my
God!—to sleep. She was done with matrimony, but matrimony
was not done with her. Sometimes she felt as if she was branded
with marriage as they used to brand convicts with irons.

She had done everything she could to shake herself free.
When she had—escaped, when the law had set her free, she had
left the city where he and she had lived and she had gone to
another city—far away. There she had assumed her maiden
name, and as plain Ella Hume—Miss Hume—she had sought
work. For she had shaken off the money with all the rest. She
had come out of marriage as poor as she went in. She wanted
nothing from the man she had lived with but to be free of him.
Free! She was free. After eight years that intolerable burden had
fallen off her—and she could live again.

But what a life! She worked for her money, and what she
earned she lived on. She earned enough to have a tiny bachelor
flat to come home to. When she put her key in the door there

was no one on the other side—no man—no marriage to be free of any more—just loneliness. She came in at night and she took off her things and got her supper and ate it. And then perhaps she read, or she sewed a little, or she busied herself about some household task—and then she went to bed and hoped she wouldn't dream of Jay. And the next morning she got up and had her bath and got her things on and made her breakfast and ate it and went down to business; and when she came home again there was the same loneliness and the same bed and the same dream she hoped she might escape from. On Sunday she didn't work—and it seemed long. There were moments when she was inclined to doubt God's wisdom in setting aside the seventh day so that women might have more time to think in it.

Work. That was her life. And nothing to work for. For what is the good of working for yourself? There isn't any good. It is dull. It is poor. It has no reward of any kind to give. You just do it because it is your duty—and duty is poor comfort to any of us. She knew very well that the daily round *wasn't* enough for her, that she asked more than that. Far, far more. But what?

Yes, what? She knew very well she had nothing to ask—for everything was gone. Jay had taken everything she had to give and more besides. He had taken her strength and made it impossible for her to have children of her own—and, oddly enough, she cherished no resentment against him for this. But he had taken away her illusions. He had hacked at life till she could only see the mess he had made. The good world that the girl she dimly remembered had seen long ago didn't exist any more. What Ella Hume saw now was a distorted world—a world where men had mistresses, not openly and decently, avowing their needs, but secretly and falsely—creeping away to their women as a dog sneaks in at a back door. She didn't believe in men's honour any more—and it was Jay's fault. And he had done worse than this to her. He had taken away her trustfulness—in the world round about her—in everything. She couldn't look at another life now and not say to herself: "Is it what it seems? Aren't there falsenesses and meannesses and skeleton hatreds there too?" She had lost her trust in things. It seemed to her a base world—a world full of cries and miseries and injustices . . . and once she had seen it shining in the sunlight and exquisitely pure and beautiful.

When her marriage was dissolved she had hoped to see it like that again. But no. Somehow she couldn't. Things came back on her—and she thought of things. The world wouldn't be just sunny any more.

She wondered if Jay ever thought of her—and she knew he didn't. He had chucked her away as a boy throws a stone into the distance, and he would think of her as much as the boy thinks of his stone. She knew it. She knew it and she had a passionate feeling that it wasn't *fair* that Jay should have this advantage too. Why should he have the privilege of forgetting, while she had to feel his hands on her for evermore? Sometimes she felt inclined to argue with God about the way He had made woman—to argue with Him and to show Him how unfair it was. Jay could go on to other women—and enjoy them. He had enjoyed them even while she was there. But she . . . she didn't want other men. She never had wanted them. She wanted—

She stopped.

Yes, she wanted Jay. She wanted him. She wanted the feel of his hands on her; she wanted to hear his voice. She wanted the physical joys he had taught her and given her—she who had only longed for freedom!—and she wanted them from him. She knew just what he was. She realised just how mean and how petty and how low-down he had been. But he was her husband. She had gone to him a girl and he had made her a woman . . . and she knew that if she could have a child she would want him to be its father.

How inexplicable! "Are all women made like this?" she asked herself. "Are we all cursed with this foolishness? Must we all be bound to one man—and to him only?"

She looked down at her finger. She had discarded her ring with the rest. She was Miss Ella Hume—no ring, no man, no anything. And as she sat there she longed passionately for her ring, for her married name, for her wedded life—that wedded life that had been such a cataclysm of failure and disgrace.

Down at the office where she worked they didn't even know she had been married. She passed as a single woman and she ranked as a single woman—and in her heart she despised single women; she who had taken such pains to be in all appearance one of them again. "What do *they* know?" she would ask herself impatiently. "What's life to *them*?" And she would have to bridle her tongue lest she should catch herself dropping out the word to betray her story. She had to keep watch on herself—be quiet—reserved. She didn't dare to join in discussions—for you so easily betray yourself if you're a woman.

Miss Ella Hume.

She hated the name. She hated her—

But *did* she hate her freedom? Would she, if she could, go back to that intensity of misery? She sat there thinking.

No. She wouldn't go back. She had had enough of it. But—

She thought.

"I'm done either way," she said to herself. "I'm done. I can't be contented. I—"

She thought.

"There's one thing," she said. "I wouldn't be without it. It's bad. It was wicked while it lasted. But—I wouldn't be without it."

She thought of the single women she knew—their narrowed views—their impossible fences and prohibitions. She thought of the incompleteness of their lives. She thought of their little angularities of mind—their primnesses of thought. Their misunderstandings of many of the most beautiful things of life. She remembered how one of them had said to her, taking her for another spinster: "How *can* women marry?" And she remembered how—

As she sat thinking, suddenly her life—as our lives do—seemed to unroll itself. She saw clearly enough that she had had a bad time; but she also saw that if she hadn't had that bad time she might have had a worse in not having any time at all. "It's better to suffer than not to *feel*," she said to herself. "It's better even to be maimed than never to have had an instinct." And then—quite suddenly and unexpectedly—she realised that she had not stopped loving her husband. "Why, I love him," she said to herself. "I love him!"

She felt comforted.

How *could* she love him? How could she love a man who had debased and degraded her? How could she feel anything but loathing for the creature who—? She wouldn't think of that. The fact remained. She had escaped from him, feeling as one would feel escaping from a shower of offal. She had shaken off his name—the ring he had given her—she had refused his money, everything that was his. And she knew that she had always loved him. She knew that nothing he ever had done or ever could do would make any difference. She knew that she always would love him. She felt as if her love was in every separate cell of her body and as if they must vivisect her to get it away from her—and if they vivisected her she knew she would escape from them with her love still in her soul. "How *can* I love him?" she asked herself. Her reason told her she loved a scoundrel—worse than that. Her reason told her she was a fool. But she knew that if she could save him from death she would throw her body between him and the danger. She knew that if she could save him from the wrath of God she would interpose her soul between her lover and damnation.

Her lover! That was why. He had wakened up in her body and in her soul something that but for him would have slumbered through her lifetime. She felt as if he had brought her to love—as if she might never have found love but for him—and she loved him because he had aroused love in her. She felt the love he had aroused go quivering through her body. "What is equal to that?" she asked herself. "What comes near it?"

And in her—was it in her soul?—she deified her love. It had broken her. But she felt it worth while for all that. "What would life feel like *without* this love?" she kept asking herself. "What should I be if Jay and I had never met?"

The old feeling of—of entirety—came sweeping over her. She felt this single life, that she had struggled so to get back again, falling away from her. She knew that just as she had once belonged—and she rejoiced in the word "belonged"—to her husband, so she belonged to him now. She felt that rather than belong to any other man she would destroy herself . . . and it came over her as the wind comes curling and twisting over the plains that she was—bound. "What is the Law?" she asked herself. "How can it cut between man and wife? I am Jay's. And Jay may forget—but he's mine. One day we shall meet and the past will all be blotted out between us—except that we used to love." And words that she had cast out of her mind with violence and resentment came back into it again and filled it: "Whom God has joined together let no man put asunder." "God is love," she said to herself. "Love joined us—we are one."

The thought came to her that she was the keeper of their love and that, in that day to come, she would have his share to hand

back to Jay. "He'll take it out of my hand," she said to herself—
and she smiled. "And we'll lie together again—and sleep."

When she went back to her work next day wore a symbol of
her change of heart. And they noticed that, in the intervals of
her work, she played with her symbol—twisting it round and
round her finger.

EPILOGUE

"**O**H!" he said.
He puffed.
"*Oh!*" said he.
Then after a second: "It sounds simple."

"Yes," I said, "it sounds simple, doesn't it?"

"So that's all," he said, after another pause, "that's all that women want?"

"Speaking at broad and large," I said, "I think so."

"Oh!" he said again.

We sat a bit.

"Then that's the lot!"—relief was in his voice. "That's all you have to say," he said complacently.

"*What!*" said I.

I was startled, and I confess I raised my voice a little.

"All," he said—this time there was hesitation in his voice—"you have to—"

I drew a breath.

"Why, I'm not even started yet," I said.

"Oh!" said he.

"I . . ." I positively stammered in my hurry—"I've got reams and reams and reams to say," I said to him. "Oh, so you think it's simple, do you? Well, let me tell you what we women want is simple—but the world isn't simple. Don't you see," I said, "you've got to start the world again if—*We* can't fight the world the way it is. You—you've got to . . ."

I stopped for breath. He sat there saying nothing for a bit. At last he said: "When you've got started, let me know."

I ran my fingers over the typewriter keys—and felt them lovingly. . . .

Biocritical Context

Sandra Campbell
Introduction: Biocritical Context for
J. G. Sime and *Sister Woman**

In 1922, the popular Toronto magazine *Saturday Night* published an article about a "gifted and versatile" woman writer:

> She brings to our country new gifts of mind and the culture of the Old World. And better still, supplementing and crowning her talents, there is the love of humanity that stands out in her sympathetic writings and shows in her expressive, mobile face. ("Canadian Women" 31)

The writer in question was J. G. Sime, author of *Sister Woman*, whose powerful work Canadians are only now rediscovering. In 1919, twelve years after her arrival in Canada from the British Isles, Jessie Georgina Sime published this book of short stories strongly rooted in gender and place. The stories focus on female protagonists—lower and lower-middle class women who are usually alone, bereft of male companionship and support for a variety of reasons, and who experience the joys and sorrows, the travails and consequences of sexual and maternal feeling.

Many of these women are depicted at work in the occupations open to women in the Montreal of the First World War: they struggle to survive as seamstresses, shop clerks, factory, office and domestic workers, and even as prostitutes. In their struggle, they experience the evolving psychic and social pressures brought to bear on women as a result of the rapid industrialization and urbanization that Georgina Sime witnessed between 1907 and 1919 in Montreal, then Canada's leading city.[1] Moreover, many of Sime's characters are immigrant

---

* Revised version of "Introduction" to J. G. Sime, *Sister Woman* (Ottawa: Tecumseh, 1992) vii-xxxv. All page numbers in the following articles referring to *Sister Woman* now harmonize with the text in this edition.

women from England, Scotland, Ireland, France, and Eastern Europe. As a result, the multicultural, occupational, and immigrant realities for women in early twentieth-century Canada are central to the stories.

As I have discussed elsewhere ("Gently Scan"), *Sister Woman* is structured as a cycle of thematically linked stories framed by a Prologue and an Epilogue. The twenty-eight stories are told by a woman writer to her male companion to illustrate women's multifaceted need for self-realization and the support of men in changing a society whose norms have been strictest for women, in particular single, working-class or lower-class women. The narrator's perspective echoes Sime's own—that of an independent, expatriate intellectual woman of some means, with an empathy for "sister creatures" in the spirit of the work's epigraph from Robert Burns's "Address to the Unco Guid": "Then gently scan your brother man, / Still gentler, sister woman."

Within the Prologue and the Epilogue, Sime creates a nameless female narrator—a writer—to "gently scan" woman's lot by means of stories told to a male interlocutor—an Everyman. When the man demands an answer to the "Woman's Question," the woman writer insists that it is really the "Man's and Woman's Question." Her answer is indirect, as we learn in the Prologue:

> "When," I asked him—"when shall I begin?"
> "Now," he said, "this minute. State your grievance, madam!"
> I took the cover off my typewriter and sat down before it.
> . . . (8)

The woman's answer is thus embedded in short stories that breathe compassion. As the Prologue ends, we enter the world of the stories, which focus on women's experience of life, on empathy between women, and on their struggle to affirm life and love in the face of suffering, loneliness, and betrayal. It is striking how seldom direct interaction or dialogue between men and women occurs. Instead, the stories present women's thoughts about love and motherhood, often in reverie or in a recounting of their lives to or by a sympathetic female

narrator. Although the stories are told to a man, the real communication in them is usually between *woman* and *woman*. This
gynocentric dialogue transcends differences in age, education,
ethnic origin and social status between the women involved.

In fact, the primacy of women's rapport with their own sex
is stressed throughout *Sister Woman*. For example, in the story
"Love-O'-Man" a poor Scots cook reminds the narrator that

> "Ye're a leddy born, it's true . . . but ye're a woman
> too. And gin woman meets wi' woman, mem, she'll
> clash o'whit lies neist her heart . . . and there's nae
> eddication'll stand atwixt the twa o'them." (38)

In "Alexine," a seamstress is welcomed by her middle-class
employer regardless of her history:

> I have a shrewd suspicion that in her own country
> Alexine used to be all things to all men, or a good
> many things to a lot of them—but I don't know that
> that specially matters. What does matter is that I like
> to see her come in at the door and am sorry to see her
> go out again. (39)

The *persona* of the narrator in *Sister Woman* and many of
its thematic concerns are rooted in Sime's own life. An Anglo-
Scot who arrived in Quebec City in 1907 on the eve of her
fortieth birthday, Sime, in her four decades of residence in
Montreal, came to see herself as a "near" Canadian, as she
called herself in an interview ("Canadian Women" 31). She
once described an immigrant as "a person who has definitely
fallen between two stools, and, whether he likes it or not, has
to stay there" (*Canada Chaps* 177). As an immigrant, as a
woman alone, and as a writer, she was always conscious that
she had a unique and marginalized perspective on the country
that had so fascinated her.

Sime was born in Scotland on February 12, 1868 (New
357).[2] Both her mother, Jessie Aitken Wilson, and her father,
James Sime (1843-1895)—described in his entry in the
Dictionary of National Biography as the author of books on
German literature and history—were writers. James Sime

wrote lives of Schiller, Lessing and Goethe and was a well-known journalist for the magazines *Pall Mall Gazette*, *Athenaeum*, and *Saturday Review*, among others. Georgina, an only child, grew up in London with several intervals on the Continent in a world of books and literature and such family friends as George Meredith, Thomas Hardy, and W. B. Yeats. Her childhood included visits to the popular Victorian novelist Mrs. Margaret Oliphant, a distant relative of her mother. Such youthful influences are recalled in Sime's *Brave Spirits* (1952), a book of memoir-essays.

Sime was educated at home and at Queen's College, London, a college for the education of women. She then studied singing in Berlin for a year, a period about which we know little, although, according to Jane Watt's research, Sime appears to have had her first love affair during this time, with an artist. At the age of eighteen, she returned to London, and her interests shifted from music to writing. In *Brave Spirits*, she recalled that at this period, she was fascinated by the debate over the "New Woman" and interested in the ideas of George Bernard Shaw and William Morris. Shaw was a family acquaintance, and Sime found his iconoclasm, Fabian socialism, and interest in the role of women intriguing. William Morris lived not far from the Simes in London, and Georgina remembered hearing him address a group of workers on his socialist ideas (*Brave Spirits* 9-15).

Sime began to write at this time: a column for the *Pall Mall Gazette*, book reviews for the *Athenaeum*, and editorial work for publishers in London and Edinburgh, some of it under a male pseudonym, "Jacob Salviris" (New 357). Sime and her mother moved to Edinburgh after the death of her father in 1895. Sime had viewed her father as a mentor, "the person whose opinion I valued more than any other in the world," a writer with a natural sympathy for other writers (*Brave Spirits* 60). The loss of her father was one blow; the years 1895 to 1907 brought the sorrow and financial hardship of her mother's long illness and death. To earn money Sime worked as secretary to Dr. Freeland Barbour, an eminent Edinburgh gynaecologist. There, according to scholar Jane Watt, in an event that shaped her life and work, she met a young Canadian, Walter William Chipman (1866-1950), a

Nova Scotia–born medical student who was winning academic honours at the University of Edinburgh (M.D. 1898). Henceforth their lives were to be intertwined in a love that Georgina Sime cherished all her life.

In 1907, after her mother's death, Sime came to Canada. She had family associations with the country: her mother's brother, Sir Daniel Wilson (1816-1892), had been a long-time professor and chancellor at the University of Toronto (*Brave Spirits* 42). However, it was not to Toronto but to Montreal that she came.[3] By her own account, she initially worked for Walter Chipman, who had returned to Canada in 1900 and begun to make his name as Montreal's premier obstetrician-gynaecologist, becoming a leading professor and surgeon at McGill University's Medical School and the nearby Royal Victoria Hospital. Married since 1889 to Maud Angus (d. 1946)—the daughter of one of the wealthiest men in Montreal, the financier and CPR Director R. B. Angus—Walter Chipman moved in the most exclusive circles of Montreal society and lived in a mansion on Drummond Street, near the upper reaches of Montreal's fabled and fashionable Square Mile.[4]

Intellectually, Sime and Chipman had interests in common: he had worked briefly as a journalist before medical school and was interested in literature, publishing a monograph on Kipling about 1910. For her part, Sime, in many of the stories of *Sister Woman*, focuses on pregnancy, childbirth, and women's health issues, topics in which she would have been immersed while doing office work for Chipman. Several of the stories are set in hospitals and maternity wards. Chipman was, for his part, a well-known authority on women's health whose writings are scattered with literary references from Ruskin to O. Henry. For example, Chipman's article "Sociological Aspects of Medicine" appeals to Ruskin in attacking the working conditions for shopgirls: "Ruskin rightly tells us that the worth of any civilization may be measured by what it makes of its girls—its potential mothers" (15). There are obvious affinities with the themes of *Sister Woman*. Even more importantly for her life and art, Sime's association with Chipman seems to have been personal as well as professional. Available evidence points to a lifelong liaison between them, an emotional tie that perforce placed Sime in a rather isolated social position.

Given such a liaison with a prominent married man, and the constraints it would have placed on Sime, a middle-class woman, it seems probable that the vivid descriptions in such stories as "Motherhood" and "An Irregular Union" of a woman office worker's suffering and isolation in a clandestine love affair owe something to Sime's own life. (In addition, there are various portrayals of physicians in the stories, from the casual kindness and later dismissiveness of a young surgeon, to the elderly woman patient who adores him in "Waiting," to the mockery of the lofty status of physicians in the satirical "Livin' Up to It.") Only through fiction could Georgina Sime discuss an important aspect of changing sexual mores—the increasing frequency of what she terms "irregular unions"— and symbolically break a seal of silence that the rigid conventions of the day imposed on her in relation to her own liaison. (Indeed, by contrast, Sime is conspicuously silent about her romantic life in such autobiographical works as *Brave Spirits*).

At one level, therefore, many of the stories of *Sister Woman* are a form of autobiographical fiction, where Sime displaces and disperses elements of her own personal situation onto certain sexual and social dilemmas of some of her characters, simultaneously bringing such issues and situations before the reading public while protecting her personal reputation. Theorists of women's autobiography point out that women writers commonly use such fictional strategies to protect their own reputations (Morgan and Hall 11), protection Sime would have needed to avoid ostracism in the moralistic world of English Montreal. Moreover, in my opinion, Sime's own marginalization in her romantic life gave her increased empathy with women who were socially marginalized or socially isolated in other ways—unwed mothers, prostitutes, immigrants, and the poor, all staple characters in *Sister Woman*.

In her own life, Sime achieved through professional activities the status and social validation impossible in her romantic life. She became known in Eastern Canada as a lecturer on women's writing, giving talks on Bronte, Austen and others in Ottawa, Toronto, Quebec, and elsewhere. Lorne Pierce, editor of Ryerson Press, wrote in his diary on October 12, 1921: "Heard Miss J. G. Sime—Can. authoress at Vic[toria College] this evening on 'Women in Men's Novels.'" A gifted and expressive speaker, her lectures were praised for their eloquence and "great charm" ("Canadian Women" 31). Sime was also active in literary organizations, P.E.N. in particular. She served in various positions nationally and in the Montreal chapter, and attended its lectures and readings. A fellow member, May Lamberton Becker, remembered Sime's prominence at a Vienna conference: "I met Miss Sime just once, in Vienna some years since, and heard her put into a five-minute speech as representative of Canada at the World Congress of P.E.N. Clubs, more of the essential spirit of the Viennese and what it meant to the rest of the world, than any other delegate had been able on that occasion to do in far more time" (Becker 114-15). Yet Georgina Sime felt her aloneness keenly at times. One catches the note of wistfulness in a remark in a memoir of her childhood at age eleven:

> So, when we got to Chiswick, my mother, wisely suggesting to me the possibility that I might be alone, quite alone, later in life and that I had better get accustomed to going about independently and becoming used to my own company, encouraged me to make little expeditions from home, see people and things and tell her about my adventures on my return. (*Brave Spirits* 3)

Here we see the germ of the storyteller, and an echo of the tales of lonely and isolated women Sime is moved to tell.

Indeed, even before the publication of *Sister Woman* in 1919, Sime had made women—and women's changing roles—her theme. For example, in 1916, she published *The Mistress of All Work*, a housekeeping guide for the single working woman, complete with basic advice on cooking and cleaning. Early in the First World War, she was commissioned to write *Canada Chaps* (1917), part of a series of patriotic stories of wartime life in each of the Allied countries issued by the English publisher John Lane. Undaunted by the coercive masculinity of "chaps," Sime included war nurses and waiting wives in her stories of Canada's part in the Great War. The inclusion prompted one critic, Peter Donovan of *Saturday Night*, to

complain that "the publisher would have been better to have
the stories written by a man." He further attacked Sime's
credentials to write on Canadian life:

> . . . she is obviously a stranger to the finer points of
> Canadian life. Her notion of Canadian speech, for
> instance is a weirdly wonderful thing—the sort of
> notion a visiting English woman might get by listen-
> ing to the talk of brakeman and coloured porters
> during a transcontinental trip. (Donovan 1917)

This criticism was to have its effect on *Sister Woman*. One
remarks the frequency with which Sime (perhaps a little
tongue-in-cheek) points out to a British reader distinctively
Canadian speech or usage, for example, in the story "Mr.
Johnston":

> Altabelle—for that, I am sorry to say, is her name—
> serves in a drug store; one of the kind that is called
> "cut-rate"—cheap, cheap and exceedingly nasty at
> the price. She is a young lady clerk there (pronounce,
> please, just as it is written), on a salary of five dollars
> a week. She is due at the drug store at eight-thirty in
> the morning, and there she stays till six-thirty p.m.,
> with a short space of time off for her dinner—or her
> lunch, as Altabelle prefers that it should be called.
> (82)

There is another link between *Canada Chaps* and *Sister
Woman*. In the latter, Sime again uses the short story mode to
portray contemporary life. Her choice arose out of her conviction, discussed in her criticism, that the short story form
captured the "rapid tempo of transformation" and "the unsettled
character of the psychic atmosphere" in cities like Montreal in
the grip of social change (*Orpheus* 37, 35). Short fiction could
capture the discontinuities of urban female life in Montreal in
the early twentieth century:

> . . . one feels in the cities, I think, the potentials of
> quite another kind of art—disjointed, disconnected

art that finds its expression in thumb-nail sketches, short stories, one-act scrappy plays and the like. There is material without end for this sort of interpretation. (*Orpheus* 34-35)

Accordingly, the stories "scan" a mosaic of Montreal women typical of the day. Young, middle-aged, or elderly women are presented, and the main occupations of working women—domestic service, office work, factory work, the retail trade—appear in different stories. In such stories as "Alexine" and "Adrift," immigrant women talk about women's lives in the new country from the perspective of other cultures.

Despite the range of characters and settings, there is nothing "scrappy" about the overall design of *Sister Woman*. The book is a short story cycle—an interrelated group of stories linked by subject matter, imagery, narrative tone, and complementary plots. The short story cycle has long been a significant form in Canadian writing—one that includes, for example, Duncan Campbell Scott's *In the Village of Viger* (1896) and Alice Munro's *Who Do You Think You Are?* (1978). Sime's contribution to the form is constructed with great artistry. The stories are framed by the Prologue and Epilogue, and they present variations on theme, plot, character, and tone. For example, "Mr. Johnston" and "The Cocktail" both deal with shopgirls, but the former is young and able to escape this life, while the protagonist in "The Cocktail" is middle-aged and trapped. In "The Child," a young maid miscarries her illegitimate baby, whereas in "Motherhood," a single mother successfully gives birth. In "Last Hope" and "The Wrestler," it is the mothers who die. A woman's despair in "Alone," the first story in the volume, is juxtaposed with a lonely woman's affirmation of life in "Divorced," the last story in the volume.

The settings of many of the stories are also linked: women often brood in lonely rooms. Like many women writers, Sime uses spatial imagery to suggest the isolation and restrictions of her characters' lives. In "Alone," the protagonist's feelings of entrapment and despair are symbolized by her claustrophobic room at the top of the house. In "Waiting," an elderly woman who slips into senility is at last confined, blind and forgotten, to a room in the alms-house. She has moved from fruitless vigils in a surgeon's waiting room to another limbo—the antechamber of Death:

> There she sat day-long and week-long and month-long —waiting. There was nothing else to do. She sat in her room alone and waited.
> . . . So she sits, loving life away. One day Death will remember. (52)

In addition to spatial imagery, three principal elements unify the stories: the "gentle scan"—to use the words of the epigraph—by which the stories realistically document the lives of working women to urge empathy and the sisterhood of women, a frank (for the time) consideration of sexual mores, and an overall valorization of women's sexual and maternal love, even given suffering and betrayal.

Sime's "gentle scan" encompasses a realistic picture of conditions for working women in the Montreal of her time, one drawn with empathy and compassion but without political activism. There is a pervasive and uncannily accurate social documentary aspect to many of the stories. The protagonist of "Munitions!," for instance, has gone from domestic service to munitions work, because she prefers the greater independence and social contact of factory life, exhausting as it is. Women by the thousands were in fact making just such a transition, as women's historians tell us:

> By 1913 women in Ontario and Quebec factories still routinely worked 55-60 hours a week and up to 70 hours in rush seasons. But at least the hours were defined and at the end of the working day the time remaining was a worker's own. Factory work also seemed more "modern" and therefore more exciting than domestic employment. It usually provided the opportunity to talk and make friends with other women. In the factory, and during free time after work, a young woman was able to meet young men. . . . (Prentice et al. 126-27)

Other stories document the poor wages and exploitative working conditions of retail workers, seamstresses, domestic servants, and office clerks. Sime presents her readers with the ethical dilemmas posed by the poverty of working-class women, and refuses to censure or condemn. In "Mr. Johnston," Altabelle, a pretty young shopgirl, is at risk of destitution or prostitution, given her precarious material existence. The narrator is empathetic:

> Young women who look dainty and charming and tempting and delicious don't have a very easy time of it on life's journey if they have nothing to protect them but their own sense of decency and fairness. And young women in stores who also serve by standing and waiting all day long suffer not only from sore and swollen feet—they suffer in their self-respect too. They get bumped up against and hustled and hurtled: they are either too sharply or too sweetly spoken to. If they don't get themselves into a mess they deserve, to my mind, everything that is going—for, take it all in all, they have a pretty poor time. (81)

Even when the social proprieties are violated, the stories valorize empathy and compassion towards the transgressor. This is made clear when the narrator of "A Woman of Business" learns that her neighbour is a 'kept' woman, finally able to retire on her illicit earnings to live with the daughter whose virtue her income has protected:

> The snatches of her life, as she gave them to me . . . were bald and bad and low and mean and unspeakably sordid—they were the life of a loose woman from her own lips. Madame Sloyovska had had lovers galore, and when she had one lover's money she had gone on to the next one and she had had his money. Could there be anything more definitely against the moral code? And yet—explain it how you will—I felt no rancour against Madame Sloyovska as she told me—things. I felt even that no special blame attached to her.

"I most haf mooney," she said simply. "How, if I
haf not mooney, can I keep my daughter pure?" (143)

Given Sime's youthful admiration for George Bernard Shaw,
the parallels between this story and his play *Mrs Warren's
Profession* (1893) are striking. The defiant dictum in Act One
of Shaw's Mrs. Warren, a madam who also raises a daughter
innocent of her mother's real profession, could be put in the
mouth of Madame Sloyovska: "The only way for a woman to
provide for herself decently is for her to be good to some man
that can afford to be good to her" (197). Unlike Shaw, however, Sime keeps her criticism of the exploiters themselves
implicit rather than explicit in these stories. She invokes
compassion and the sisterhood of women rather than advo-
cating direct political action, a result of her conviction that
"the great sin against art" was writing "to the order of a
philosophy of life instead of to the order of life itself"
(*Thomas Hardy* 45).

Sime documents women's emotional lives as realistically
as she scans the world of women's work. Women's sexual
mores were shifting in tandem with their work, and *Sister
Woman* is remarkable in its treatment of female sexuality.
Sime's stories touch on female sexual awakening with a frankness rarely found in Canadian stories of this period, a fact the
book reviewers of 1920 noted a little uneasily, as we shall see.
In "Divorced," a woman agonizes over her sexual longing for
her ex-husband:

Yes, she wanted Jay. She wanted him. She wanted the
feel of his hands on her; she wanted to hear his voice.
She wanted the physical joys he had taught her and
given her—she who had only longed for freedom!—
and she wanted them from him. (201)

In "Motherhood," the central character muses on the awakening of her desire:

She thought of it, lying there. She thought of their
physical union—her surprise. Her surprise at herself
—at this undiscovered life she felt surging up and up

in her. "Where is this leading me?" she would ask
herself. There were moments when she used to feel
afraid of these waves of life that surged up in her—
and came back and back on her. (66)

In fact, "Motherhood," like many of the stories ("Alone,"
"An Irregular Union," "The Child"), deals with the problems
of extra-marital sexuality, referring forthrightly to changing
sexual mores:

They had entered perfectly open-eyed into an irregular union: into one of those unions with which our
whole society is honeycombed today. Marion Drysdale
had gone on working. She had taken nothing from
David Winterford but his love. As a free gift, she gave
herself—he gave himself. They were two to the bargain—they loved one another—they came to meet
each other freely. So they had united. They had become
one. (65-66)

The stories show how such women must struggle to reconcile
love and convention as they attempt to juggle the demands of
morality, feeling, and tradition. Sime was acutely aware that
"new women" had to cope with new difficulties as well as old
models and rules of conduct that could still censure them.
Accordingly in "Motherhood," Marion Drysdale, already con-
strained by the tensions and secrecy of an "irregular union,"
must struggle to retain ambition and a sense of autonomy in
her work. When she becomes pregnant, she must face the
stigma of her baby's illegitimacy and the difficulty of supporting her child. In other stories, women characters experience
isolation, poverty, disgrace, abortion or even death by suicide
as the price of venturing outside traditional moral boundaries.

Sister Woman, therefore, illustrates the disproportionate
suffering of women in an era of social change. But, on balance,
the stories also valorize women's sexual and maternal love
despite the high cost such love exacts. The fidelity, the self-
abnegation, and the self-sacrifice of women is a continuing
theme. Marion Drysdale, for example, vows to keep her baby:

. . . she loved her son as one loves the future. She saw
the possibilities of the future in that tiny creature that
she had carried in her womb for nine long months. She
saw in him the possibilities that long ago, as it seemed
now, had dimly stirred in her for herself—and she felt
that everything she had to give was not enough to
give, if only it could help those possibilities to grow
into actual fact. She lay counting and calculating.
What does a child need? How can I do what is best for
him? . . . The difficulties in front of her were plain but
she felt in herself the strength to override them. (71)

The stories exalt woman's capacity for fidelity and affirmation,
her spiritual power and her idealism in the face of suffering
and loss. Male-female unions, whether legal or unsanctioned,
can bring no secure happiness, but woman's enduring love is
affirmed in *Sister Woman*. Even characters who refuse sexual
or maternal commitment acknowledge that to love and to
suffer is preferable to celibacy. In "The Damned Old Maid,"
such a character asks: "Isn't it better to be sore and live with a
man than to live safe and sound with yer past behind ye and
no future to come?" (131). The answer the stories point to is
affirmative—but the affirmation is hard-won.

Furthermore, stories like "Union" and "Love-O'-Man"
express the hope that female love, given its power and fidelity,
may find fulfilment beyond the grave, even if that love has
been frustrated in life. This mystical exaltation of women's
love culminates in the last story in the cycle. In "Divorced,"
Ella Hume has obtained a divorce, rejecting victimization by
her unfaithful husband. She will not return to him, but she
affirms the inviolability of the love itself:

She felt the love he had aroused go quivering through
her body. "What is equal to that?" she asked herself.
"What comes near it?"
    And in her—was it in her soul?—she deified her
love. It had broken her. But she felt it worthwhile for
all that. "What would life feel like *without* this love?"
she kept asking herself. "What should I be if Jay and
I had never met?" (203)

She espouses a mystic fidelity to the husband she loves sexually and spiritually, even though the two will never be reunited in this world.[5]

The affirmation in these stories of a female love that transcends suffering derives from Sime's type of feminism, one typical of her time. Her handbook *The Mistress of All Work* (1916) expresses her conviction that "the central desire of the normal woman is to please some one of whom she is fond, and the more normal she is, the more will that desire occupy the inmost place in her heart" (137). Twenty years later, in *In a Canadian Shack* (1937), a memoir of the Laurentians, she was equally emphatic:

> . . . whatever we [women] say and however feminist
> we become, it is woman's nature to serve, and I think
> we are never happier than doing so. (206)

Such a viewpoint was shared by many of Sime's Canadian contemporaries. Women's historian Deborah Gorham has pointed out that early twentieth-century feminism in Canada was infused by a "spirit of reconciliation," a maternal feminism in which "self-sacrifice was central to woman's role and the key to her psyche" (43-44).

The ironic ending of *Sister Woman*, moreover, makes it clear that Sime believed that the struggle for reconciliation—and a better rapport between the sexes—was still perforce women's work, not men's. When the stories end, we are presented in the Epilogue with continuing male incomprehension of women's lot. The Epilogue makes it clear that women must continue to struggle to be understood and valued by men. Having heard the stories, the male of the Epilogue remains politely puzzled:

> "Oh!" he said.
> He puffed.
> "*Oh!*" said he.
> Then after a second: "It sounds simple." (205)

The male is clearly unable—or unwilling—to interpret what he has heard, and complacently leaves the task of reordering the world to the woman. In the final image of *Sister Woman*, Sime subverts the conventional "happy ending" of romance with an ending that emphasizes quest. The woman writer embraces not the man, but her typewriter, her real companion in the quest for a better world for women:

> At last he said: "When you've got started, let me know."
> I ran my fingers over the typewriter keys—and felt them lovingly. . . . (205)

Following its publication in 1919, reviewers of *Sister Woman* were, on the whole, just as unsure what to make of the stories as the male of the Epilogue. This is understandable. Canadian fiction, like the country as a whole, took time to assimilate the rapid and radical social change of early twentieth-century Canada. Canadian writers like Nellie McClung and Kit Coleman were publishing stories of women and their conflicts over labour and love, but no other writer of the day matched Sime's urban focus, documentary style, and sexual candour.[6] In the *Literary History of Canada* (1973), Desmond Pacey rightly points to Georgina Sime as a pioneer in dealing "fully and accurately with the contemporary life of a Canadian city" (175) in *Sister Woman* and her 1921 novel *Our Little Life*.

In the middle-class and decorous Canadian literary world of 1920, it was unusual—and a trifle unsettling—to read fiction that dealt with the sexual and occupational problems of urban, lower-class working women. Reviewers of the book tended to be uncomfortable with its candour and therefore ambivalent about it. In his 1920 review, Peter Donovan of *Saturday Night* praised the grace and sympathy with which Sime wrote of clerks, munitions workers, and charwomen—but then he added "especially those [women] whose histories are somewhat unconventional, let us say," thereby scanting the book's documentary style and sexual candour in just one prudish phrase. He was also critical of the narrative strategy of the book without explaining its rationale, complaining that "the constancy of the point of view in the tales gives a certain monotony" (9). This criticism (which was, alas, repeated by Pacey) overlooked Sime's subtle interweaving of theme and point of view.

Sister Woman fared somewhat better in the April 1920 *Canadian Bookman*, which, along with its review, reprinted the story "An Irregular Union," a daring choice of topic and treatment in a Canadian periodical of this time. But while the anonymous reviewer in *Canadian Bookman* admired Sime's "wonderfully moving presentation of unmarried love," the reviewer was clearly uncomfortable with Sime's "enormous sympathy with all the great primitive motives and feelings which probably form a larger part of the structure of life among scrubwomen . . . ." Despite this mixed reaction, the reviewer, unlike Donovan, did accept Sime as a "near-Canadian" writer inasmuch as it was clear from the book that "Montreal has had to do with the shaping of the author's attitude towards life." But the review quite prophetically acknowledged that, although the "characters and episodes of the book belong to Montreal," *Sister Woman* was too avant-garde to be immediately appreciated in Canada, lacking as it did the "sentimentality and optimism, which we seem to demand from purveyors of fiction on the North American continent" (57-58). There was indeed a commercial cost to being avant-garde in tone and subject matter: according to Jane Watt, sales of the book in Canada totalled less than 250 copies by June 1920 (Introduction xviii).

Clearly, Georgina Sime's stark, socially aware, feminist short fiction was remarkable for its time, unrivalled until the fiction of Mary Quayle Innis, Irene Baird, Dorothy Livesay, Gwethalyn Graham and others in the thirties and forties.[7] In the Prologue to *Sister Woman*, the narrator, poised before her typewriter, vows that women are "learning to be articulate" about women's needs and vision of life. *Sister Woman* is compelling proof of that—a landmark in women's writing in Canada.

Endnotes

[1] In the first two decades of the twentieth century, the industrial, retail, and clerical sectors began to be a major source of employment for women, albeit one with difficult working conditions and low wages. By 1921, only eleven percent of working women were in domestic service, whereas nearly half of working women had been domestic servants just thirty years earlier. Between 1901 and 1911, the female paid

labour force increased by fifty percent. By 1921, over seventeen percent of Canadian women over the age of fifteen were
in the paid labour force. The social change was rapid, particularly in an urban centre like Montreal (Prentice et al., 113-41).
For Montreal, a historical overview can be found in Terry
Copp's study of Montreal urban poverty of the day.

   [2] Some revealing facts about Sime's life have been
uncovered by W. H. New and by Jane Watt. Jane Watt, whose
doctoral thesis deals with Sime, has done extensive research on
Sime in England, and has recovered an important collection of
her correspondence.

   [3] Montreal city directories and other sources list various
addresses for Sime during the period 1907 to 1947. Through
interviews, Jane Watt has learned that Sime was in Montreal at
the time of Walter Chipman's death in 1950. Sime did spend
periods of time in England and returned to England to live after
1950; she died in England in 1958 (New 357).

   [4] Chipman's career was illustrious, as his *Montreal Star*
obituary and entry on him in Beasley's *McGill Medical
Luminaries* (70-73) make clear. Chipman was born in Wolfville,
Nova Scotia. He received a Bachelor of Arts from Acadia
University in 1890, and a B.M. (1895) and M.D. (1898) from
Edinburgh University, followed by postgraduate study in
Edinburgh, London, and the Continent. After his return to
Canada in 1900, he quickly advanced in the McGill Medical
Faculty, becoming Professor and Head of the newly created
Department of Obstetrics and Gynaecology in 1912. His wife,
Maud Mary Angus, was the daughter of R. B. Angus, a CPR
director and sometime governor of McGill University and
president of the Royal Victoria Hospital, the latter two positions
held by Chipman himself. As director of the Women's Pavilion
of the internationally known Royal Victoria Hospital, Dr.
Chipman oversaw its amalgamation with the Montreal
Maternity Hospital in 1926. The Women's Pavilion benefited
from major donations by Maud Chipman in the years after her
father's death in 1922.

   [5] Sime's later fiction also treated this theme. The enduring, giving love of a suffering, lonely woman is exalted in two
very different novels: the realistic *Our Little Life* (1921) and
the mystic *Inez and Her Angel* (1954).

⁶ The journalist Kit Coleman (1856-1915) also wrote short fiction. Two of her stories treat a woman journalist's conflicts over career and extramarital love. For her part, Nellie McClung (1873-1951) valorized female spirit in the exuberant Pearlie Watson stories set in the rural and small town West in *Sowing Seeds in Danny* (1908). See Campbell and McMullen.

⁷ Some of the socially aware short fiction of Livesay and others is collected in Donna Phillips, ed., *Voices of Discord: Canadian Short Stories from the 1930s.*

Works Cited

Beasley, E. H. *McGill Medical Luminaries.* McGill University: Osler Library, 1990.

Becker, May Lamberton. *Golden Tales of Canada.* 1938. Rpt. Freeport, New York: Books for Libraries Press, 1972.

Campbell, Sandra. "'Gently Scan': Theme and Technique in J. G. Sime's *Sister Woman* (1919)." *Canadian Literature* 133 (Summer 1992) 40-52.

Campbell, Sandra and Lorraine McMullen, eds. *New Women: Short Stories by Canadian Women 1900-1920.* Ottawa: University of Ottawa Press, 1991.

"Canadian Women in the Public Eye: Miss Sime." *Saturday Night* 18 February 1922: 31.

Chipman, Walter William. *Kipling: An Appreciation.* Montreal: Author, n.d.

—. "Sociological Aspects of Medicine." *McGill News* 11 (June 1930): 15-20.

Copp, Terry. *The Anatomy of Poverty: The Condition of the Working Class in Montreal 1897-1929.* Toronto: McClelland and Stewart, 1974.

"Dr W. W. Chipman, Former President of R.V.H., Dies." Montreal *Star* 4 April 1950: 1.

Donovan, Peter ("Tom Folio"). Review of *Canada Chaps. Saturday Night* 7 April 1917: 9.

—. Review of *Sister Woman. Saturday Night* 28 February 1920: 9.

Gorham, Deborah. "The Canadian Suffragists." In *Women in the Canadian Mosaic.* Ed. Gwen Matheson. Toronto: Martin, 1976. 23-56.

"A Montreal Woman on Women." *Canadian Bookman* April 1920: 57-58.

Morgan, Janice. "Subject to Subject / Voice to Voice." In *Redefining Autobiography in Twentieth Century Women's Fiction.* Ed. Janice Morgan and Colette Hall. New York: Garland, 1991. 3-18.

New, W.H. "Jessie Georgina Sime." *Dictionary of Literary Biography.* Vol. 92. Ed. W. H. New. Detroit: Gale Research, 1990. 356-361.

Pacey, Desmond. "Fiction 1920-1940." *Literary History of Canada.* 2nd edition. Ed. Carl F. Klinck et al. Vol. I. Toronto: University of Toronto Press, 1976. 168-204.

Phillips, Donna, ed. *Voices of Discord: Canadian Short Stories from the 1930s.* Toronto: New Hogtown, 1979.

Pierce, Lorne. Diaries. Lorne Pierce Papers, Queen's University Archives, Kingston, Ontario.

Prentice, Alison, Paula Bourne, Gail Cuthbert Brandt, Beth Light, Wendy Mitchinson and Naomi Black. *Canadian Women: A History.* Toronto: Harcourt Brace, 1988.

Shaw, George Bernard. *Mrs Warren's Profession* in *Plays Pleasant and Unpleasant.* Vol. I. London: Constable, 1908.

Sime, J. G. *Canada Chaps.* London: John Lane, 1917.

—. *In a Canadian Shack.* Toronto: Macmillan, 1937.

—. *The Mistress of All Work.* London: Methuen, 1916.

—. *Orpheus in Quebec.* London: Allen and Unwin, 1942.

—. *Our Little Life: A Novel of To-Day.* New York: Stokes, 1921; London: Richards, 1921. Rpt. Ottawa: Tecumseh, 1994.

—. *Sister Woman.* London: Grant Richards; Toronto: S. B. Gundy, 1919.

—. *Thomas Hardy of the Wessex Novels.* New York and Montreal: Carrier, 1928.

Sime, J. G. and Frank Nicholson. *Inez and Her Angel.* London: Chapman and Hall, 1954.

Sime, J. G. and Frank Nicholson. *Brave Spirits.* London: Privately printed, 1952.

Watt, Jane. Introduction. *Our Little Life: A Novel of To-Day.* 1921. Ottawa: Tecumseh, 1994. vii-xl.

—. "Passing Out of Memory: Georgina Sime and the Politics of Literary Recuperation." Diss. U of Alberta, 1997.

Documentary

Peter Donovan ("Tom Folio")
Review of *Sister Woman* (1920)[1]

It is always pleasant to see the scenes of stories laid in localities with which one is familiar, and Canadian readers may take a special interest in this collection of short tales by Miss Sime — at least I think it is Miss Sime. The stories, which are nearly all extremely short—there are about thirty of them in the volume—deal with women and life in a Canadian city. While there is considerable variety in the stories themselves, they are bound together by a governing thought—the needs of women. The central figures of the tales are nearly always working women, studied from the point of view of their instinctive longing for a happiness beyond their circumstances. Clerks, munition workers, charwomen—the author knows them all and writes of them gracefully and sympathetically, especially of those whose histories are rather unconventional, let us say. It is an attractive and clever book, but the constancy of the point of view in the tales gives a certain monotony. But one doesn't need to read them all at once.

---

[1] Peter Donovan (pseudonym "Tom Folio"). Review of *Sister Woman*. *Saturday Night* 28 February 1920: 9.

Canadian Women in the Public Eye: Miss Sime (1922)[1]

Miss J. G. Sime, the author of that clever, arresting book, *Our Little Life* [1921], which Prof. Pelham Edgar pronounced to be the best novel that has appeared for a decade, is a Canadian by adoption, and a [niece] of the late Sir Daniel Wilson, Chancellor of Toronto University. She was born in Scotland and was brought up in London.

Miss Sime indeed belongs to the veritable aristocracy of letters. Mrs. Oliphant was her [relative], and both her mother and her father, Mr. James Sime, historian and biographer, were noted writers. A maternal uncle, Prof. George Wilson of Edinburgh University, was the author of the best seller of his day, *The Five Gateways of Knowledge*, which was also the first popular scientific book to be published. She grew to young womanhood in a literary atmosphere that included in its circle such distinguished writers as Thomas Hardy and George Meredith, both intimate friends of her father. So surrounded was she with celebrities of the pen that when a young girl she decided she would never try to write herself. However, what is bred in the bone will come out, and Miss Sime presents a strong argument for the claim that talent is inherited.

About ten years ago she came as a tourist to see Canada, and liked it so much she decided to remain a year or two. At the end of this period she found herself so fond of Canada that she resolved to cast in her lot with the new country and become a Canadian, or a "near" Canadian as she calls herself, which is the next thing to being born here. She says the youth of Canada appeals to her. Its bigness and newness probably provided her with the necessary stimulus and caused her to take up her pen. During the War she wrote *Canada Chaps* [1917]. *The Mistress of All Work* [1916], a series of little essays . . . [was] the result of her own struggles with housekeeping in a flat. As the aim of this book is to show women who have to do their own work the great possibilities underlying it, it should make a wide appeal

[1] This unsigned article appeared in *Saturday Night* 18 February 1922: 31.

in this age of the disappearing domestic help. Creating a home is a woman's supreme contribution to art, and into that work all her culture can be used, is the belief of Miss Sime.

Sister Woman [1919] followed and then came *Our Little Life* [1921], her latest contribution to literature.

Miss Sime is a lecturer of great charm, and has everywhere met with deserved success in this work. Out of the dim and storied past she makes historic and celebrated persons live again, and invests her recitals with real eloquence and beauty of diction. Her voice is very pleasing in its flexibility and expressive modulations. Miss Sime recently lectured in Toronto, and will shortly speak in Quebec and Ottawa. One of her lectures is entitled "The Wit, Humour and Tragedy of Dickens." Another one deals with the great pioneer women writers who blazed the trail for women scribes of today, Fanny Burney, Jane Austen, George Eliot and Elizabeth Browning. Under the title of "An 18th Century Entanglement," she makes Dean Swift, and his Stella and Vanessa, so real we feel we have met them.

This gifted and versatile woman is emphatically the type of citizen that Canada needs and is glad and proud to possess. She brings to our new country gifts of mind and the culture of the Old World. And better still, supplementing and crowning her talents, there is the love of humanity that stands out in her sympathetic writings and shows in her expressive, mobile face.

Criticism

Misao Dean
Sister Woman as New Woman Fiction in Canada*

. . . This hierarchy [of women as subordinate in the power structure] is inscribed in the common formulation of gender issues at the turn of the century by the phrase 'woman question.' This 'question' is often vague: "What do women want?" or "What should the social position of women be?" However, in order to determine why woman should be a "question" [at] all, it is necessary to discover who asks the woman question, and who answers. The New Woman novel often self-consciously presents itself as a response to this question, and foregrounds the circumstances of its asking. The Prologue to Jessie Sime's *Sister Woman* dramatizes the situation which is the beginning point of all these novels — a man complains, "You women don't know what you want," and suggests that the narrator "be articulate" (7) in order to explain women's lives to him. The narrator responds by creating the vignettes of character and action which explain women to her male hearer.[1] The fact that the question is asked of woman implies her authority to answer; but it also suggests the power of the male examiner, who listens and in the end pronounces dismissively: "Then that's the lot" (205). As Jane Tompkins remarks, "The impassivity of male silence suggests the inadequacy of female verbalization, establishes male superiority, and silences the one who would engage in conversation" (59).

This does not necessarily imply that all New Woman novels self-consciously address a male reader: the majority of readers of these novels were female. However, the novels exist as a reply to an implicit demand of patriarchy, to "be articu-

---

*   From *Practising Femininity: Domestic Realism and the Performance of Gender in Early Canadian Fiction* (Toronto: U of Toronto P, 1998) 72-76. Reprinted with the kind permission of University of Toronto Press. Editor's Title.

late" within the bounds set by patriarchal language. In Jessie Sime's *Sister Woman*, the male listener is made explicit: the main action is framed by a question posed by a man, and its narration is explicitly an answer to the question. The Prologue to *Sister Woman* ends as the woman journalist "t[akes] the cover off [her] typewriter and s[its] down before it . . ." (8). Thus the collection of twenty-eight stories which follows is offered as a reply to the man's command: "State your grievance" (8). The stories are marked as New Woman fiction immediately as the protagonist of the opening story, "Alone," a housekeeper who has chosen to live secretly as her employer's lover, prepares to make their relationship public by expressing her grief at his death. Many of the stories recount such "irregular unions" of married men and their mistresses, or single men and their employees who choose not to marry, and some involve illegitimate children. Most focus on women who work for a living, though they differ from much New Woman writing in including the experience of working-class women and prostitutes as well as the middle-class "business woman" (secretary). These stories, however, insist that despite the newness of the style of life chosen by some of the protagonists, and the sordid details of exploitation endured by others, the biological 'womanhood' of the women described remains eternal, unchanging, and essentially defined by their roles as heterosexual lovers, caregivers, and mothers.

Several of the stories describe women who, despite life choices which are presented as unconventional, still conform to the domestic ideal. The protagonist of "Alone" falls in love with her employer as she invests more and more of her emotional life in her job as his housekeeper. "The folding of his clothes, the putting them away, the little mendings and darnings that she used to do for him . . . she remembered that sometimes she was puzzled at her joy in doing them. There was something new in all of it; and yet, behind, somewhere, it all felt infinitely old" (11). The "joy" she feels in something "infinitely old" is a result of her natural desire to perform the role of domestic help to a "good man," a desire which, the stories make clear, is common to all women, not just those who choose Domestic Science as a career. As Sime herself argued, "the central desire of the normal woman is to please some one of whom she is fond, and the more normal she is, the more will that desire occupy the inmost place in her heart" (cited in Campbell xxv). In "An Irregular Union," Phyllis Redmayne, "the ubiquitous Business Girl of our time" (53), sees her relationship to her employer as exactly comparable to that of a wife: "For all that was unexpected in her ideas, her typewriter might just as well have been a kitchen stove—or a cradle. She looked on Dick Radcliffe as Eve looked on Adam. She thought the same old things that women have always thought, though she gained her own living and imagined she was independent and free and modern and all the rest of it" (54). While Phyllis takes no money from Dick for her services as his mistress, a circumstance which she feels guards her independence, "there are moments when she almost certainly does want" (55) to be his wife.

"Love-O'-Man" addresses the issue of sexual desire in women, offering a narrative of feminine life in which the characteristics of a universal Woman in individual women are awakened by intense sexual love and/or the birth of a child. Elsie, an elderly Scots cook, explains to the narrator that now that her husband is dead and her child married, she looks forward to a reunion (in this life or the next) with her true love, Jamie, whose intense sexual love made her a woman. "Ye'll mind . . . how the woman sleeps i' ye at the first?" asks Elsie of the narrator, and goes on to explain how the experience of childbirth wakens the "mither 'at sleeps in the lassie" (35) for some women, but that for other women, "it's the sweetness o'whit the man has tae gi'e her" (36) that awakens her knowledge of herself. Elsie calls upon the narrator to own the truth of her words as common to all women: "'gin woman meets wi' woman, mem, she'll clash o' whit lies neist her heart . . . and ther's nae eddication'll stand atwixt the twa o' them'" (38). The narrator confirms Elsie's reliance upon an essential womanhood by referring to the "eternal feminine way" (38) they share. As Sandra Campbell has argued, this "gynocentric dialogue transcends differences in ages, education, ethnic origin and social status" (Introduction ix), but at the expense of reducing women to their heterosexual reproductive and sexual histories.

Motherhood is the third eternal in feminine behaviour

which the stories address. In "Jacquot and Pierre," a childless woman laments, "How strange is this longing that we have for children! . . . Life is an empty thing without a child. Life is without reason if one has not got a child" (77-78). In "The Child" and "Motherhood," the love of the protagonists for their illegitimate children changes their lives, giving them renewed ambition and a sense of self-worth. In "A Page from Life," a childless woman greets the son her husband unexpectedly brings home from the orphanage: "My child, my child . . . have ye come to me, have ye come at last?" (139). Even Donna, the elegant and aimless protagonist of "A Social Problem," feels a desire for a baby (150-51).

While stories such as "A Social Problem" and the familiar anthology piece "Munitions!" suggest that women need productive work and are strong enough and capable enough to enjoy it, *Sister Woman* reiterates the theme that despite the social changes implied by these narratives, Woman herself is eternal and unchanging, and marked by an innate desire for union with a man, love of domestic life, and a drive to have children. The stories accommodate the practices of sexual relations outside of marriage, of women's desire for careers and productive work, and of sexually expressive behaviour in women to an inner self who is biologically determined to be mate and mother. The Epilogue expresses the male hearer's "relief" that women's desire "sounds simple" (205); the act of articulating the feminine self has allowed the male hearer to objectify and contain women's desire in predictable and traditional forms. While the narrator attempts to evade this containment by protesting, "I'm not even started yet" (205), the collection ends here; though the last words of the "Epilogue" describe an action performed by the narrator, in a sense, the man has had the last word.

While these texts refer to practices which are in many ways feminist, they construct such practices as ephemeralities in evolutionary time and signify as "real" a radically conservative view of the feminine inner self. Like the French naturalists, they draw upon popular understandings of heredity and evolution to signify humans as primarily material beings whose essence is determined by their biology and their physical conditions of life. By signifying as real the feminine self as constructed by science, they grant authority only to those aspects of femininity which are authorized by biological and evolutionary theories, that is, to those aspects of femininity which define woman as the sex whose legitimate social function is reproduction. Significant dissent from this position harks back to domestic ideology by constructing women as idealized guardians of spiritual ideals in an increasingly materialist society. While New Woman fiction represents the dramatic social changes of this period in the actions of female characters, it also represents these changes as ephemeral, a distraction from the eternal and unchanging inner self of women.

In taking the definition of Woman herself as its focus, and in laying bare the mysteries of Woman to the penetrating gaze of the reader, New Woman fiction inscribes itself in the gender hierarchy as the subordinate term and marks itself as feminine textual practice. In purporting to "explain" woman, these texts implicitly acknowledge the authority of patriarchy and respond to its demand that Woman remain the ultimate object of both knowledge and narrative. In adopting the metaphors and the discourse of evolutionary and biological science of the turn of the century, New Woman texts like [Joanna Wood's] *Judith Moore*, [and] *The Untempered Wind*, [Lily Dougall's] *The Madonna of a Day*, [Maria Amelia Fytche's] *Kerchiefs to Hunt Souls* and *Sister Woman* redefine and reconstruct women in the role of passive partner in heterosexual reproduction with a relentless and predictable reiterative force. Rather than representing a step into a liberatory narrative of subjective agency, they reiterate women's subjection to linguistic norms.

Endnotes

[1] Lyn Pykett also argues that the New Woman novel is a self-conscious response to the woman question (7). Sandra Campbell argues that because each of the characters in the stories seems to be telling her story to the narrator, the "real communication in them is usually between woman and woman " (ix). I would argue, in contrast, that this technique allows the reader, male or female, to overhear the intimate conversation between women, which is usually protected, and thereby to witness women more fully revealed to the male listener.

Works Cited

Campbell, Sandra. Introduction to *Sister Woman*. By J. G. Sime. Ottawa: Tecumseh, 1992. vii-xxxv.

Dougall, Lily. *The Madonna of a Day*. New York: D. Appleton, 1895.

Fytche, Maria Amelia. *Kerchiefs to Hunt Souls*. 1895. Introduction by Carrie MacMillan. Rpt. Sackville, NB: Ralph Pickard Bell Library, 1980.

Pykett, Lyn. *The 'Improper' Feminine: The Woman's Sensation Novel and the New Woman Writing*. London: Routledge, 1992.

Sime, Jessie Georgina. *Sister Woman*. 1919. Introduction by Sandra Campbell. Rpt. Ottawa: Tecumseh, 1992.

Tompkins, Jane. *West of Everything: The Inner Life of Westerns*. New York: Oxford UP, 1992.

Wood, Joanna E. *Judith Moore; or, Fashioning a Pipe*. Toronto: Ontario Publishing Company, 1898.

Gerald Lynch
Fabian Feminism: Sime's Short Story Cycle*

Sister Woman comprises twenty-eight stories framed by a very brief prologue and epilogue. The first feature of its organization as a story cycle worth remarking is the actual number of stories, twenty-eight, which corresponds both to the time for the moon, traditionally associated with the female, to make one orbit, or cycle, of the earth (with a bit to spare), and also with the period of a woman's menstrual cycle. It is too odd and large a number of stories for Sime to have arrived at it randomly, so twenty-eight may indeed have been chosen for its associations with women and the completion of natural cycles. Such associations complement Sime's continual recourse to a maternal feminism grounded in nineteenth-century natural science, the maternal feminism which essentializes women as mothers and mates, though much more as mothers in *Sister Woman*. (The radical aspect of Sime's feminism rests in this priorizing of the maternal over the spousal role, as well as in her refusal of the happy, compromising endings of New Women novels.[1]) Further, there is some evidence that the volume as a whole is indeed organized to reflect either the phases of the moon or the flux of hormones (estrogen and progesterone) in the progression of a woman's menstrual cycle (not to say that there is any one pattern for women or that Sime would have been aware of the clinical-scientific explanations of menstruation, though she did spend her working life as secretary to Montreal's leading gynaecologist; but interestingly, in a cycle of twenty-eight stories that treats of a great many aspects of women's lives, from abortion to prostitution to sexual longing to coquetry, there is no reference to menstruation). The moon does wax and wane from new to full, and Sister Woman moves from a despairing first two stories of women brutally victimized, through a developing arc of endurance stories, to a

---

*   Adapted by the author from *The One and the Many: English-Canadian Short Story Cycles* (Toronto: U of Toronto P, 2001) 65-73. Used by permission. Author's title.

closing return story of a woman who struggles to redefine the words "marriage" (in the absence of a husband) and "love" in a triumph for which the words "gynocentric" and "full" are accurately descriptive.

But the primary structuring principle of *Sister Woman* as a story cycle is framing: by the prologue and epilogue, by the fairly consistent frame-narrator who provides the opportunity for most of these women's stories, and by the framing of the twenty-four interior stories by the first two ("Alone" and "Adrift") and the last two ("The Bachelor Girl" and "Divorced"). The last story, "Divorced," also constitutes the definitive return story of Sister Woman as a story cycle by taking the recurrent theme of women's freedom within patriarchal capitalism and moving matters to a higher level with a vision of idealized love that would appear to be identical with and exclusive to women, or at least to the childless woman of this return story, "Divorced." I use the conditional voice here not only because "Divorced" is finally but one of twenty-eight stories, however paramount its role as the return story of *Sister Woman*, but also because there is another story, "A Page from Life," the only story that adopts a male point of view, where a man proves himself capable of a similar kind of mystically intuitive love.

Having touched on the aesthetic aptness of numerological matters, I might also remark here again that the excessive number of stories in *Sister Woman* also contributes most to its few aesthetic flaws. There are simply too many short stories. Some strain for effect and others are sketchy pieces that do little but justify the charge of repetitiveness that the mostly confused reviewers levelled at the book (Campbell xxvi-xxvii). *Sister Woman* has other faults: frequent dialect fiction in thick stretches that makes the reading more a chore than a pleasure (she had thought at one time of doing a whole novel in dialogue [Sime, *Thomas Hardy* 56]), and seem to have little point other than to display the writer's considerable skill at rendering brogue phonetically; a recurrent tendency towards sentimentality (Pacey 185), especially as regards babies (perhaps the pitfall of a writer who never married, was childless, and had a decades-long affair with a prominent Montreal gynaecologist); a repetitive recourse to the idealization of maternal feminism that, whatever the reader's biases, becomes at times but a metaphysically signifying tag and is, quite simply, too simple a solution to the socio-economic issues which *Sister Woman* engages. Those are by no means minor flaws, but in *Sister Woman* they are the sort of faults that a powerful imagination and intellect sometimes allow in an otherwise excellent work of literary art.

Of course, such criticisms—of style, of repetitiveness, dialect, sentimentalism, and gestural mysticism as regards motherhood—must be understood in view of the feminist didactic intention that dictated the style of these stories, the (as I will argue) mild socialist-realist aesthetic that eschews ornamentation and features directness and clarity for the sake of wide accessibility and influence. It could even be said that the stories of *Sister Woman* are hardly modern short stories at all; but for "Divorced," the return story (and one or two others to a much lesser degree), they achieve few moments of insight or Joycean epiphanies for their subjects; they are not especially interested in the well-made plot or unity of impression and effect, apart from the dominant impression that these are sympathetic representations of working-class women's generally drab lives. What they are preponderantly are biographical sketches statedly (by the frame narrator) for illustrative-educative purpose, in a way that recalls the eighteenth-century story and, before that, medieval exempla and parable. Mary Louise Pratt, quoting H. S. Canby, is especially helpful on this aspect of the form of *Sister Woman*'s stories:

> The exemplary or illustrative trend in the short story traces back not just to the medieval exemplum or the biblical parable, but to the use of the short narrative in eighteenth century periodicals like London's *The Spectator* and *The Rambler*, where it merges with the essay. In the eighteenth century, says H.S. Canby, "the novel developed freely. But the short story, by custom, remained a pendant to the essay, was restricted to the purposes of illustration. In this age, as never before or since, it was bound up to the service of didacticism. Its range was small. Its success was remarkable " [Canby 26]. . . . Outside literature, the exemplary narrative is always a fragment of a larger discourse, never a complete whole. (Pratt 103).

Where the pre-modern Duncan Campbell Scott exercised a range of nineteenth-century story forms in *In the Village of Viger* (1896), Sime reaches back to earlier practices, in a manner that is yet typically modern in its participation in the myth of discontinuity, its rejection of immediate predecessors in favour of earlier and more austere craftsmen (T. S. Eliot's relation to the metaphysicals, especially Donne, is the obvious example; in Canada, A.J.M Smith and F. R. Scott enact similar leaps of literary faith).[2]

In *Sister Woman* the biographical stories serve as exempla in a total design that is as powerful as it is compelling. The external "larger discourse" to which Pratt refers is, as I've been hinting, the discourse of socialism. Perhaps the best evidence of this is simply that most of the stories of *Sister Woman* persistently establish and keep attention focused on the working conditions of their subjects, and their themes are always bound up with exploitative economic circumstances. Two of Sime's later books are especially useful for the light they cast on the form and intent of her story cycle, *Orpheus in Quebec* (1942) and *Brave Spirits* (1952; Frank Nicholson is given as co-author). *Orpheus* is a musing upon the kind of art that may arise in the aftermath of the Second World War, and *Brave Spirits* is a memoir that might usefully have been subtitled "Famous Writers I Have Known and Their Influence on Me." In *Orpheus* Sime speculates that Quebec's and Canada's indigenous art form will be music, a music inspired by the St. Lawrence River (suggestively an extension into aesthetic matters of Donald Creighton's "Laurentian Thesis" of 1937).[3] She also considers what new forms of literature may arise, and one is a form that sounds very much like the short story cycle Sime had fashioned in *Sister Woman* some twenty years before: "[O]ne feels in the cities, I think, the potentialities of quite another kind of art—disjointed, disconnected art that finds its expression in thumb-nail sketches, short stories, one-act scrappy plays, and the like" (34). That is an aesthetic which also suits such of her literary descendants in both Montreal and the short story cycle as the Hugh Hood of *Around the Mountain: Scenes from Montreal Life* (1967) and the Mordecai Richler of *The Street* (1969). Sime observes further that modern Canadian society itself lacks the coherence necessary to the novel as it was understood in the eighteenth and nineteenth centuries (45); and she prognosticates, long after her own dealing with the theme in *Sister Woman* and her novel *Our Little Life*, that for Canada explorations of the subject of immigration could prove to be its original contribution to world literature; and concludes by suggesting further that the divided loyalties and lives of immigrants and modern women have much in common (42-43).

Brave Spirits is the more interesting work, though, as in it Sime remembers the most influential people in her life as a writer. For those few readers acquainted only with Sime's fiction, her memoir reveals her to be an even more fascinating figure than they may have projected. She was personally acquainted with an impressive array of mid- and late-Victorian writers. And with early modern writers too: to take but one instance, she participated as subject in some failed experiments in mysticism with the young William Butler Yeats (and Sime's father was one of a very few to encourage the young poet). But of all the literary luminaries she met, the two most influential were William Morris and Mrs. Oliphant (the mid-Victorian popular novelist who was also a distant relation), and these two neatly contribute to the shaping of Sime's thinking on social-political matters and on women's lives respectively. The portrait of Mrs. Oliphant is engaging in itself, but for present purposes its most significant feature is the somewhat cold and independent woman's last words of general advice to Sime:" 'Marry the first man who asks you and get yourself a baby as soon as you can. For that is the only thing that matters in this world'" (55). It may strike present-day ears as comically retrograde, that kind of maternal feminism, until readers notice the cavalier way in which the male of the species is dispensed with altogether. Any man will do, motherhood's what matters. Such advice could be interpreted as promoting as radical a feminism, what amounts to a sorority of self-sufficiency, as any since. Oliphant's are last maternal words which Sime put into practice, if not in her own life, then in *Sister Woman*'s ultimate picture of woman alone and as keeper of the ideal of love.

As important as Mrs. Oliphant was to Sime as the model of an independent woman writer and as wise woman, the legacy of William Morris influenced her at least equally through the period of *Sister Woman*. In "A Whiff of William Morris as a

Socialist," she recounts meeting Morris when she was eleven years old as he was speaking to a group of workers. She was immediately fascinated (1952, 7), and it was a lasting impression repeatedly fortified through the late 1880s and 1890s by frequent attendance at Morris's Sunday evening lectures for his Hammersmith Socialist Society in the Kelmscott stable of his house outside London. On first encounter, she describes him as "pointing out how we might all, if we only would, share with each of our fellow creatures the comforts and conveniences that were within our reach"(7). She concedes that initially she could not connect Morris's vision of love with the romantic love she had read of in novels: "I couldn't recognize the kinship between that love and the love with which my novels had made me familiar." But she makes clear that Morris was a prime, perhaps *the* prime, and lifelong influence on her thought. And if she is frustratingly non-specific about just what it was she took from Morris, she reveals in the following statement that it may well have been Morris's well-known championing of the value of work as the foundation of art and social justice: "He set before us a vision of the sort of life that anyone with a morsel of the artistic build in him would like to lead and to see his fellowmen leading. It seemed a simple proposition (not so very unlike that of the early Christians)"(12).[4]

Fabian Socialism was so called after Quintus Fabius Maximus, the second-century B.C. Roman general who, with his tactic of avoidance, of wearing the opposition down slowly, defeated Hannibal in the second Punic War. In Fabian Socialism this avoidance tactic translates into its first principle of gradualism as opposed to communist (Marxist-Leninist) revolution. Besides having been the political affiliation of her hero Morris, Fabianism possesses a number of features that would have appealed to Sime. It was very much a middle-class and intellectual social movement of the late nineteenth century; and its two prime directives of gradualism and permeation didn't make overly taxing demands on its adherents (Weintraub 10). As Margaret Cole describes the essentials of the movement, "the main characteristics of Fabian thinking . . . are, first, that it is eclectic . . ."(27), second "democratic"(28), and third "gradualist"(29); she adds endearingly that its adherents are optimists and enthusiasts (32). As Rodelle Weintraub observes in his introduction to *Fabian Feminist*, middle-class professional women were among those groups especially attracted to Fabian Socialism (10). The history of Fabian Socialism and of Morris's involvement in it requires no rehearsal here. Suffice it to say that the history of British socialism itself and of Fabianism constitutes a sequence of factionalisms into various societies that seems most to prove nothing so well as Freud's concept of the narcissism of small differences. Regardless, as Cole, who had deep and personal ties to the Fabian movement, attests, despite his early setting up of his own socialist shop, "William Morris remained a Fabian" (3). The main point of contention between Morris and the Fabians was that Morris, something of a lifelong anarchist, never wanted a political party, but rather saw his prime duty in teaching, and teaching through art (Cole 20). In this, he was in sympathy with the Fabians' most popular proselytizer, George Bernard Shaw—to whom Sime also had a close connection, and whose own Fabianism contained—or didn't contain rather, but expressed explosively—a strong strain of radical feminism.

It was at a Morris lecture that Sime first became aware of Shaw (and Oscar Wilde, H. G. Wells, and others). For a time she boarded with Shaw's sister, Lucy, and an essay in *Brave Spirits* recalls her close association with the Shaws.[5] It is not difficult to make a case for the influence that Morris's talks and his arts-and-crafts movement had on *Sister Woman*, especially as regards Sime's continual valorization in her story cycle of woman's domestic work as art, and particularly the repeated recognition of the art-craft of seamstresses: in *Brave Spirits* she writes of her acquaintance with embroideresses from Morris's workshops, one of whom was Yeats's sister Lily, whom, she says, Yeats considered a real artist (62). It is only a little more difficult to imagine the impact on Sime of Shaw's histrionic addresses to the Fabian Society, yet such an interchange must surely have occurred. Shaw's radical feminism is best appreciated in his *The Quintessence of Ibsenism* (1891), which began as a talk to the Fabian Society in 1890 and was repeatedly published. So it is possible to picture, if somewhat fancifully, the impressionable Sime sitting spellbound through Shaw's performances of Shavian wit. Whatever the actual case may have been, biographical and circumstantial evidence indicate that Sime would surely have encountered, quite likely in person and surely in print, volleys of Shaw, such as the following bulleted gems (bullets mine) from the *Quintessence*'s "The Womanly Woman" chapter:

- Now of all the idealist abominations that make society pestiferous, I doubt if there be any so mean as that of forcing self-sacrifice on a woman under pretence that she likes it; and, if she ventures to contradict the pretence, declaring her no true woman (124).

- The truth is, that in real life a self-sacrificing woman . . . is not only taken advantage of, but disliked as well for her pains (125).

- The sum of the matter is that unless Woman repudiates her womanliness, her duty to her husband, to her children, to society, to the law, and to everyone but herself, she cannot emancipate herself . . . . In that repudiation lies her freedom; for it is false to say that Woman is now directly the slave of Man: she is the immediate slave of duty; and as man's path to freedom is strewn with the wreckage of the duties and ideals he has trampled on, so must hers be (130-31).

There are numerous other, and sometimes quite specific, Shavian influences in the stories of *Sister Woman* (I don't doubt but there were many other influences in the life and writings of such a well-read woman, though I doubt that they were equally formative), but for the present I must conclude this detour by recalling that the primary influences on Sime are the conservative Mrs. Oliphant for a form of maternal-radical feminism, William Morris for the valuing of women's domestic work, and Shaw for a witty form of firebrand Fabian Socialism permeated by an unequivocating radical feminism. The gradualist and permeative character of Fabianism was expressed practically in an educative thrust, which can be seen in the framing epilogue and prologue of *Sister Woman*, where the intention also is clearly to educate the male interlocutor in (pace Freud) what modern women want. Thus the mode of the stories within the frame is illustrative exempla, and Sime's intention is didactic in a way that anticipates later socialist realist aesthetics (see Doyle). Unsurprisingly, all three of her primary influences—Oliphant, Morris, Shaw—viewed literature as their main tool for educating the masses and achieving their ends, as did Sime.

Ultimately, though, in *Brave Spirits* (in 1952, that is) Sime declares her differences from Morris and Shaw in their socialism (though never from Mrs. Oliphant as a model of an independent woman writer [6]). In retrospect she rejects Morris's utopian vision, believing that it lacks the vital sharpness necessary to true literary art, and dismisses any art tainted by a programmatic ideology. In her brief monograph on Thomas Hardy, she already criticizes his later novels "for committing the great sin against art—that of writing to the order of a philosophy of life instead of to the order of life itself " (1928, 45). Always with Sime, as is evident much later in *Orpheus in Quebec* and the numerous recollections of writers in *Brave Spirits*, the implied aesthetic is an eclectic mixture; here, of the modernist-realist and the didactically engagé that has affinities with the high Victorian moral-aesthetic. As Watt describes it, though, the *Sister Woman–Our Little Life* period was suggestively a socialist-realist stage through which the middle-aged writer Sime passed: "At this stage of her career, at least, Georgina Sime believed in a direct link between literature and the realm of the political. Her work was not only about formal experimentation, about the possibilities of differing engagements with genre and form, but was about saying something [in reference to Sime's criticism of a novel], about moving literature away from a decadent artfulness into an engagement with contemporary society through an exploration of individual situations" (x).

Sime's reputation may well have been low, then, because of the implied socialist politics that underlies *Sister Woman* and *Our Little Life* (though in the end "politics" may be the wrong word; "attitude" may be more vaguely accurate). It is likely that *Sister Woman*'s challenging view of patriarchal systemic unfairness and capitalist-consumerism/commodification made and makes the story cycle at least as threatening today as when it was first published. As the frame narrator (a Sime persona) of the stories declares in frustration to her smug male interlocutor in the Epilogue, "'you've got to start the world again'" (205)—that is, tear it down and start over—if the injustices to working women that her stories body forth are ever to be rectified. That is the most extreme statement of Sime's exasperated narrator, at her most threatening-challenging. Thus *Sister Woman*'s socialist-feminist critique, with its disturbing mixture of a conventional maternal feminism and insistence on women's independence, would have contributed significantly to Sime's continuing undervaluation. And historically, Sime would have suffered under the conservatively Canadian response/lack of response to a woman writing powerfully and frankly about working women's lives. In her two works of fiction, and more so in *Sister Woman*, her subject matter is highly risqué and dealt with more frankly than anything in Grove or Callaghan, whose later introduction into Canadian fiction of such taboo subjects as women's sexual desire and prostitution (in *Settlers of the Marsh*, 1925, and *Such Is My Beloved*, 1934, respectively) gave them much censorious trouble. Still, such material would have been more acceptable in male-authored fiction. Furthermore, though Sime lived in Montreal for some forty-three years and didn't begin writing till moving there, she seems to have been viewed, at worst, with critical suspicion, when included at all in surveys and Canadian literary histories, and at best as providing an immigrant woman writer's view of Canada (Logan and French 305; see Campbell Introduction in this volume, 207).

It is understandable that Sime's few critics have focused attention on the feminist aspect of *Sister Woman* on what Campbell calls Sime's "gynocentric empathy"(43), abundant and obvious as it is. The stories are so stridently about the lives of working women that it would be as critically irresponsible not to give due emphasis initially to a feminist reading as it would be to ignore the question of identity posed by Alice Munro's *Who Do You Think You Are?* New accurately, if yet only partially, describes the form and function of *Sister Woman* this way: "Sime's remarkable work adopted an interrupted narrative form in order to expose the inadequacies of a normative social pattern that consigned women to second-class status and abandoned them to penury, divorce, stillbirths, single parenthood, and domestic service" ("Back to the Future" 257). Watt is closer to the mark with her description of the story cycle as one dealing with "women's varied and conflicting relationships to power, and the economic and social consequences of any divergences from the path of 'normal' morality" (ix). But once this has been observed, we are left to wonder what *Sister Woman* and Sime have to say about the material causes of such conditions.

The "normative social pattern" operative in the world of *Sister Woman* is clearly and primarily patriarchy. But what should become apparent is that this story cycle, with but a couple of exceptions, focuses attention as relentlessly on the various economic conditions of its female protagonists. It repeatedly presents even its sympathetic female narrator in an employer-employee relationship with her subjects, and frames its twenty-eight stories between an epilogue and prologue that has the narrator wanting to enlist her male interlocutor in a campaign to right the wrongs of women's lives. It is only when that invitation to a co-operative war on systemic injustice fails that she calls him to a revolutionary effort to "start the world again" (205). Interestingly, in New's series of victim positions above, "penury" begins it and "domestic service" ends it, and of the three coming between, "single parenthood" also elicits associations of unfavourable economic circumstances. With the exceptions of the Prologue and Epilogue, and a few money complaints of characters in the stories, Sime is never obvious in the way of most socialist-realist fiction. She insists that her stories and their implied critiques speak for themselves. Still, in its "gentle scan" (*Sister Woman*'s epigraph from Robert Burns) of economic conditions for working women around the time of the First World War in Montreal, Sister Woman implicitly indicts capitalism as much as patriarchy.

Endnotes

[1] As to the number of stories, though, I would even go so far as to speculate that Sime must have had either a higher or a lower number of sister-woman stories on hand and either subtracted from or added to that number to arrive at twenty-eight. Such purported numerological design may explain why a few of the stories of the cycle, and they are later ones, should have been omitted. "The

Wrestler," "Livin' Up to It," and "A Page from Life" are trite, condescending, and sentimental respectively.

2 In the form of its stories, *Sister Woman* also carries traces of Sime's first book, *Rainbow Lights: Being Extracts from the Missives of Iris* (1913), which is generically a sketch book, a miscellaneous collection of pieces (Watt viii). But of course the eighteenth- and nineteenth-century sketch book was one source of the modern story cycle, as the sketch was one of the forms from which the short story itself developed.

3 Hugh MacLennan's *Seven Rivers of Canada* (1961) presents not only another innovative use of story cycle form (complete with "L'Envoi") in a non-fictional genre but, in the context of Sime's prophecy, a fellow Montrealer's more formal approximation of the kind of literary art she forecast.

4 Frederick Kirchoff offers a compelling picture of Morris as proselytizer for the Fabian cause, giving a better idea than does Sime herself of what would have won her to his teaching:

> Morris discusses "work" in such an unabashedly personal fashion that it is difficult to argue with his premises. Here, as elsewhere, the voice that emerges from these lectures and essays is very much that of a man speaking to men. Few literary spokesmen for revolution have argued in such down-to-earth terms. For Morris, socialism was not a matter of political theorizing, but one of the plain facts of human experience. He makes his case most cogently when he makes his audience most conscious of the complex, responsive personality behind his words. He is analytic without being obstruse, plainspoken without being condescending. And the result is the deep sincerity that characterizes the writings of his final twenty years. (117)

5 In *Bernard Shaw's Sister and Her Friends: A New Angle on G.B.S.*, Henry George Farmer quotes liberally from Sime's recollection of Shaw's sister.

6 Sime's relations with her own mother appear to have been cool and distant, though she does say of her, "I don't know that my mother was a feminist, but she nearly always did take the woman's part" (1952, 90). The appraisal sounds oddly like that of the more radical feminist and socialist: one is either for or against; the particulars of the issue are irrelevant.

Works Cited

Campbell, Sandra. "'Gently Scan': Theme and Technique in J. G. Sime's *Sister Woman* (1919)." *Canadian Literature* 133 (Summer 1992): 40-52.

Campbell, Sandra. Introduction to *Sister Woman*. By J. G. Sime. Ottawa: Tecumseh, 1992. vii-xxxv.

Canby, H. A. *A Study of the Short Story*. New York: Holt, 1913.

Cole, Margaret. *The Story of Fabian Socialism*. Stanford: Stanford UP, 1961.

Doyle, James. "'Just Above the Breadline': Social(ist) Realism in Canadian Short Stories of the 1930s." In *Dominant Impressions: Essays on the Canadian Short Story*. Ed. Gerald Lynch and Angela Arnold-Robbeson. Ottawa: U of Ottawa P, 1999. 65-73.

Farmer, Henry George. *Bernard Shaw's Sister and Her Friends: A New Angle on G.B.S.* Leiden: E. J. Brill, 1959.

Hood, Hugh. *Around the Mountain: Scenes from Montreal Life*. Toronto: Peter Martin, 1967.

Kirchhoff, Frederick. *William Morris*. Boston: Twayne, 1979.

Logan, J. D., and Donald G. French. *Highways of Canadian Literature: A Synoptic Introduction to the Literary History of Canada (English) from 1760 to 1924*. Toronto: McClelland and Stewart, 1924.

MacLennan, Hugh. *Seven Rivers of Canada*. Toronto: Macmillan, 1961.

Munro, Alice. *Who Do You Think You Are?* Toronto: Macmillan, 1978.

New, W. H. "Back to the Future: The Short Story in Canada and the Writing of Literary History." In *New Contexts of Canadian Criticism*. Ed. Ajay Heble et al. Peterborough, ON: Broadview, 1997. 249-64.

Pacey, Desmond. "Fiction 1920-1940." *Literary History of Canada: Canadian Literature in English*. 2nd edition. Ed. Carl F. Klinck et al. Vol. I. Toronto: U of Toronto P, 1976. 168-204.

Pratt, Mary Louise. "The Short Story: The Long and the Short of It." In *The New Short Story Theories*. Ed. Charles E. May. Athens: Ohio UP, 1994. 91-113.

Richler, Mordecai. *The Street*. 1969. Rpt. Toronto: Penguin, 1985.

Scott, Duncan Campbell. *In the Village of Viger*. 1896. Rpt. Toronto: McClelland and Stewart, 1996.

Shaw, George Bernard. *Shaw and Ibsen: Bernard Shaw's The Quintessence of Ibsenism and Related Writings*. Ed. J. L. Wiesenthal. Toronto: U of Toronto P, 1979.

Sime, J. G. *Orpheus in Quebec*. London: George Allen and Unwin, 1942.

—. *Our Little Life*. 1921. Rpt. Ottawa: Tecumseh, 1994.

—. *Sister Woman*. 1919. Rpt. Ottawa: Tecumseh, 1992.

—. *Thomas Hardy of the Wessex Novels: An Essay & Biographical Note*. 1928. Rpt. Folcroft, PA: Folcroft Library Editions, 1975.

Sime, J. G., and Frank Nicholson. *Brave Spirits*. London: privately printed, 1952.

Watt, K. Jane. Introduction. *Our Little Life*, by J. G. Sime. Ottawa: Tecumseh, 1994. vii-xl.

Weintraub, Rodelle, ed. *Fabian Feminist: Bernard Shaw and Woman*. University Park, PA: Pennsylvania State UP, 1977.

Lindsey McMaster
The Urban Working Girl in Turn-of-the-Century Canadian Fiction*

The eyes of the women met. They smiled at one another.
Fellow-workers—out in the world together. That's what their
eyes said: Free!
—J. G. Sime, *Sister Woman* (29)

At the turn of the twentieth century, the relatively new figure
of the independent urban "working girl" represented for many
writers the modern city: its opportunities but also its potential
for immorality and cultural disruption. At a time when
women—in particular young single women—were entering
the paid workforce in unprecedented numbers, there emerged
in social commentary and fictional narrative the recognized
figure of the working girl—the representational counterpart of
society's new female wage earners. It is to this culturally constructed figure that I refer in the following discussion of the
working girl in Canadian literature. While many American
writers seized upon the working girl as a heroine through
which to explore the dubious social repercussions of modernity, Canadian writers were more hesitant to address this
female harbinger of change. In a literary market dominated by
historical romance, the texts of social realism more likely to
depict the working class were often neglected, but a more spe-
cialized suppression seemed to apply to representations of the
urban working girl. Subject to exploitation both economic and
sexual, the working girl had the potential to take on universal
meaning as the innocent working-class victim of unprincipled
capital, and in some texts this is her role. But the confidence
and enthusiasm with which young women were entering the
urban fray in Canada significantly undermined the appraisal of
them as unwilling sacrifices to industrialism. Not easily fixed
in categories of innocence or corruption, the working girl's

---

*   Originally published in *Essays on Canadian Writing* 77 (Fall
      2002) as winner of the George Wicken Prize. Reprinted with the
      kind permission of *Essays on Canadian Writing*.

elision from Canadian literature may in part reflect an unwill-ingness to face the complex social changes that she embodied. Notably, the works of the few writers who did take up the fig-ure of the working girl seem to fall into two distinct genres: either issue-oriented social realism or light-hearted popular romance, both often neglected in criticism then and today. While journalists and social reformers of the day voiced concern about the plight of working women, it seems that literature directed at the middle-class literary audience was not expected to foreground social injustice too insistently, and it is this literature that entered the canon. There are, of course, myriad reasons for one text to be canonized and not another, but the coincidence that saw urban themes, working-class issues, and gender politics all frequently sidelined suggests a palpable resistance to acknowledging precisely those cultural conditions epitomized in the working girl. Those works that do address this figure were thus engaged in a politics of represen-tation wherein even to depict the working girl was to invest meaning where it had long been denied. Just as working women were contributing to the industrial economy in a whole new way, so too working girls in literature were doing cultural work in figuring social transformation and gender transgression, and, considering the momentous changes in gender expecta-tions occurring in the twentieth century, the narratives that lent meaning to the wage-earning woman are social documents of great importance.

Social Realism and Working Women in Canadian Literature

And so, by force of cruel fate, as it seemed, this girl was as truly chained by invisible fetters to her daily toil among those relentless wheels and pulleys, as if she were a galley-slave.
—Agnes Maule Machar, *Roland Graeme, Knight* (67)

In 1919, Jessie Georgina Sime published *Sister Woman*, a col-lection of short stories that addressed the "Woman Question" by portraying, in stark realist mode, the struggles of Montreal's working-class women. Reviews of the work were not hostile, but they betray a marked ambivalence: "It is an attractive and clever book, but the constancy of the point of view in the tales gives a certain monotony. But one doesn't need to read them all at once" (Donovan). More intriguing than mere dismissal, however, is the opening statement of the anonymous *Canadian Bookman* review, which situates its evaluation in terms of the national literature: "There are qualities about the collection of short sketches entitled 'Sister Woman,' by Miss J. B. [sic] Sime, which make us hesitate to describe it as belonging to Canadian literature" ("A Montreal Woman" 57). The reviewer admits that the writer has lived in Montreal for several years, and the setting is likewise Canadian, but "it is not a book for a young country. It is lacking in sentimentality and optimism, which we seem to demand from purveyors of fiction on this North American continent" (58). Despite these reservations, the review is not otherwise negative; the reviewer describes the story "Munitions!" as "one of the most effective presentations in modern literature of the desire of the modern woman for economic independence" (58) and the whole volume as one "which should take rank among the best of the current work of English writers" (58). The hesitation to embrace the text as part of Canadian literature, then, seems to be based not on any lack of quality but on a feeling that, partly because of its dearth of optimism and sentimentality, the work was atypical of Canadian literature and unlikely to be appreciated by Canadian readers. The degree of ambivalence betrayed by these reviewers, and in particular the articulation of that ambivalence in terms of the national literature, are indicative of the reluctance to accept social criticism as part of Canadian literature. But that nationalist bent further suggests a reluctance to acknowledge contemporary social problems in Canada or to see fiction as one part of the debate needed to address social inequity.

In her introduction to the 1892 novel *Roland Graeme, Knight*, Carole Gerson notes that "In nineteenth century Canada . . . realistic social fiction was generally rejected in favour of historical romance inspired by the example of Sir Walter Scott. So rare was the literary acknowledgment of social problems that for *Roland Graeme*, one of the most sustained examinations of socio-economic issues to appear in Canadian fiction before the First World War, Machar chose an American setting" (xiii). Gerson explains that this may have been careful planning by Machar, who knew that America and

Britain would likely hold the majority of her audience, while Canadian readers would more readily accept a social critique set outside Canada. *Roland Graeme* appeared in the late nineteenth century, but the Canadian distaste for socially engaged fiction persisted into the twentieth century as "scores of writers produced lyrical tributes to place and youth . . . or penned tender historical romances" (New 140). As William H. New points out, this predilection for historical romance was concomitant with a rejection of urban narrative. Despite the rapid expansion of Canadian cities, literature remained rural in setting and theme. Representing problems of social inequity may not demand an urban setting, but in literature of social critique the city, as the spatial manifestation of modernity, often provides the milieu in which questions of social injustice are represented in most detail. Furthermore, the most sustained challenges to the social order in terms of gender configuration were taking place in the city as women's increasing entrance into the paid workforce brought about fundamental shifts in gender relations. As New points out, there was also a gendered aspect to the taste for rural themes in Canadian literature: "The general resistance to 'city themes' was perhaps a refusal to recognize social inequities in Canada, perhaps part of a continuing rejection of women's newly visible role in literature and (urban) politics. The city was in some sense figuratively theirs, just as received versions of 'Nature' were extensions of male myths of control" (140). The rejection of urban social themes in Canadian literature, then, was not merely a genre preference but a refusal of those media that might allow for gender contestation. As one of the most visible and troubling figures of urban modernity, the working girl embodied precisely those conflicts that Canadian literature sought to avoid. It is not surprising, then, that Sime's *Sister Woman*, despite its acknowledged merit and its realist innovation, was excluded from established notions of what constituted Canadian literature, for it centred on the urban working girl.

While feminist critics such as Sandra Campbell and Lorraine McMullen have brought to light writers such as Sime who have often been neglected in the canonization of Canadian literature, novels of socially engaged fiction are still largely marginalized, meaning that narrative representations of

Canada's urban working women have been all but buried. In the United States, the tale of the working girl is a much more recognized institution, with landmark texts such as Theodore Dreiser's *Sister Carrie* and Dorothy Richardson's *The Long Day* standing out from a crowd of lesser-known popular works and serialized fiction. Indeed, at the end of the nineteenth century in America, the prolific serial-fiction writer Laura Jean Libbey made the working-girl story into a formula romance and guaranteed best-seller, and her works may have influenced to some degree the Canadian writers who did portray the working girl in their fiction. In fact, the few texts that do revolve around this figure reveal a degree of class tension and social turbulence that is all the more fascinating for its Canadian context. One 1912 novel even has its working-girl heroine suddenly awaken to class hierarchy as she looks for work: "It had never before occurred to her that in applying for this place she had forfeited some of the rights of caste. Social distinctions had troubled Christine as little as they trouble most sensible Canadian girls. She had thought as little about her position as a Duchess might: now, for the first time, she felt troubled and uneasy" (Mackay 66). This passage draws on the Canadian myth of a classless society, a myth that often went unchallenged by mainstream literature, which curtailed class commentary by excluding social fiction. As Christine's troubling realization demonstrates, the struggles of the working girl are inextricably bound to class inequity, and the Canadian reader of working-girl fiction was likely, like Christine, to feel "troubled and uneasy" when literature brought that conflict to light.

The four texts that I discuss in detail here feature themes of gender and labour, and, though they differ greatly in their treatment of the social questions involved, the various depictions of the working girl suggest her representational power. Since the texts are seldom read today, what follows are brief summaries to clarify the content and genre positions of the texts.

As with the Canadian working girl's realization of class in the quotation above, Agnes Maule Machar's *Roland Graeme, Knight* is a novel designed to elicit precisely this kind of awakening to social injustice. Published in 1892, it centres on a young, middle-class woman, Nora Blanchard, who comes to sympathize with her working-class sisters and subsequently embarks on a number of philanthropic projects to help them. The catalyst in her moral awakening is Roland Graeme, a member of the Knights of Labour and a Canadian, who introduces Nora to labour politics and thus educates the reader. With its focus on middle-class characters, the novel clearly addresses a middle-class reader as well, urging sympathy for the working class in the form of maternal feminist philanthropy for women and fair labour practices for men. Two minor characters are working girls employed at the town mill: Lizzie Mason, who supports an ailing mother and a wayward brother, is chronically overworked and on her way to an early grave by the end of the novel; Nelly Grove, meanwhile, the more spirited incarnation of the factory girl, displays the good looks and fancy dress that portend her fate as a fallen woman. These two versions of the working girl are recognizable tropes in both fiction and social commentary of the day, figures meant to evoke the pity and humanitarian impulses of a middle-class readership.

While the novel remains largely conservative in that class hierarchy is not overtly challenged, the way in which Machar executes her moral project is interesting in terms of gender politics. While the title character and ostensible hero is male, the central character is undoubtedly Nora, whose awakening to class inequity provides her character with the most development; Roland, by contrast, is virtuous but static. In this narrative of labour unrest, the presence of the Knights of Labour and the event of a strike suggest a male conflict, but the only working-class characters of any prominence are the working girls; meanwhile, what causes the major reforms for the mill workers are the complaints to the mill owner by his wife and daughter, who, like Nora, are appalled by the working conditions of the young women. The working girls, then, appear to stand in for the whole working class, since their exploitation is the most visible and the most likely to elicit middle-class moral indignation; and the middle-class women, albeit by pestering their men, are the primary agents of social change. The novel is thus very much about the role of women in labour politics, even though in 1892 a relation between these two would seldom have been thought to exist.

Novels aimed at a more popular audience represented the working girl differently. Bertrand Sinclair's most popular novel,

North of Fifty-Three (1914), and Isabel Ecclestone Mackay's *The House of Windows* (1912) both depict the working girl as adventurous and capable. *North of Fifty-Three*'s Hazel Weir is twice subjected to unwanted physical advances by men, and both times she successfully slugs the offender and proves herself both physically and morally superior. The novel sold 340,000 copies, and Sinclair followed it with several more novels also set in British Columbia, few of which, however, featured female characters so prominently or sold so well. In many ways, *North of Fifty-Three* depends on gender stereotypes, but a major part of Sinclair's project is a critique of urban industrialism, and it is significant that for this Sinclair chose the working girl as the pivotal figure. Hazel Weir starts the novel as a stenographer in an eastern city and is engaged to a young man in real estate, who breaks their engagement when he believes a false rumour that she has had an affair with her boss. Hazel moves out to British Columbia to teach, where she gets lost in the woods and is found by Roaring Bill Wagstaff, who promptly kidnaps her to spend the winter in his isolated cabin. In many ways, this episode echoes the rumours of brideship girls brought out from Britain and whisked off by wilderness men to backwoods weddings; it is as though the novel's working-girl formula is being highjacked by western Canadian folklore. Wagstaff, ever the gentleman, does not lay a finger on Hazel, and come spring he yields to her demand to be released, escorting her to Vancouver and leaving her there. Hazel plans to pick up where she left off by finding work as a stenographer, but the bustle of the city is now alien to her: "She had her trade at her finger ends, and the storied office buildings of Vancouver assured her that any efficient stenographer could find work. But she looked up as she walked the streets at the high, ugly walls of brick and steel and stone, and her heart misgave her" (158). Just as the city thus threatens to overwhelm her, on the corner of Seymour and Hastings she encounters her ex-fiancé, Jack Barrow, who is full of apologies for his past behaviour and begs her to take him back. Hazel cannot resist comparing him in her mind to Wagstaff: "And she could not conceive of Bill Wagstaff ever being humble or penitent for anything he had done. Barrow's attitude was that of a little boy who had broken some plaything in a fit of anger and was now woefully trying to put the pieces together again. It amused her" (161). Soon after, Hazel makes her way back to Wagstaff's cabin, and she and Wagstaff are married instantly. Her moral choice between the rugged wilderness life, considered here to be more honest, and wage work in the city is represented as a romantic choice between the hypermasculine mountain man and the vacillating city boy. As a working girl engaged to a real estate man, Hazel begins the novel as a representative of the corrupt urban life: subject to harassment in the economically and sexually exploitative workplace and a victim of false innuendo, she is betrayed by her fiancé and ostracized by a hypocritical society. Here the working-girl figure is clearly the touchstone for judgements on city life and the moral cesspool of urban industrialism. Her journey to the West Coast, then, is a moral one as well as a physical and romantic one. However, since redemption here is contingent upon rejection of city and workplace hypocrisies, and valorization of the explicitly masculine wilderness life, Hazel must renounce her role as a worker and become the devoted backwoods wife. The romance, of course, naturalizes this transition, but an extended section of the novel involves her reluctance to give up the pleasures of the urban social scene for the isolation of rural B.C. By positing her redemption, figured as romantic fulfil-ment with Wagstaff, on renunciation of city life, the novel demonstrates the tendency for moral arguments on urban life to coalesce around the working girl, whose independence in a setting of moral indeterminacy is considered unmanageable and so demands containment.

Also aimed at a popular audience, Mackay's *The House of Windows* shares many attributes with the formulaic working-girl romance, including sinister plots and kidnappings, a hidden family lineage, an almost thwarted romance, and a heroine whose flawless beauty is exceeded only by her perfect virtue. While still a baby, Christine is discovered abandoned in the Angers & Son department store. One of the shopgirls takes her home and, together with her blind sister, raises the child as if she were their younger sister. When she is sixteen, Christine and her adoptive sisters fall on hard times, and Christine also becomes a shopgirl at Angers & Son. Meanwhile, a fallen-woman subplot rises to unusual prominence, incorporating strong judgements on women's wages and labour conditions: before Christine appeared as a baby at Angers & Son, a shopgirl there had turned to prostitution because of overwork, low wages, and the need to support an ailing mother. The shopgirl died, but her mother recovered and swore vengeance upon the owner of Angers & Son, Adam Torrance, whose indifference to the plight of his shopgirls indirectly caused the downfall of the daughter. The avenging mother therefore kidnapped Torrance's baby girl and left her in the department store, the child being none other than our heroine Christine. Sixteen years later, with Christine a shopgirl, the old woman fulfils her scheme of poetic justice by kidnapping Christine and imprisoning her in a brothel, where she is every moment in danger of experiencing the same fate as the hapless daughter. The ensuing detective narrative has Christine rescued by Torrance's nephew, who has loved her all along. The novel concludes with a merging of upper and lower classes: Christine engaged to the nephew and the blind adoptive sister engaged to Torrance. Although the novel is set in an unnamed city in eastern Canada, Mackay wrote it in Vancouver, and she includes a subplot that sends the shop owner's nephew to Vancouver, where he comments on the charm and sophistication of the city's young women. The romance formula tends to have the hero sent away as an obstacle to the eventual union with the heroine, and it is interesting that Mackay uses this convention to add a commentary on life in her own city of Vancouver, lending the tale a degree of West Coast character.

Undoubtedly the most serious work of fiction regarding the working girl in early twentieth-century Canada is J. G. Sime's *Sister Woman*, set in Montreal and published in 1919. As Sandra Campbell points out, Sime intended the form of her writing to reflect the character of modern urban life, and for this reason she used the short story: ". . . one feels in the cities, I think, the potentials of quite another kind of art—disjointed, disconnected art that finds its expression in thumb-nail sketches, short stories, one-act scrappy plays and the like" (qtd. in Campbell 43). In *Sister Woman*, the stories revolve around the many incarnations of the urban working woman: seamstresses, secretaries, munitions workers, domestic workers, and so on. Many of the narratives also explore female sexuality by representing the relationships of working women with men, drawing special attention to illicit relationships popularly known as "irregular unions": a secretary's secret relationship with her boss, a housekeeper's with her employer, an unwed couple faced with an unplanned pregnancy. All of these relationships are represented with a sympathetic yet unapologetic candour very unusual for the time. Employing the fragmentary form of the short story, Sime's writing carefully connects the tone of urban life with the struggles of the working woman, and, by further focusing on gender relations, her fiction places the working girl at the forefront of cultural transformation.

All four of these texts depict the working girl in narratives of social unease, with economic exploitation and sexual danger everywhere. In fact, as with the boss who gets socked in the teeth in *North of Fifty-Three*, or the mill owner's son who flirts with factory girls in *Roland Graeme*, the two are often conflated. In stories of the working girl, the pressures of the labour economy are closely bound to a coercive sexual economy fraught with shifting implications for gender politics in urban society. The working-girl narrative as the subplot for a middle-class morality tale in *Roland Graeme* works in a very different way than it does as the centre of popular romance in *The House of Windows*, in which working-class virtue guarantees wealth and happiness. The fact that the figure of the working girl can act as a recognizable trope in a variety of texts, yet a trope with multiple possible meanings, is indicative of the cultural significance of this neglected figure of Canadian literature.

Class Cross-Dressing in *The House of Windows*

> Again he took the small hand extended to him and again it seemed to change miraculously from the hand of Miss Brown into the hand of some delectable princess.
> —Isabel Ecclestone Mackay, *The House of Windows* (180)

Isabel Ecclestone Mackay moved to Vancouver in 1909 and wrote a number of novels, primarily romantic in tone and aimed at a popular audience, but she was better known for her poetry, which was grouped with that of Pauline Johnson. Published in 1912, *The House of Windows* draws on the dime novel tradition of the working-girl romance, a formula popularized in late-nineteenth-century America by Laura Jean Libbey, whose serialized narratives were devoured by America's female working class. In Canada, a writer of comparable popularity was May Agnes Fleming, but her romances featured primarily middle-class characters, while the working-girl romance always had a working-class heroine. So, while the works of Libbey and her counterparts were likely read in Canada, there was no equivalent trend in Canadian literature. *The House of Windows*, then, was unusual for Canadian literature of the day; with its urban setting and shopgirl characters, it represented a side of Canadian life not usually addressed in literature. Far from Sime's direct realism, however, Mackay's novel mixes realist depictions of working women's hardships with romantic fantasies of danger, adventure, and wealth. Nan Enstad examines the genre of working-girl fiction at length in her book *Ladies of Labor, Girls of Adventure: Working Women, Popular Culture, and Labor Politics at the Turn of the Twentieth Century*, and these plots of mystery, intrigue, and Cinderella romance characterized the working-girl formula popular in America: "The stories invoked the difficulty of working-class women's lives—toiling at jobs that offered little hope for advancement—and offered them fabulous fantasies of wealth, fashion, success, and love" (19). In some ways, this popular-culture form, closing with wealth and marriage, which remove the young heroine from the working sphere, seems to re-inscribe a traditional vision of female success. But as critics of the genre have pointed out, there is a noticeable current in such narratives running counter to readings that would thus circum-scribe the meaning of the texts, especially as representations of class.

In *Roland Graeme*, the factory girl, Nelly, engages in a flirtation with the mill owner's son, Harold Pomeroy, already engaged to another girl. This relationship signifies the moral degradation of both characters, but it is Nelly who fares worse in the end with the implication that she becomes a fallen woman. Working-girl narratives often feature an involvement between the working girl and the boss's son, sometimes repre-senting the latter as hero but more often as wicked seducer. As Michael Denning points out in *Mechanic Accents: Dime Novels and Working-Class Culture in America*, such narratives render class conflict as the direct, personal confrontation of sexual intrigue or harassment (196), but how that conflict unfolds may also indicate the social agenda of the writer: "Unlike the seduction novels that occasionally occur in middle-class fiction, which focus on the fallen woman, the Libbey stories [working-girl dime novels] are tales of the woman who does not fall, despite drugs, false marriage, physical violence, and disguise. Against middle-class sympathy for the fallen is set working-class virtue" (192). *Roland Graeme* is very much a novel of "middle-class sympathy," in which working girls are pitiable victims of industrial and sexual exploitation; while middle-class philanthropy might ease their suffering, there is no question of their class position changing or of the women themselves successfully resisting their treatment. By contrast, in the popular working-girl narrative established by Libbey and played on by Sinclair and Mackay, the sexually charged class confrontation of working girl and upper-class man unfolds quite differently. In *North of Fifty-Three*, Hazel capably punches her boss in the nose and even somewhat enjoys it: "It seemed unwomanly to strike. But the humour of the thing appealed to her most strongly of all. In spite of herself, she smiled as she reached once more for her hat. And this time Mr. Bush did not attempt to restrain her" (21). Hazel's able self-defence here is a precursor of her ultimate rejection of class exploitation, represented through her relationship with the socialist hero. In *The House of Windows*, the gentleman seducer hovers around the heroine's workplace, virtually stalking her, until Christine confronts him: "'I do not know you,' she said quietly, 'but if you are a gentleman you will annoy me no further. I do not wish to appeal to the police.' . . . It was a defeat as complete and unexpected as Waterloo!" (151). Christine is the embodiment of working-class virtue, and the introduction of this would-be seducer seems to be almost an offhand way to highlight the impossibility of her being tempted. She does, however, strike up a romance with the boss's adopted son, here the hero, who must actually masquerade as a working-class piano salesman so that her initial attraction to him remains unsullied by questions of class aspiration. These popular depictions of the working girl appealed to a working-class readership, who might well have been insulted if the working girl were represented as morally weak. Where narratives aimed at the middle class may invite sympathy for the downtrodden working girl, her vulnerability to seduction and her exploitation in the workplace seeming to go hand in hand, they nevertheless leave class divisions intact. The moral and physical strength of the working girl who ably fights off her assailants, meanwhile, suggests a working-class resistance to exploitation, sexual or class based. The endings of working-girl novels in turn reward their feisty heroines with secret inheritances and propitious marriages that defy class boundaries.

What both the middle-class and dime novel modes of fiction demonstrate, then, is that, in narratives of working-class womanhood, class identity and sexual purity are inextricably intertwined: in *Roland Graeme*, Nelly's vulnerability to sexual degradation is a product of her class-specific environment, while in *The House of Windows* Christine's unassailable purity is, depending on one's reading, a testimony to working-class virtue or evidence that Christine is really a "lady" all along. This connection between class and sexuality, and the dual readings that arise from it, are part of a debate central to the working-girl narrative. As Denning points out, "in the rhetoric of the late nineteenth century bourgeois culture, a working woman could not be virtuous, regardless of her virginity" (191). To contend, as working-girl novels did, that the working woman was indeed a figure of unquestionable virtue was to assert that she was as good as any "lady." Hence the central question in these narratives: "Key to the dime novel plot is the question: Can a worker be a lady? That is, does work indeed degrade, spoil one's virtue, make one coarse and masculine?" (Enstad 74).

Concerned with the proper deportment in public of the working woman, a 1903 article by Annie Merrill in *Canadian Magazine* dispensed the following fashion advice for the "Serious Woman in Business": "She is careful to avoid being conspicuous in her manner. Dresses plainly. Does not try to ape the 'lady,' with gaudy imitations in gowns and jewels" (408). Accompanying this admonition is an illustration of the modestly dressed working woman, the caption reminding us that "She dresses plainly" (408). Merrill's advice manifests the middle-class desire to clarify class divisions, especially when working-class women were at issue, and fashion was a major system of signification for female class hierarchy. In fact, the tendency of working-class women "to ape the 'lady,'" as Merrill puts it, was a common middle-class complaint about working girls. Enstad documents working women's consumer culture and describes turn-of-the-century working women who were notorious for their fashion sense, choosing clothes that many thought were inappropriate for their class: "Working women dressed in fashion, but they exaggerated elements of style that specifically coded femininity: high-heeled shoes, large or highly decorated hats, exceedingly long trains (if trains were in style) and fine undergarments. . . . By appropriating and exaggerating the accoutrements of ladyhood, working women invested the category of lady with great imaginative value, implicitly challenging dominant meanings and filling the category with their own flamboyant practices" (78). Enstad draws a connection between this fantasy of ladyhood enacted through dress and the fantasies afforded to working women in novels, in which the working girl similarly becomes a lady. The heightened femininity of their attire, meanwhile, responded to the notion that work was masculinizing for women: class and gender definitions, then, were clearly both at stake. Mackay describes the shopgirls in *The House of Windows* engaging in this exaggerated and decorative femininity through their hairdos:

> The fashion in hairdressing had also changed, and the young ladies behind the counters, who in Celia's day had been content with neatly coiled or braided tresses, were now resplendent in towering structures which held the eye with the fascination of the wonderful. It was all simple enough to one who understood the mysteries of rats and buns and turbans and puffs and curls, but to the uninitiated the result was little short of miraculous, for even supposing that Nature, in lavish mood, had supplied such hair—how did they get it to stick on? (123)

That the hairdos here are extravagant, defy nature, and include fake stick-on hair demonstrates the trend towards excess described by Enstad. Shopgirls, in fact, whose work had everything to do with fashion and display, were thought to be particularly guilty of this kind of accessorizing overkill. In *Counter Cultures: Saleswomen, Managers, and Customers in American Department Stores 1890-1940*, Susan Porter Benson describes how shopgirls, working in the world of style and consumerism, often displayed their expertise through their dress, a practice that also narrowed the class gap between them and their customers, sometimes to the dismay of the latter (235). For Christine in *The House of Windows*, it is interesting that, even before she starts working in the stores, she is categorized with shopgirls because of her appearance. Following her failed attempt to get work in a home reading to the lady of the house, the maid sums up her chances elsewhere:

> "She'll have some trouble getting anything respectable with that face," she remarked. "In her walk of life I always say that beauty is a drawback as often as not." . . . "And what would you say Miss Brown's walk in life might be, Martha?"
>
> The maid shook her head slowly. "Oh, she's got airs and graces enough! But you never can tell. Shopgirls are getting very dressy, these days, what with their false hair and all! And ladies don't go about looking for work." (75)

In other words, Christine resembles either a lady or a shop girl, according to her good looks (her hair in particular is often mentioned), her dress, and her demeanour; the only reason not to classify her as a lady is that ladies do not need work. This scene has everything to do with identity and the class and gender markers that supposedly reveal that identity, but the working-girl figure poses a significant challenge to her interpreters; undermining the maid's apparent accuracy here is the dramatic irony—though the characters are not aware of it, the reader knows that Christine really is a lady. Mackay is thus deliberately playing on the class and fashion ambiguities that make the shop girl hard to distinguish from the lady, foregrounding class indeterminacy and so gesturing to the possible breakdown of class division.

Enstad has examined the frequent objections made by middle-class commentators such as Merrill to the "tastelessness" of working women who were thought to be aping the lady through their fashion choices. In fact, turn-of-the-century social critics, especially those concerned with prostitution, such as John Shearer, not only judged fashionable working women's attire as tasteless but also predicted that it was the first step towards immorality—where class ambiguity led, aspersions of sexual impropriety followed. At the end of *Roland Graeme*, the fate of the factory girl who flirted with the boss's son is rendered in a shorthand that the nineteenth-century reader would have understood instantly when Roland says "I met that poor Nelly, the other day, very much overdressed. I don't think she works in the mill, now" (283). In *The House of Windows*, the stores have a policy of "employing only such girls as have homes and other means of support" (144). When questioned about this, the owner, Torrance, explains: "Because long ago I investigated and found out that, as a matter of fact, a girl, entirely alone and dependent upon herself, would find it hard to get along comfortably upon her wage. This, in the cases of some girls more fond of display, etc., etc., led to a—ah—deplorable state of things. Things which I need not discuss" (144). Here, once more, a taste for clothes or a fondness of display essentially stands in for the less mentionable sexual downfall of the working woman. But in addition, this assumed connection between dress and sexuality influences not only attitudes towards the working woman but labour policies as well. Mackay's is an informed depiction here, for in Vancouver and elsewhere it was common business practice to hire only girls who lived at home and had other means of support, a policy that drew on the prevalent view that young women worked for "pin money" and thus did not deserve or require a living wage (Kealey 36). This practically institutionalized pre-occupation with working women's consumer habits, especially in the heavily symbolic area of dress, suggests the widespread anxiety over their potentially transgressive desires. In the scene noted above, Torrance is upbraided by his sister, who mocks his euphemism ("fond of display, I think you said" [145]), and his redemption in the novel involves a reformation of his labour practices. The way in which working girls' fashion was considered indexical of their morality signals the conceptual bond between class position and sexual purity:

dressing above one's station was a moral failing. With working women's dress signifying so much, it is no wonder that, like the novel, it became one terrain on which questions of lady-hood and respectability were repeatedly played out.

In the class narrative of *The House of Windows*, Mackay seems to oscillate at certain points between extolling working-class virtue and reinscribing class essentialism by reminding us of Christine's hidden birthright. When Christine is kidnapped by the evil old woman who intends to make a fallen woman of her, the detective assures the girl's rich long-lost father that Christine will never fall because "blood tells. Don't you ever believe but that good blood tells" (195). Yet her goodness is elsewhere ascribed to the devoted upbringing given by her working-class adoptive sisters. She herself never thinks of her own class position until she looks for work, and the class indif-ference ascribed to Christine, who "thought as little about her position as a Duchess might" (66), is also used to describe Vancouver girls, mentioned in a letter by the travelling hero, Mark: "One's notions of caste get a sharp knock out here. . . . These girls, for instance, whose mother waited at table and whose father worked as a navvy, would be quite undismayed in shaking hands with a princess. It would not occur to them that there was any reason for undue diffidence" (138). Mackay's repeated representation of young women whose self-respect defies class distinctions suggests her endorsement of this tendency ascribed to "most sensible Canadian girls" (66). Meanwhile, the upper-class characters such as Mark and Torrance have interactions with such women that shake their class-defined assumptions, and Torrance eventually marries one of Christine's poor sisters, thereby transcending class divi-sion. Mackay seems to relish the moment when class distinctions are unexpectedly rendered visible and through that visibility shown to be unnatural and undesirable. By endorsing the views ascribed specifically to young Canadian women, even to shopgirls, Mackay destabilizes class categories while giving her novel a Canadian specificity. To lend the working girl the voice of authority in matters of class was bold for Canadian literature, and perhaps the contradictions and incon-sistencies in the class terminology of the novel indicate a hesitancy to fully challenge a conservative readership. Nevertheless, by situating the working-class woman at centre stage of her narrative, Mackay was already defying convention for Canadian literature, and by choosing the highly visible shop girl as the heroine, and titling the novel *The House of Windows*, perhaps Mackay sought to lend greater social recognition to the working girl and her struggles. Considering Merrill's admonition to avoid being "conspicuous," and the moral imputations concerning those "fond of display" or "making a spectacle of themselves," to insist that women and especially working women deserved greater social prominence was to protest against codes of both gender and class. And in this way, the project of writers such as Mackay and Sime cannot be underestimated.

Sex and the City

There was the Factory—the Factory, with its coarse, strong, beckoning life—its noise—its dirt—its men. Its men! And suddenly into Bertha Martin's cheek a wave of colour surged.
                    —J. G. Sime, *Sister Woman* (32)

Representations of the working girl are often mediating figures through which the cultural transitions of urban industrialism are negotiated. As Suzanne Mackenzie points out, "It is not a simple coincidence that periods of urban transition happen simultaneously with periods of gender role alteration. . . . Changes in the city and in women's activities are inextricably linked" (24). Literature that represented the urban working girl took a great interest in her social life, for, despite long hours and low wages, young working women were known for their pursuit of leisure, and the city offered new kinds of pleasures, many targeted at the growing demographic of single working women. One area of leisure that underwent rapid change soon after the turn of the century was the practice of dating. Not surprisingly, Annie Merrill had advice on this activity as well:

> This Serious Woman in Business will not allow men to squander money upon her, remembering the admonition of her good old grandmother, that such a course would be vulgar. She insists upon bearing her share of the expense when going about with her men friends, and the nice man

will appreciate her position, amiably permitting her to feel
a comfortable independence which to-day is making real
comradeship between men and women such a delightful
possibility. . . . It proves to him that she values his friend-
ship and companionship for its own worth; that she is not
accepting his attentions merely for the "good time" he is
able to give her, in the way that the mercenary girl "makes
use of" many a generous-hearted and blindly-devoted man.
(408)

Two versions of the working girl appear here: the "Serious
Woman in Business" who listens to her grandmother's advice,
and "the mercenary girl" who uses men to have a good time.
Meanwhile, the question of who pays for dinner was clearly as
much an object of debate one hundred years ago as it is today.
Merrill was reacting to the changing codes of dating, which
may have been dictated in part by young women eager for
amusement but low on spending money; Joanne Meyerowitz
documents the habits of American "women adrift" living on
their own and working in the city: "Adopting new urban dating patterns, they relied on men for entertainment, luxuries,
and sometimes necessities. By the early twentieth century,
many 'women adrift' belonged to urban subcultures in which
women gave men sexual favours in return for limited economic support" (xviii). These may have been the mercenary
girls of whom Merrill speaks; however, whether exchanging a
few favours with men or insisting on paying their own way,
working women were playing an active role in changing the
rules of dating and the associated rules of gender relations.
Merrill even makes a utopian gesture in her assertion that
women who pay for themselves will enable a "real comradeship" to exist between men and women. Her advice signals the
interest taken in the social practices of single working women
and the dual vision that opposed the morally upright woman
who shuns vulgarity to the mercenary vixen out for a good
time—a contradiction that fuelled the imaginative fire surrounding the sex life of the working girl.

North of Fifty-Three's Hazel Weir has no family in the
novel, and she manages all of her relationships on her own,
without chaperones or advice. Working girls in literature tend

to lack the traditional family and so have to fend for themselves. This was increasingly typical of actual single working women, who came from the countryside or from overseas to find work in the city. Often living on their own in rooming houses or hostels, they conducted their social lives free of family structure and according more to their own preferences than to conventional standards, and their influence on social codes was unmistakable: "By the 1920s, young middle-class flappers romanticized and imitated the working-class women who lived on their own and socialized with men. And popular movies and pulp magazines used the overt sexual behaviour of some 'women adrift' to spread a new stereotype of women as sexual objects. In these ways, the wage-earning women who lived apart from family were a vanguard in the decline of Victorian culture" (Meyerowitz xxiii). Signalling society's familiarity with the independent working girl as a romantic figure, Sime opens one of her stories with "A bachelor girl! What visions of cigarettes and latch-keys—and liberty!" (191). The reader here is expected to recognize the "bachelor girl" instantly along with the accessories that symbolize her independence. The unconventional relationships of single working women made possible by this independence feature in many of Sime's stories, and the intentionality of the female characters in entering into these relationships is often reaffirmed—they are not innocents seduced but women whose social circumstances afforded them new choices: "And so they had—not drifted into it, not at all. They had entered perfectly open-eyed into an irregular union: into one of those unions with which our whole society is honeycombed to-day. Marion Drysdale had gone on working. She had taken nothing from David Winterford but his love" (66). In a literary context in which the depiction of women engaging in illicit relationships was either completely absent or couched in the assertion of moral imperatives, to represent this choice in such an unflinching way was bold. But there is a series of choices represented here, the connection of which is noteworthy; Marion will engage in a socially unsanctioned sexual relationship, she will keep working, and she will remain financially independent. In a sense, then, the basis of the relationship and the suggested equality of Marion and David are posited on the economic independence of the woman, made possible by her work. Women's wage work was thus a determining factor in new types of relationships between men and women, and the immediate connection in this passage between work and sexual choices demonstrates the profound influence of women's work in the cultural handling of gender.

Sime elaborates on how working women conceived of their relationships and distinguished their behaviour from that of socially stigmatized mistresses or "kept women," and the difference has everything to do with their position as workers. In "An Irregular Union," a secretary who has a secret relationship with her boss makes a point of continuing to work and taking nothing material from her lover:

> In plain words, she didn't take any money for the gift of herself.
>
> It is queer how a little practical fact like that can make an old episode seem new—a new thing in the history of the world . . . . The little insignificant fact that she was able to "keep herself," as it is called, changed for her the whole complexion of her love episode. It gave her confidence and self-respect. She could feel with perfect accuracy that she was not a "kept woman." (55)

For this character, the fact of working colours her view of sexual relationships. Yet her need to justify her actions in her own mind and to separate herself from traditionally censured versions of female sexuality also demonstrates the difficulties faced by women who challenged social codes of gender and sexuality. Working women may have been pioneering new kinds of relationships, but destabilizing gender systems was not work to be taken lightly. The working classes may have readily rejected a certain degree of middle-class prudery, but enduring codes of female chastity and working-class honour still had influence and in many cases contributed to working women's self-definition. Given middle-class administrators eager for evidence of moral degradation among working women, often the affirmation of purity was important not only to working women's pride but to their political activism as well. The niceties of an irregular union or the degrees of supposed impropriety, then, were considerations of some importance. Sime, though she often focuses on the sense of liberation and independence among working women, also represents some of the subtleties and contradictions that beset women who took advantage of new-found freedom. The secretary in "An Irregular Union," for instance, spends the story in her room waiting for the phone to ring because her lover is in the hospital, and, unable to visit him because of the nature of their relationship, she has to await news of his condition from a nurse. The new world of urban dating was an important manifestation of the desires of working women, but it was also a world of many pressures and constraints.

The freedom to enact new kinds of desire as well as the challenges involved in so breaking with tradition were both linked in important ways to working women's residence in the city. In "An Irregular Union," the single working girl rents her own room and is therefore able to engage in her secret relationship unchaperoned and unnoticed; the narrative likewise depends on the telephone, a relatively new form of technology that came first to urban centres and thus marks the urban setting of the story. As in "Munitions!," which takes place on a streetcar carrying women to the factory, Sime's other stories lend prominence to urban technologies, suggesting their significance to her representation of modern women. In "A Woman of Business," the narrator repeatedly mentions the electric light beneath which she hears the life story of a woman who made a career of wealthy lovers:

> Madame Sloyovska has led what we call a bad life. She is thoroughly disreputable from head to heel. She has walked in the shadiest paths, and there are few dirty tricks that her hands haven't dabbled in. The snatches of her life, as she gave them to me hurriedly in the glare of that unprotected light, sounded like something you might read in a dime novelette. . . . Madame Sloyovska had had lovers galore, and when she had had one lover's money she had gone on to the next one and she had had his money. (143)

Sime emphasizes the electric light here perhaps as a metaphor for the illumination of things usually kept dark and hidden. But it is striking that she specifically uses a modern technology to provide her metaphor, for in this way she links Madame

Sloyovska's way of life to the conditions of modern urban settings. That her way of life depends on a type of sexual conduct
wholly condemned by polite society thus suggests a link
between urban life and illicit sexuality. The use of this
metaphor is another instance of a writer highlighting the existence of figures usually rendered invisible by both social
custom and literary convention. In fact, the mention in this
passage of the "dime novelette" is telling. The realist short-
story genre in which Sime is working is far from the dime
novel, yet by using this reference she signals the only other
literary milieu in which Madame Sloyovska might be encountered. This gestures subtly to the exclusion of certain
women—working-class women or in this case sexually suspect women—from mainstream representation. Sime was
highly aware of the form of her writing, choosing the short
story for its ability to mimic the fragmentation of urban life, so
her thematization of technology is perhaps part of her insight
into her own technology of writing. In a sense, then, her story,
like the electric light that figures in it, renders suddenly visible
what was previously thought too sordid for exposure.

Sime's writing reveals the critical links between modern
technology, urbanism, and women's work, and in this way her
writing is highly sensitive to the social transformations taking
place in part through the agency of working women. Sime
could clearly imagine that the urban conditions allowing working women a wholly new independence could lead to the
creation of wholly new kinds of women. Although some of her
characters fall into feminine stereotypes in their relationships,
evincing a self-sacrificing devotion to their lovers that is somewhat essentialized by Sime as a woman's nature, one story
depicts a woman wholly separate from the heterosexual system. "The Bachelor Girl" focuses on a single working woman
named Tryphena, whose way of life has always been free of
men. Orphaned early, raised by a maiden relative, and educated in a convent, Tryphena now earns her own living as a
masseuse for female clients only. The result, we are told, is a
total indifference towards men:

> Men for Tryphena really don't exist. She does not so much
> dislike them—she simply feels an absolute indifference for

and about them. They don't exist for her. . . . This liberty to look past men she buys with work—hard, honest work. Her work is, as she says herself, "just rubbing arms and legs.". . . She knows her work—and she is popular. Women like her quiet ways . . . . And they admire her too—Tryphena is emphatically a woman's woman. (192)

For this character, the ability to support herself and live on her own has made possible a way of life and a perception of reality that render traditional gender relations completely obsolete. The narrator points out that "Old Maid is what they would have called her fifty years ago" (191), but old maids tend to be defined as women who have failed to find a husband; Tryphena, however, is not just indifferent to men but even finds the thought of marriage preposterous. Seeing her excited one day, the narrator wonders if she has a suitor: "'Oh *no*,' she said. 'Not that.' She looked at me reproachfully. 'How *could* you think,' she said, 'I'd ever marry!' I felt a positive criminal" (193-94). The narrator's embarrassment here signals her feeling that she has blundered, her mistake being the heterosexist assumption that Tryphena would ever be interested in men or marriage. Although the narrator does not draw further attention to it, this moment of realization—that not all women want men—takes place as Tryphena is giving her a massage, suggesting a more sensual level to this female dialogue. But the desire that Sime elaborates on in the remainder of the story is more maternal in nature; Tryphena is excited because she has bought a baby from the nuns, who were watching for an appropriate orphan for her to adopt. Now that they have found her a baby girl ("'A *boy*! No, sir! What do you take me for. . . ?'" [195]), Tryphena is engrossed in making financial plans for single motherhood. Sime closes the story with Tryphena's intention to name the baby Tryphosa, alluding to the twin sisters from the New Testament. The reference is perhaps a suggestion that Tryphena will raise the child in her own image to relish sisterly female bonds and dismiss heterosexual conventions. Although many of Sime's stories address unconventional relationships of various kinds, this is the only one that suggests the possibility of rejecting heterosexuality outright, and it is striking how explicit the link is—almost cause and effect—between earning one's own living and the "liberty to look past men." Here work provides a degree of freedom that will influence women on fundamental levels of identity and sexuality. Moreover, in 1919, the idea that a woman might intentionally set out to become a single mother would certainly have been unfathomable to many people; indeed, it remains so to many people today. By representing the many possible forms that the working girl might take, Sime shows an awareness of how subtle shifts in gender norms would give way to profound upheavals in the social fabric.

In *Toronto's Girl Problem: The Perils and Pleasures of the City, 1880-1930*, Carolyn Strange describes how "The issue of sexual morality loomed like a dark cloud over discussions of woman's work in the industrializing city, casting waged labour as a test of chastity rather than an economic or political issue" (22). Sime, however, resolutely sees the silver lining here, and, in a society eager to condemn any increase in the sexual licence of women, she demonstrates in the tone of her writing a way to recognize women's sexual choices without castigating them. In a similarly utopian way, where many women virtually drew knives over who could be deemed a lady, Sime advocated a feminist sisterhood that would cross class boundaries. Although Mackay does not write with the same degree of political conviction, her working-class heroine similarly suggests the possibility of transcending class divisions. In fact, it seems that, where representations of the working girl lead, sexual trans-gression, class breakdown, and gender instability soon follow. A denizen of factories, city streets, and department stores, the single wage-earning woman represented to her contemporaries everything that was unnatural and unnerving about modern life. Those who were watching closely could see her potential to unravel social codes and critically redefine what it meant to be a woman in Canadian society. This is where writers entered into the cultural work initiated by these women: by representing this often disregarded figure, they insisted on new distributions of social respect, and they validated the cultural innovations of independent women. Middle-class critics may have wished Sime's characters were not quite so "extreme" in their reactions to economic freedom, but her unapologetic heroines were as striking in their realism as in their actions, making Sime's book a prescient social document.

Works Cited

Benson, Susan Porter. *Counter Cultures: Saleswomen, Managers, and Customers in American Department Stores 1890-1940*. Chicago: U of Illinois P, 1986.

Campbell, Sandra. "'Gently Scan': Theme and Technique in J. G. Sime's *Sister Woman* (1919)." *Canadian Literature* 133 (Summer 1992): 40-52.

Campbell, Sandra, and Lorraine McMullen, eds. *New Women: Short Stories by Canadian Women 1900-1920*. Ottawa: U of Ottawa P, 1991.

Denning, Michael. *Mechanic Accents: Dime Novels and Working-Class Culture in America*. New York: Verso, 1987.

Donovan, Peter ("Tom Folio"). Review of *Sister Woman*, by J. G. Sime. *Saturday Night* 28 February 1920: 9.

Dreiser, Theodore. *Sister Carrie*. 1900. New York: Norton, 1970.

Enstad, Nan. *Ladies of Labor, Girls of Adventure: Working Women, Popular Culture, and Labor Politics at the Turn of the Twentieth Century*. New York: Columbia UP, 1999.

Gerson, Carole. Introduction. *Roland Graeme, Knight: A Novel of Our Time*. Ottawa: Tecumseh, 1996. vii-xx.

Kealey, Linda. *Enlisting Women for the Cause: Women, Labour, and the Left in Canada, 1890- 1920*. Toronto: U of Toronto P, 1998.

Machar, Agnes Maule. *Roland Graeme, Knight: A Novel of Our Time*. 1892. Rpt. Ottawa: Tecumseh, 1996.

Mackenzie, Suzanne. "Building Women, Building Cities: Toward Gender Sensitive Theory in the Environmental Disciplines." *Life Spaces: Gender, Household, Employment*. Ed. Caroline Andrew and Beth Moore Milroy. Vancouver: UBC P, 1988. 13-30.

Mackay, Isabel Ecclestone. *The House of Windows*. Toronto: Cassel, 1912.

McMullen, Lorraine, ed. *Re(Dis)covering Our Foremothers: Nineteenth-Century Canadian Women Writers*. Ottawa: U of Ottawa P, 1990.

Merrill, Annie. "The Woman in Business." *Canadian Magazine* 21 (1903): 407-10.

Meyerowitz, Joanne. *Women Adrift: Independent Wage-Earners in Chicago, 1880-1930*. Chicago: U of Chicago P, 1988.

"A Montreal Woman on Women." *Canadian Bookman* April 1920: 57-58.

New, W. H. *A History of Canadian Literature*. London: Macmillan, 1991.

Richardson, Dorothy. *The Long Day: The Story of a New York Working Girl*. 1905. Women at Work. Chicago: Quadrangle, 1972.

Sime, J. G. *Sister Woman*. 1919. Rpt. Ottawa: Tecumseh, 1992.

Sinclair, Bertrand. *North of Fifty-Three*. [Toronto]: n.p., [1914].

Strange, Carolyn. *Toronto's Girl Problem: The Perils and Pleasures of the City, 1880-1930*. Toronto: U of Toronto P, 1995.

Ann Martin
Mapping Modernity in J. G. Sime's *Sister Woman**

In *Sister Woman*, as in her novel of 1921, *Our Little Life*, Jessie Georgina Sime presents characters who must renegotiate class and gender roles that have been destabilized by the Great War, by industrialization, and by urbanization. Building upon her earlier depictions of single women living in the city (*The Mistress of All Work*), and men and women living through the First World War (*Canada Chaps*), Sime's collection portrays the flux of urban life in the wake of widespread cultural upheaval. In presenting varied responses to an altered social and physical landscape, Sime maps the experience of a twentieth-century modernity, and suggests the possibilities as well as the limitations of the metropolis in the forging of modern subjectivity.

Both men and women in Sime's texts are defined according to the locations in which they live and work, as the hierarchically organized spaces of the modern city—its boarding houses, factories, shops, and mansions—reflect the classed and gendered social system. Rooms within these structures seem to indicate "the isolation and restrictions" of modern life (Campbell xvii), and the sense of alienation that has become associated with the experience of modernity. However, as Sime observes, "Life in the cities of the New World is fluid, restless, like a kaleidoscope to which someone is perpetually giving a shake" (*Orpheus* 37-38). This constant destabilization indicates the potential for resistance, and indeed, even from marginalized positions, Sime's characters subvert official, established mappings of both the city and identity. For Sime, rooms—bedrooms, sitting rooms, studies—are the grounds upon which men and women revise the social geographies of their times. What Sime emphasizes is the tactical use of space, which Virginia Woolf addresses also in *A Room of One's Own*. With an inheritance of £500, Woolf's speaker becomes inde-

---

* Written especially for this critical edition of *Sister Woman*.

pendent: "Food, house, clothing are mine forever. . . . I need
not hate any man; he cannot hurt me. I need not flatter any
man; he has nothing to give me" (34). As Julie Solomon
argues, it is a highly pragmatic approach, where "the acquisi-
tion of capital and 'a room of one's own' will allow women to
wield power within the system" (333). Rooms do not allow
their inhabitants to escape the power structures of the urban
society; however, private space allows for certain trespasses of
the boundaries that divide neighbourhoods, sexes, and social
positions. It is not an idealistic vision of modernity that Sime
embraces, then, in which the individual transcends material
conditions; but it does signal the potential of local resistance.

The gender and class hierarchies that organize the city, the
workplace, and the family home are the primary objects of
critique in *Sister Woman*. In "Alone," for example, the house
is a microcosm of the society, where patriarchal order is both
affirmed and resisted. Hetty Grayson, a housekeeper, has been
the long-time lover of her unmarried employer. Instead of
securing her position, however, this boundary crossing has
increased Hetty's emotional and financial subordination to the
master: as she acknowledges, even her bedroom "was his room
really, not hers" (9). Hetty has internalized the class and
gender divisions of the society through the relationship, "clois-
ter[ing]" herself in the house in an almost religious devotion to
her man (13). Though her happiness has been disrupted by an
unwanted abortion, Hetty's love has remained constant, and
the story opens with her grief at the loss of her lover, whose
death has left Hetty alone and lonely in her room.

Hetty's situation reflects the inequities of the patriarchal system: with the death of the master and thus of the male
gaze that has given her a sense of self, she is now "deprived of
identity and a life of her own worth living" (Lynch 81). But the
story concerns the reassertion and not just the loss of identity, for
the master's death allows Hetty to clear a space for herself within
the room that represents their relationship. Here, Hetty reconsid-
ers her place, and betrays a subtle but increasing resistance to the
power structures of the household and the society itself. The
stilted style and ambiguous diction suggest the difficulty of
Hetty's assertion of voice, and indicate the traumatic kernel that is
at the heart of her grief and that resists articulation: "If she hadn't

ever . . . had to lose it . . . there needn't ever have been any trouble. But that changed everything" (14). The "trouble" here is the tension surrounding the abortion desired by her employer, which has made overt Hetty's subordinate position in the house. The deeper resistance, however, is to the master's desire for secrecy, signalled by his prohibition of the child—a tangible sign of their love—as well as by the ellipses, which suggest the silences by which the relationship has operated. The master's complicity with the society in his enforcement of silence has prevented Hetty from being "his *openly*" (15). Over the course of the story, Hetty comes to acknowledge that she is "sick" of this secrecy; that she wants to "cry out, as loud as she could, to the whole world, 'I'm his. Do you hear?'" (15).

The disjunction between the force of her own desire and the patriarchal prohibition of its expression prompts Hetty's epiphany; that is, her momentary but highly disconcerting glimpse of the unrepresentable that lies behind the existing social fabric. The narrative of the master's power, which she has shored up, has been proven false by his death; but this realization is coupled with the equally unsettling recognition of the fiction's continuing effects in both the house and the larger society. In other words, Hetty must deal with both the loss and the persistence of the master narrative, which leaves her in a divided position, symbolized by her dissociation before the bedroom mirror:

> . . . in the glass Hetty Grayson saw the figure raise its arms and coil up the heavy hair that hung all about, and made itself neat . . . rapidly . . . unself-consciously. She seemed to be just watching it; she had no connection with it. And then she saw it pause a moment with its closed hand at its mouth. And she saw its lips move, and she seemed to see—or was it hear?—the words somewhere: "And then it'll not be a secret any more!" (16)

Her radical split in subjectivity is sutured over when Hetty verbally rearranges her identity here. She then descends to the room in which the dead master is lying in state, and lies beside him, wearing a wedding ring. Her gesture is, perhaps, a statement of desperate love and loyalty; but Hetty's resignification of her identity also signals a moment of resistance to the power dynamics of the household. The master's desire to keep their relationship silent and confined to the bedroom is countered by her action. She subverts his law through a gesture that will be seen, if not acknowledged, by his sister, who is staying in the house for the funeral.

Hetty's ruptured identity suggests the pitfalls of domestic space, where the power of the master represents the power of the society that, if challenged, leaves the individual divided and conflicted. While the housekeeper's local resistance suggests a larger critique of the systems by which she is enmeshed, her actions are accompanied by an almost inevitable marginalization. It is a common theme in Sime's stories. Ella Hume in "Divorced," for instance, feels both liberated and isolated in her own apartment: she has "no one on the other side—no man—no marriage to be free of any more—just loneliness" (200). Even a sense of independence and self-reliance does not compensate for the absence of community or "companionship" in Sime's view (*Mistress* 137), though the sense of "satisfaction" (139) that arises from the single woman's autonomy may lead to an "unlooked-for happiness that she finds in her own self" (143). The question is how to establish not just an autonomous self, then, but a new and different sense of connection within the power structures of the city.

In "Munitions!" the alternative to the patriarchal household is the rented room; but domestic isolation is countered by workplace camaraderie, where irreverent exchanges amongst equals replace the hierarchies associated with other occupations. The women who talk and joke with Bertha Martin in the munitions factory have previously "spent their lives caged . . . in shop or house" (26). Though such service has been "comfortable" (27), their freedom has been restricted by surveillance. Where before Bertha was "liable to be questioned" by her superiors if she returned to the house late on her day off (28), now, unsupervised, she goes "home at night, dead-tired" to her "own" room (31). The only official restriction on the working woman's freedom becomes "the necessity to go on earning money to be free with" (191). The unofficial restriction, however, is love, which poses a more serious problem in this new economy. Phyllis Redmayne in "An Irregular Union," for instance, only "imagine[s]" that she is "independent and free and modern and all the rest of it" (54). Her apparent autonomy is undercut by her real attachment to Dick Radcliffe, though she has no official status in his life. Many of Sime's characters are divided socially and physically from their partners: married men, neglectful lovers, distant authority figures, ex-husbands. Prostitutes, such as Alexine, deliberately embrace such divisions, rejecting poor-paying jobs or the restrictions of marriage for the control they seem to exert over their bodies (24). But independence must, in Sime's vision, be accompanied by some sense of connection, whether to men or to children or even to other women. To lose these immediate social networks is to experience, as Phyllis does, anonymity and powerlessness, rather than autonomy and empowerment. Madame Sloyovska in "A Woman of Business" becomes an interesting figure for this reason: her temporary sexual alliances with men have made her financially independent, but her daughter signals the personal connection that gives her life meaning. (In contrast, the less positive figure of Tryphena in "The Bachelor Girl" regards her baby as a commodity to be shopped for in magazines [196]).

The autonomy of businesswomen, those writers who either narrate or play inspirational roles in Sime's texts, represents another alternative. In their independence they do not just survive the society, but begin to change it, and their rooms are where this transformation takes place. In *Our Little Life*, for example, Eileen Martyn's career and salary enable her to alter domestic power structures. She overturns class and gender barriers by inviting her seamstress's friend, Robert Fulton, into her flat. She controls the conversation; but in this "interview," her professionalism and "friendly" authority (292) make Robert feel that he has "come home" (289). Their shared love of literature and their common desire to write about the new Canada connect Eileen and Robert. Eileen Martyn's rooms signal her social, financial, and moral independence; but they indicate also the possibilities of a different kind of community, in which men and women can meet in order to exchange and discuss and refine their views of the society together. As we see in the frame tale of *Sister Woman*, it is a dynamic predicated upon conversation and dissension rather than silence and control. The woman and the room she earns speak to an alternative system of exchange, in which the official divisions of the society are resisted through personal connections and movements towards understanding.

There is a lack of closure in many of Sime's stories, where women are left on the cusp of decisions or at the edge of revelations. These liminal endings indicate the difficulty of crossing boundaries and challenging traditions. Sime suggests, however, that an ongoing negotiation with social normatives is necessary if the individual is to create a sense of identity and community that responds to the shifting experience of modernity. In this sense, modern subjectivity does not involve a transcendence of society, where the individual can disregard the limitations of existing class or gender or economic barriers. Rather, Sime shows how official mappings of identity must be countered and changed by local engagements with the power dynamics of the home, as well as of the workplace and the city itself.

Works Cited

Campbell, Sandra. Introduction to *Sister Woman*. By J. G. Sime. Rpt. Ottawa: Tecumseh, 1992. vii-xxxv.

Lynch, Gerald. *The One and the Many: English-Canadian Short Story Cycles*. Toronto: U of Toronto P, 2001.

Sime, J. G. *The Mistress of All Work*. London: Methuen, 1916.

—. *Orpheus in Quebec*. London: George Allen and Unwin, 1942.

—. *Our Little Life: A Novel of To-Day*. 1921. Rpt. Ottawa: Tecumseh, 1994.

—. *Sister Woman*. 1919. Ottawa: Tecumseh, 1992.

Solomon, J. R. "Staking Ground: The Politics of Space in Virginia Woolf's *A Room of One's Own* and *Three Guineas*." *Women's Studies* 16.3-4 (1989): 331-47.

Woolf, Virginia. *A Room of One's Own and Three Guineas*. Ed. Michèle Barrett. London: Penguin, 1993.

K. Jane Watt
Cadences of Canada: Georgina Sime's
Sister Woman *

It has been a few years since I have read *Sister Woman* and my
return to it has been one of great pleasure mixed with wonder
at the textual subtleties that I have hitherto overlooked. *Sister
Woman* is a powerful read—a messy, provocative modernist
text that offers a palimpsestic, disharmonious reading of
Canadian nationhood in the immediate post–First World War
era. For me, this collection is unsettling and wonderful because
it refuses to be taken at face value: formally, the narrator's
promise to work towards a place of articulation from which the
multiple truths of women's lives in Canada might be spoken
appears to be being fulfilled through a realist mode, yet
powerful and compelling strains of sentimentalism percolate
into, and mix with, this critically valued mode, often carrying
what's closest to the heart of Sime's colloquy of speaking
women—the essence of their lives. This parliament of women
builds home truths from the heart, individually through reflection, collectively through dialogue, and always through poring
over in private, and discussing in public, the pluses and
minuses of complex philosophical, economic, ethical, and
emotional issues that repeatedly prove the uselessness, even
absurdity, of morally sanctioned fix-all answers.

This collection of twenty-eight "storiettes" (*Orpheus* 44),
declared by publisher Grant Richards to be "a book that really
gives you Canada," is allied in purpose (through the opening
invocation) with the Scottish poet Robert Burns who sought to
sing the songs of his people. If Burns's words suggest the
parameters of Georgina Sime's ambition with regard to creating literature in and of Canada, they also hint at her means,
promising a "gentle scan" in a spirit of good fellowship.
Sime's narrator further underlies this quest for harmonious
plain speaking about the "woman's and the man's" question
(8) because according to her, "It's the same thing. There's no
difference" (8). *Sister Woman* is a deeply nationalistic, if

---

* Written especially for this critical edition of *Sister Woman*.

exploratory and tenuous, project to write Canada in a form appropriate to the cultural terrain of the New World, to represent what Sime described in *Orpheus in Quebec* as "life in the cities of the New World [which] is fluid, restless, like a kaleidoscope to which someone is perpetually giving a shake" (38-39). It's an ambitious aspiration predicated on experimentation—to rattle old literary standards while carrying indisputable, if conflicting, truths about immigrants and how "this changing life might reflect itself in art" (38). Sime believed the novel form was a kind of distillation of established culture appropriate to settled nations and that in Canada an altogether different kind of literary art had to be developed, suited both to the kaleidoscopic quality of culture and to the project of coalescing a nation. In *Orpheus in Quebec*, Sime exhibits a simultaneous yearning for the development of a uniquely Canadian literature and a belief in the possibility of a literature built from the ground up in response to the cultural and regional exigencies of Canada. However, she sites herself as a writer in a curious middle ground, like other "recent arrivals who have brought with them methods suited no doubt to the land they have left, but not altogether to the land they have come to" (44). Writing, like living, demanded constant adaptation.

If her goal is to capture not only the present realities of immigrant women's experience in this country in rapid change, it is also to articulate a new range of choices for women in the shaping of their lives. Her domestic politics, influenced in part at this time by the writing and life of Edward Carpenter, worked from belief in the power of love and of individual choice outward to others, privileging humanity and partnership of the sexes: she writes in a letter dated May 9, 1913, to her lifelong friend and collaborator, Frank Carr Nicholson, that "I don't care when they lived, or what they wear, or how they speak so long as they are *human*." Unimpressed with the public campaigns that were the hallmark of the women's movement of her time because, in part, they turned attention away from "true affection," she complains to Nicholson that "last night I was so sick of breathing the Atmosphere of Woman and her Rights, and worse still, her Civic Conscience, that I went to the theatre in self-defence. May God preserve me from an uninterrupted week of Woman for a very long time to come."

Edward Carpenter (1844-1929) poet, essayist, and lecturer, is described by biographer Keith Neild as "a major Socialist propagandist in the twenty years after 1885" (88). Ordained deacon in the Church of England, Carpenter gave up his orders in search of a simpler, more honest intellectual life which he eventually created at his market garden and retreat at Millthorpe south of Sheffield in the Derbyshire hills. Carpenter was a disciple of Walt Whitman, peer of William Morris, friend of Havelock Ellis and Olive Schreiner, "early advocate of birth control, especially as a partial solution to chronic poverty" (90), a speaker who could draw "as many as two thousand people to a Sunday meeting of a Labour Church or to a lecture in The Sheffield Hall of Science" (89). Yet despite being a public figure in the years before the First World War, by the end of the war his "once substantial influence in the Labour movement had all but vanished" (90), leaving as his legacy his popular theories on domestic and sexual politics. "From the 1880s," according to Neild,

> Carpenter succeeded where others, including Oscar Wilde, had failed. He managed to combine with a life partly lived as a public figure his unconcealed homosexuality; and while the social influence of this prolonged act of propaganda by deed cannot be evaluated accurately, it can only be supposed that it was considerable. In matters of sex and sexuality Carpenter was unquestionably one of the earliest contributors to the wholesale reconsideration of these questions in the present century. It was his books on sex reform alone that continued to sell, even in paperback in the 1950s. (91)

The need to rethink truths about relationships between the sexes is all over *Sister Woman*; indeed, women choose life outside the parameters of the "normal" by entering into long-standing affairs, by refusing to marry, by rearing children out of wedlock. In a letter to Nicholson dated June 10, 1913, Sime delights in the fit of her present life with the life theories of Carpenter:

> I had a lovely time this morning. A lady I know here is moving to the States, and this morning I went to her house and

bought all her kitchen things. It did make me happy to go over pots and pans and dishes and think that really and truly I was going to have my own home again, and be able to use them for myself and my guests. No ornamentation of whatever period, no old china, no priceless gem of art could have given me the warmth at my heart that those granite-wear saucepans did. I felt that for once Carpenter would have approved of me, for these pots and pans were sacred to me and the root of all good.

Eschewing ornamentation and falsity in her life, Sime demanded that neither be present in her fiction. She pondered the difficulties of rendering matters of life, especially those of the heart, faithfully in art in a letter of March 3, 1914, to Nicholson:

Art, it seems to me, having only the power to shadow forth reality, cannot deal with the central facts of life en plein milieu, as it were . . . Love birth, and death are the three facts I have in my mind. In art, it seems to me that you have to take all these three things for granted, as it were, and play round them (or work round them, if you like it better) but [make] no attempt to present them in their full reality, as if it were a true presentment of what would happen in real life. If you attempt to do that you are bound to fail, it seems to me, for these things in life must always be fifty thousand times as real and as overwhelming as they can be in any presentment.

Later in the same letter, she concludes that "it is not the sense of completeness—of something finished and done with that Art must give: but the suggestion of something exquisitely beautiful that it doesn't try to portray in so many words, or sounds, or colours, or lines, but suggests—as something unfulfilled yet to come."

How then, is this fictional world made true by suggestion created in *Sister Woman*? And upon what logic is it organized? In *The One and the Many: English-Canadian Short Story Cycles*, Gerald Lynch insists that this collection must be read in the context of the emerging genre of the Canadian short story cycle because such a conception allows readers to see the significant interplay between the short stories, and to understand that together they are more than the sum of their parts. A complementary reading of form might draw on Sime's prodigious musical background and on her suggestion in *Orpheus in Quebec* that "the medium in which that art may find its most valid expression will be music, not painting or literature" (46). "I have always thought," she writes,

> that when the musician who is to interpret Quebec makes his appearance, he will take the St. Lawrence, as Smetana took the Moldau, for one of his great tone-poems; and when his river flows past the reaches of St. Anne de Beaupré or past Tadousac [sic] or Cacouna, it will take on a key, a motive, perhaps a scale, of its own, and all the history of this long stretch of river-bordered land will be evoked in sound—the Indian life breaking into the utter loneliness, the incursion of the French, the fraternization of Red and White, the long, calm, labourious [sic] life that followed, and the gradual peaceful merging of this life into the soil again; and when it flows past Montreal we shall hear the hum and stir and harmonized complexity of a great world-city. I have often thought that Quebec may be best interpreted to other lands by way of sound and that it may become most familiarly known to the world through some future musician's presentation of the St. Lawrence, as Czechoslovakia has become through Smetana's 'Moldau.' So best, it seems to me, could the cadences of Canada come in the realm of art. They are very difficult to render or even to suggest in words. (46-47)

The possibility that *Sister Woman* might be arranged in a loosely symphonic form would be a natural one for Georgina Sime, a woman for whom music was as much a part of her life as writing. In *Brave Spirits* and in an unpublished typescript, "This Girl Was I," she writes of her operatic training in Berlin in the 1880s, and the loss of her singing voice and consequently of any chance of a professional career in music. In a letter of March 3, 1914, she tells Nicholson of her recent turning away from the music of Wagner, an icon of her time and surely an integral part of her musical training over twenty years previously:

> Wagner for others certainly, but never for me again. I like it less and less as I think of it. There *is* something coarse underlying all of Wagner's music—really coarse I mean,

not conventionally. He looked on things detached, as it were—the physical as physical without the suggestion of its only being one of a holy trinity, and he makes his appeal to your physical nature without touching any other part of you. I *don't* like him, and I don't want to hear any more of him. But I am not ungrateful enough to forget the many, many happy hours he has given me, and for them I thank him heartily. But no more for me!

To conceive of *Sister Woman* as having an organizational structure related to symphonic form would be to understand symphonic form as a structure of essentially three parts sometimes with an introduction and a coda added to its basic shape. The exposition lays the thematic groundwork upon which the piece will be based (and in *Sister Woman*, the striking paired stories "Alone" and "Adrift," which set out the parameters of women's social isolation, might be considered to function in this manner). The development explores material presented in the exposition in a number of keys, and the recapitulation suggests a return marked by change to the material of the exposition (in *Sister Woman*, "Bachelor Girl" and "Divorced" are two stories which restate the idea of social isolation, but this time articulate it in terms of freedom).

This form would meet Sime's requirements for formal experimentation as well as for authenticity in her art. It makes possible an extended meditation on a single subject, provides a dialogic space for the articulations of many different voices, and requires movement and change. It makes possible degrees of modulation in terms of the reading experience: some stories are bold and loud, others are subtle meditations or recapitulations on themes already introduced; together the voices sometimes verge on cacophony. To illustrate this concept of the symphonic, consider Sime's development of the complex question of independence for women which ranges in timbre and breadth over the collection. In "Mr. Johnston," Altabelle, one of the many "young women in stores who . . . serve by standing and waiting all day long" (81) negotiates the very fine balance required of self-preservation and independence, and although she doesn't "have a very easy time of it on life's journey"(81), she is delighted to secure the affections—and the stability of a

marriage proposal—of Mr. Johnston. Altabelle lives determined not to step out of line as has Dolly in "The Child," who
"knew that for one moment she had stepped beyond the pale,
and she knew that if you step beyond the pale and are a
woman—you must stay there" (98). Dolly is an "easy-going,
affectionate creature" (96) who "wasn't a bad girl" (96). She
first loathes, then begins to love the child she carries:

> She adored this child that she had gained in pain and
> sorrow—she loved it with every fibre of her being—she
> would have died to give it a moment of life . . . .
> And that night it was born dead in the hospital—and
> her way lay clear again before her. She was rid of her
> enemy and she felt that she had lost her salvation. She could
> drop her stained past behind her and step out bravely into
> the future . . . and she felt that God was cruel. (100)

In "An Irregular Union," Phyllis Redmayne experiences a
different kind of imprisonment than Dolly envisions. She is
"just the old traditional woman clothed in a Business Woman's
garb" (54) who wrestles with the demands on independence as
she waits, imprisoned, by the phone for word of her lover
whom she cannot contact because of their unconventional relationship. Suddenly her pride at her independence, the fact that
"in plain words, she didn't take any money for the gift of herself" (55), loses its brilliance under the tarnish of loneliness
and worry. The theme of women's independence is explored
through a series of fictional what ifs: what if a shopgirl doesn't
marry? what if she ages? what if she becomes pregnant? what
if she marries? The interrelatedness of the stories across the
cycle allows Sime to explore in different directions the logical
extensions of multiple themes or social issues.

Sister Woman is the fictional result of quest for truth on
two levels—a form appropriate to an emerging country, and a
content appropriate to a new era of interpersonal and human
relations. It is a paradoxical, painful world. Surfaces seem to
suggest possibilities for hope: they seem to say not to worry
because time heals all wounds and *amor vincit omnia*. Clearly,
however, in this world love does not conquer all: Sime's world
of women in Canada is not a world in which love and the boun

ties of motherhood can solve all things, for beneath this super-
ficial world of making do and getting by lies a very dark vision
of women's lives in Canada in the first part of the twentieth
century. In "Motherhood," for example, Mamie Drysdale cherishes the moments after the birth of her illegitimate son, even
though his birth has come at the cost of her relationship with
his father, and remembers the tearing of her life: "Whole days
she had passed tossing between desire and fear. She had
wanted her child; it had seemed to her as if their love was
incomplete without a child . . . and she had dreaded the
moment when she might find it was coming" (68).

It is this doubleness, hope and action always in opposition
to a stifling kind of stasis, that has made me believe less and
less in Georgina Sime's alleged strategy of gentleness; in fact,
I have come to believe that *Sister Woman* is a subversive,
explosive text whose hammers of change require one to
rethink concepts of nation as embodied in the "proper" circumstances and actions of immigrant women in Canada.
Throughout the text, women speak of their lives yet, repeatedly, real hopelessness, born of making the best of straitened
circumstances—a kind of squeeze—lies beneath the brave
stories and bright exteriors of Sime's speaking sisters.

This squeeze is also present in the collection in its com-
manding feeling of space, or lack of space. Domestic interiors
press down on women, witnessing their actions and the consequences of their actions, the price exacted for choices made.
Space is a formidable, palpable presence indexing complex
issues of power and individual agency. Bertha Martin's eman-
cipation in "Munitions!" is a break out of expected hierarchies
framed by oppressive domestic interiors emblematic of power
and rank in the petty economies of women's neighbourhoods
and families. And here's the curious thing—if interior spaces
are controlled by women and if it is out of these orderly camps
that decisions are made, then it follows that the economic dis-
advantages and the drastic consequences of stepping beyond
the pale are not created or inflicted by men only. Repeatedly,
the stalwart keepers of an older order of morality, or of a newer
order of change, are women who knowingly consign their
"sister women" to hells of economic or emotional despair.
Power and control exist not merely in the great Canadian

world out there, but in its interstices, within the sisterhood of women: customers of Alexine band together and refuse to pay her two dollars per day. "They declared to a woman that ten hours' skilled labour wasn't *worth* two dollars a day, and they would rather die than pay it" (40). Jess Rivers, the aging shopwoman who glimpses beauty in "The Cocktail" is confronted by her peers at work who use their youth and cockiness to their advantage to secure a special place at dinner in the "great, bare, ugly dining room the workers had" (104). "Get out to hell," a woman levels at Jess, "that's Miriam's place" (104).

In *Sister Woman*, Georgina Sime does courageous work: she speaks the unspeakable with remarkable candour, publishing work of frankness and sexual openness within the seemingly puritanical confines of the Canadian literary establishment of the time. Her work suggests that we can't overlook matters of the heart and their relationships to larger social and political entities, from motherhood to nationhood. These women talk about their yearnings for the future and their hopes for previously undreamed-of freedoms for themselves and for those around them. That they depend on love and discuss how they build connection to stability and to the future through acts of love or self-affirmation makes their discourse problematic, uncomfortable, as modernist scholar Suzanne Clark suggests: "Episodes of love, like eruptions of the imaginary, appear in the modern, rational conversation, the discourse of our times, as something to be gotten over, grown out of, unwarranted" (2). Sime's work suggests the contrary, that issues articulated in *Sister Woman* remain relevant today.

Questions remain. Is *Sister Woman* a gentle scan? Or are we to take that ironically? Is what Georgina Sime seeks a gentle reminder or an education, or does the narrator suggest in the prologue a massive, monumental cultural remaking? These questions, and the beginning again this new edition of *Sister Woman* makes possible, are reminders of what a tenuous project this one of recovery is. They are also reminders of the fantastic kinds of possibilities various readers make of a text, fostering thinking that begins to create its own fabric of debate, the kind of debate, even mystery, that allows texts to be read and reread, each time taking on new nuances, new ideas, new possibilities for understanding.

Works Cited

Clark, Suzanne. *Sentimental Modernism: Women Writers and the Revolution of the Word.* Bloomington: Indiana UP, 1991.

Lynch, Gerald. *The One and the Many: English-Canadian Short Story Cycles.* Toronto: U of Toronto P, 2001.

Neild, Keith. "Edward Carpenter." *Dictionary of Labour Biography.* Ed. Joyce M. Bellamy and John Saville. London: Macmillan, 1974. 85-93.

Richards, Grant. Letter to Georgina Sime. 22 June 1920. Grant Richards Archive, University of Illinois at Urbana-Champaign. Cited in K. Jane Watt, Introduction to *Our Little Life: A Novel of To-Day,* by J. G. Sime. Ottawa: Tecumseh, 1994.

Sime, J. G. Letter to Frank Carr Nicholson. 9 May 1913. In the collection of the author.

——. Letter to Frank Carr Nicholson. 10 June 1913. In the collection of the author.

——. Letter to Frank Nicholson. [3 March 1914]. In the collection of the author.

——. *Orpheus in Quebec.* London: George Allen and Unwin, 1942.

——. "This Girl Was I," ts. In the collection of the author.

——. *Sister Woman.* 1919. Introd. Sandra Campbell. Ottawa: Tecumseh, 1992.

Sime, J. G., and Frank Nicholson. *Brave Spirits.* Plymouth: privately printed, 1952.

Bibliography

Sime's Principal Works
Books

I. Non-Fiction
—. *The Mistress of All Work*. London: Methuen, 1916.

—. *Thomas Hardy of the Wessex Novels: An Essay and Biographical Note*. Montreal and New York: Carrier, 1928. Rpt. Folcroft, PA: Folcroft Library Editions, 1975.

—. *In A Canadian Shack*. Toronto: Macmillan; London: Dickson, 1937.

—. *The Land of Dreams*. Toronto: Macmillan, 1940.

—. *Orpheus in Quebec*. London: Allen and Unwin, 1942.

—. *Dreams of the World of Light*. London: privately printed, 1951.

— (with Frank Nicholson). *Brave Spirits*. London: privately printed, 1952.

II. Fiction
—. [Pseudonym "A. De Silva"]. *Rainbow Lights: Being Extracts from the Missives of Iris*. London: Duckworth, 1913.

—. *Canada Chaps*. London: Lane; Toronto: S. B. Gundy, 1917.

—. *Sister Woman*. London: Richards; Toronto: S. B. Gundy, 1919. Rpt. with introduction by Sandra Campbell. Ottawa: Tecumseh, 1992.

—. *Our Little Life: A Novel of To-Day*. New York: Stokes and London: Richards, 1921. Rpt. with an introduction by Jane Watt. Ottawa: Tecumseh, 1994.

—. and Frank Nicholson. *A Tale of Two Worlds*. London: Chapman and Hall, 1953.

—. and Frank Nicholson. *Inez and Her Angel*. London: Chapman and Hall, 1954.

Articles
—. "The Spy." *National Review* (London) 113 (November 1939): 638-43.

—. "Incident in Vienna: A True Tale of a Young Refugee." *Saturday Night*, 5 February 1944: 25.

—. "Shakespeare's Dark Lady and the Death Mask of a Lover," *Saturday Night*, 3 June 1944: 29.

—. "Jane Welsh Carlyle as My Mother Saw Her," *Chambers's Journal*, 9th series, 8 (1954): 177-79.

Secondary Sources

Anonymous. "A Montreal Woman on Women." *Canadian Bookman*
April 1920: 57-58.

Becker, May Lamberton. *Golden Tales of Canada*. 1938. Freeport,
New York: Rpt. Books for Libraries Press, 1972. "A Book About
Canada," an excerpt from Sime's *Our Little Life* is included,
116-41.

Bobak, Esther Lisabeth. "The Artist and the City: Attitudes towards
the City in the Canadian Realistic Novel of the Twenties." Diss.
Dalhousie U, 1981. 286-373.

Campbell, Sandra. "'Gently Scan': Theme and Technique in J. G.
Sime's *Sister Woman* (1919)." *Canadian Literature* 133 (Summer
1992): 40-52.

—. Introduction to *Sister Woman* by J. G. Sime. Rpt. Ottawa:
Tecumseh, 1992. vii-xxxviii.

Campbell, Sandra, and Lorraine McMullen, eds. *New Women: Short
Stories by Canadian Women 1900-1920*. Ottawa: University of
Ottawa Press, 1991. Sime's "Munitions!" is included in this
selection.

"Canadian Women in the Public Eye: Miss Sime." *Saturday Night* 18
February 1922: 31.

Dean, Misao. *Practising Femininity: Domestic Realism and the
Performance of Gender in Early Canadian Fiction*. Toronto: U
of Toronto P, 1998.

Donovan, Peter (pseudonym "Tom Folio"). Review of *Sister Woman*.
Saturday Night 28 February 1920: 9.

Lynch, Gerald. *The One and the Many: English-Canadian Short Story
Cycles*. Toronto: U of Toronto P, 2001.

McMaster, Lindsey. "The Urban Working Girl in Turn-of-the-Century
Canadian Fiction." *Essays on Canadian Writing* 77 (Fall 2002):
1-25.

New, W. H. "Back to the Future: The Short Story in Canada and the
Writing of Literary History." *New Contexts of Canadian
Criticism*. Ed. Ajay Heble et al. Peterborough, Ont.: Broadview,
1997. 249-64.

—. *Dreams of Speech and Violence: The Art of the Short Story in
Canada and New Zealand*. Toronto: U of Toronto P, 1987.

—. Introduction. *Canadian Short Fiction*. Ed. W. H. New. 2nd edition. Scarborough, Ont.: Prentice-Hall, 1997. 1-14. Sime's "Art"
is included in this anthology.

—. "Jessie Georgina Sime." *Dictionary of Literary Biography:
Canadian Writers, 1880-1920*. Vol. 92. Ed. W. H. New. Detroit:
Gale, 1990. 356-61.

Pacey, Desmond. "Fiction 1920-1940." *Literary History of Canada: Canadian Literature in English.* 2nd edition. Ed. Carl F. Klinck et al. Vol. I. Toronto: U of Toronto P, 1976. 168-204.

Watt, Jane. Introduction to *Our Little Life* by J. G. Sime. Ottawa: Tecumseh, 1994. vii-xl.

—. "Passing out of Memory: Georgina Sime and the Politics of Literary Recuperation." Diss. U of Alberta, 1997.